"]

"What?" cried Marvin when he was told he could not talk to the jury. "He's not a defendant anymore. He's a convicted murderer! His mother's had her chance all through the trial to sit there and let the jury see her cry for him while I was barred. I had to sit in the press room. Now she's getting another chance? Now she's going to sit there in that witness chair and cry for her son—that murderer who killed my little girl!

"Who will cry for Staci? Tell me that, who will cry for Staci?"

Who Will Cry for Staci?

The True Story of a Grieving Father's Quest for Justice

Milton J. Shapiro
with
Marvin Weinstein

AN ONYX BOOK

ONYX
Published by the Penguin Group
Penguin Books USA Inc., 375 Hudson Street,
New York, New York 10014, U.S.A.
Penguin Books Ltd, 27 Wrights Lane,
London W8 5TZ, England
Penguin Books Australia Ltd, Ringwood,
Victoria, Australia
Penguin Books Canada Ltd, 10 Alcorn Avenue,
Toronto, Ontario, Canada M4V 3B2
Penguin Books (N.Z.) Ltd, 182–190 Wairau Road,
Auckland 10, New Zealand

Penguin Books Ltd, Registered Offices:
Harmondsworth, Middlesex, England

First published by Onyx, an imprint of Dutton Signet,
a division of Penguin Books USA Inc.

First Printing, December, 1995
10 9 8 7 6 5 4 3 2

To Staci,
a beautiful child, deeply loved,
never to be forgotten

Acknowledgments

A nonfiction book of this kind would be impossible to create without the cooperation of many people who generously gave of their time.

Prime place on the list must of course go to Marvin Weinstein, for whom the past fifteen months spent recalling the tragic events of his life have been difficult in the extreme and emotionally draining. For his daughter Hilari, too, these past many months have stirred memories of a time she would rather put aside. My thanks and my heart go out to them.

The Metro-Dade Police Department, the Office of the State Attorney of Florida and the Public Defenders Office were open and helpful with information, transcripts of official records, and interviews. My thanks go to Assistant Director, Metro-Dade Police Department, Willie Morrison; Division Commander Major Don Matthews; Sergeant Ben Hall; Sergeant Jim Ratcliffe; former police sergeant Steve Sessler, now a private investigator; Sessler & Lopez Investigations Inc.; Detective Greg Smith; Detective John King; Detective Harold Ross; Metro-Dade serologist Theresa Merritt; former police officer Earl Higginbotham of the North Miami Police, retired; dispatcher Theresa Morris; 911 Unit, Metro-Dade Police Communications Center.

Thanks to the following attorneys: Assistant State Attorney Abraham Laeser, Deputy Chief, Major Crimes Division, State Attorney's Office; Assistant State Attorney David Waksman, Major Crimes Division; Assistant Public Defender Brian McDonald; former assistant state attorney Bruce Lehr; now in private practice; attorney Kelley Finn.

Friends and neighbors of Marvin Weinstein: Bookie and David Rogers, Alan Sacharoff, Rabbi and Mrs. Klein, Paul Kallman, Audrey and Nelan Sweet of Parents of Murdered Children, funeral director Sonny Levitt.

My thanks to the many nameless but not unappreciated secretaries and receptionists for the above named police and attorneys, who skillfully fielded my many telephone calls and forwarded my messages.

To my editor, Michaela Hamilton, thanks for the patience and help in working with me and seeing this book through to its final stages, and to editor John Paine for his constructive suggestions; to my agent Bernard Kurman of Rights Unlimited, for his continuing inspiration and votes of confidence.

Thank you, my understanding wife, Jill, who tended our garden in England as she awaited my return and turn with the lawn mower as the green, green grass of home loomed taller and taller.

Finally, a special thank-you to my friends Lee and Linda Selverne, the matchmakers who introduced me to Marvin Weinstein and who from the very beginning saw the potential and depth of human interest in Marvin Weinstein's story.

Authors' Note

The following story is true. In the interests of brevity and space, trial testimony and in some instances the testimony given in depositions have been edited. For legal requirements and in respect of privacy, the names of some persons in this book are pseudonyms.

Chapter 1

North Miami Beach, Florida, October 14, 1982

On this pleasant subtropical Thursday evening, about 6:15, Marvin Weinstein parked his yellow Ford van in the drive of his ranch-style house and struggled to his front door, his arms laden with groceries. "Hilari! Staci!" he called out to his two young daughters. "Open the door for me!"

No reply. Puzzled for a moment, he then noticed that Hilari's bike was not on the front lawn, where usually she dropped it on returning home from school, and he recalled that she had told him she had swimming team practice that afternoon and would be home late. "Staci?" he called out again. Staci, his ten-year-old, a year younger than Hilari, had asked to stay home from school that day, complaining of a headache. More likely she hadn't done her homework, Marvin had thought, but he had indulged her; ever since his wife, Ruth Ann, had died in June, just four months earlier, he had indulged both his daughters as they all tried to put back together the pieces of their shattered lives.

But now where was Staci? Asleep? Gone to a friend, a neighbor? Not likely at this hour. Annoyed, Marvin placed his grocery bags on the ground and fumbled for his keys. He turned the key in the lock and opened the front door.

The ranch house was typical of this area, a quiet middle-class neighborhood. The front door opened into the living room. To the right was a den, and straight ahead a dining room that backed onto a so-called Florida room leading out via sliding doors to the patio area and small plunge pool. To the right of the dining area was a kitchen, pantry, and laundry room. To the left were three steps that led to three bedrooms.

Dumping the groceries on the couch, Marvin started up the steps, calling out once again, "Staci?" At the top he noted that the child's bedroom door was ajar and her light was on. Curious, he thought. Asleep, or what? Playing games with him, not answering his call? He approached her door cautiously, puzzled.

At the doorway, he looked into the child's room, and saw . . . he couldn't take in what he was seeing. Red. His eyes saw red, were filled with red. Blood. Marvin understood he was seeing blood.

There was blood everywhere. Blood spattered on the walls, blood on the bed. Blood on the headboard. Blood on the head and on the half-naked body of Staci that lay curled on its side on the blood-soaked sheets.

Marvin stood there, rooted to the spot, bile rising in his throat, choking him. Then he turned and fled down the hallway, down the three steps, flying out the front door and across the street to the house of his friends, Stanley and Dianne Saul.

He pounded on their front door. "Stan, Dianne, help! Help me, please! God, I must be dreaming!"

Dianne Saul opened the door. "Marvin, what's the matter, what's wrong?" Stanley Saul appeared over her shoulder. "Marvin, what's happened?"

"Help, you've got to help me! I'm dreaming! I've gotta be dreaming! It's Staci . . . there's blood . . . she's bleeding!"

He turned and ran back to the house, Dianne and Stanley Saul in his wake. When he came to his yellow van he stopped short. "Wait!" he shouted. "They might still be in there!"

"Who? what?" Stanley shouted.

Poking around on the rear seat of the van, under a bundle of clothing, Marvin withdrew a .25-caliber pistol. Waving it in the air, he cried out, "Come on!" and rushed back into the house, up the three stairs, and to the door of the child's bedroom. Dianne and Stanley were close behind him. In the doorway, Marvin held out his arm to stop them from entering the bedroom. Over his outstretched arm, they peered inside.

Dianne screamed. She put her hands to her eyes, turned away, and ran out of the house, back across the street, and into her own house, crying hysterically.

Stanley Saul stared in horror at the sight. "Marvin, we must call for help! Call 911 for help!" Together they ran to the phone in the kitchen. Marvin put down the gun, picked up the phone, dropped it, picked it up again, dropped it. "Here, give it to me!" said Stanley. He took the phone, hands shaking, and dialed 911. His voice quavering, he cried, "Help! We need help. Send an ambulance! Send police! A little girl's been hurt! She's bleeding. It's very bad!"

At the Metro-Dade Police Communications Center, the 911 complaints operator prepared her computer for input. "Please try to be calm," she said. The voice was so shrill, so high-pitched, she thought a woman was calling. "Let me have the address, please. Help will be sent immediately. Stay at the scene, please."

In the vast communications center, batteries of computers were set in front of some ninety people. To one side of the complaints operators were those for Fire/Rescue. On the other side were the dispatchers. Given the address for Marvin Weinstein, the complaints operator simultaneously fed the information to Fire/Rescue and to the computer of dispatcher Theresa Morris.

On the right-hand side of her computer screen, Theresa had a list of all police units on duty in her designated area at that precise moment. On her screen came up Marvin Weinstein's address and the coded message from the complaints operator: 32—person bleeding, possible assault in progress.

When he'd hung up the phone, Stanley Saul turned to Marvin. "Maybe she's still alive, Marvin," he said.

Marvin shook his head slowly. "It's no good, Stanley. Did you see her little body? It's all gray. It's no good, Stanley." Together they went outside to wait.

On routine patrol less than a mile from the Weinstein home, Earl Higginbotham, at forty-seven a veteran cop, got the 32 on his radio. To Higginbotham, this meant assault in progress with the possibility of a deadly weapon involved.

Headlights on, rooftop blue lights flashing, and siren on full, gun holster unsnapped, Higginbotham reached the Weinstein house in less than a minute. As he screeched to a halt Higginbotham saw two men standing outside the open front door. One of the two men was holding a gun in his right hand. Higginbotham threw open his door and pulled his own gun from his holster.

He held it out in front of him, pointing it at Marvin Weinstein as he approached.

Gun down at his side, his manner composed, Marvin said to him quietly, "It's my daughter."

"Where is she?" asked Higginbotham.

"In her bedroom."

"Show me," said the officer.

"Marvin, I'm going home," Stanley Saul said.

Higginbotham turned to him. "Who are you?"

Saul explained. Higginbotham noted his address and let him go. Then, with his gun hand, he motioned Marvin inside. "Show me which bedroom," Higginbotham said, "but before you do, put your gun down on that dining room table," he said, watching Marvin carefully. The man is calm, the officer noted. Entirely too calm, considering. Marvin looked down at the gun he had forgotten he was holding, placed it on the table.

"Okay, now show me the bedroom," Higginbotham repeated.

Instead, Marvin led him to the back door leading to the patio. "I think maybe they were burglars," Marvin said. "I think maybe they got out through the back door."

Higginbotham looked at him, curious, suspicious. Why is he showing me this? Why is he keeping me away from the girl's bedroom?

"Show me the bedroom," he said firmly. "Now."

Marvin led him to Staci's room. Stood outside. Pointed.

Higginbotham, a burly man built like a football linebacker, looked at the bloodied body on the bed and swore softly to himself. The girl was lying on her left side, naked above the waist. She was wearing what appeared to be pink terry cloth shorts. The shorts were rolled down slightly and under, Higginbotham noted, exposing the tops of yellow panties. Blood was smeared all over her back. He approached carefully, disturbing nothing, noticing a small hole in the right side of Staci's body. The back of her head showed a large, bloody contusion, and Higginbotham concluded she'd been hit hard by a flat object back there. He leaned over Staci's body and touched two fingers to the carotid artery on her neck. He turned to Marvin, standing in the doorway, eyes on Staci's body, lips pressed together, dry-eyed. He took Marvin by the arm, silently led him down to the living room, sat him down on the couch.

On his hand-held radio, Higginbotham called in to his own, North Miami Beach dispatcher. "We got a 45 here," he said to her.

A 45. A DOA. Dead on arrival.

A homicide.

Chapter 2

Two hundred years ago south Florida was Seminole country. They were not a nation as much as an alliance of several Indian tribes banded together and given the name Seminole by the Spanish (Spain owned Florida until it ceded it to the United States in 1819). The Seminole hunted and fished in the vast mangrove forest that extended from the Atlantic beaches westward some twenty miles until the forest met the sawgrass swamplands of the Everglades. There lived a branch of the Seminole called the Miccosukee.

During the Seminole Indian wars of the early nineteenth century, the Seminole were almost completely exterminated. Eventually, some survivors were moved to a reservation in Oklahoma. Another reservation was established in Dania, now called the Hollywood Reservation, where some 150 descendants of the original Seminole live on 480 acres, just a few miles north of what is today the city of North Miami Beach. The Miccosukee, who refused to live on a reservation, are content to live in the Everglades, where the few families remaining eke out a living off the land, and by wrestling alligators and selling arts and crafts to tourists.

Today, while the inhospitable Everglades remains more or less uninhabited, the mangrove forests of the Seminole have given way to a sea of ranch-style homes, sprawling acres of condominiums, and shopping malls intersected by a few turgid canals and fast-flowing ribbons of concrete highway.

When the Spanish explorer and conquistador Juan Ponce de León landed in Florida in 1513, it is said that he came looking for the mythical Fountain of Youth. Many Floridians who have moved here from the north, particularly the elderly, believe they have indeed found it.

It was here that Marvin Weinstein emigrated from Canada with his young wife and two young daughters in 1977, seeking a better life. The child of Russian-born parents, he left high school to help his ailing father and older brother run a small cigar store. The family lived above the store. To earn extra money for the family, including two other brothers and a sister, Marvin took a part-time job selling door-to-door for the Fuller Brush Company. As a passenger in a car one day, making deliveries, he was involved in an accident and suffered serious head injuries. He needed reconstructive surgery on his mouth, face, and head, could not work for many weeks, and lost his sales job. Shortly afterward his father died of cancer, and Marvin took over the store. When his older brothers married and moved on, business turned sour, the store was sold. Unable to pay the mortgage, Marvin sold the building and took a job as a clothing salesman for a retail store. He was twenty-two.

A year later, in May 1965, he married a lovely local girl named Ruth Ann Berman. She was twenty, working in the accounts department of the Hudson Bay Company. They moved into a one-bedroom apartment in a high-rise.

Marvin was not satisfied with his salesman's job. It was too confining, a dead end. He felt that the only way to earn real money was with a business of his own. He tried several, with little success. So when a friend came to him with a deal to open a pool hall, he grabbed the chance. Maybe this would pay off.

Certainly it looked better than the part-time business he had been operating with an American friend he'd met, Alan Sacharoff, a market-research analyst working in Toronto. The scheme was called Gourmet Dining. It had made a bit of money through the years, but when Alan joined Marvin and his partner in the pool hall business and Marvin's daughter Hilari was born, in April 1970, Gourmet Dining was sold. Soon a second pool hall was opened. And Staci was born, in October 1971.

Eventually this venture, too, fell apart. Marvin went to work in a furniture store. That store closed down. For several years Marvin again drifted unhappily from job to job, until finally he got a break. His American friend Alan received a letter from his mother in Florida. A Canadian-owned bakery chain, Tiffany Bakeries, she wrote, was offering opportunities for franchises in the Miami area, with full training provided. A native Floridian himself, Alan saw this as an opportunity to return, and he approached Marvin with a proposition to go in with him as a partner in a Miami franchise bakery.

To Marvin and Ruth Ann, this appeared to be a wonderful opportunity. They could own a good business backed by the reputation of the bakery chain. They discovered, too, that the overall cost of living in Florida was much less than in Toronto. The fantasy images of sunshine and swimming pools, of beaches and a resort area lifestyle, overwhelmed them. Following a period of training in Toronto and Chicago, in February 1977 Marvin and Alan moved with their families to North Miami Beach.

As it happened, Marvin did not immediately become a partner in the bakery franchise. He couldn't raise the money. Alan and his brother-in-law could, and hired Marvin as a baker when the shop opened at the Omni

Mall in Miami. Still, within two years Marvin managed to earn enough to move out of an apartment and buy a house—the house in which he lives today—and when a second bakery was opened in Cutler Ridge, he bought in as a minority-holding third partner. The picture was looking good. Marvin believed that at last his luck had turned.

Unfortunately, Alan Sacharoff and his brother-in-law soon disagreed on the running of the bakeries. Alan left and started his own bakery-supply business. The Cutler Ridge store was sold. Alan's brother-in-law took control of the Omni store, brought in family to help out, and cut the overhead. Marvin, working at the Cutler Ridge bakery, was out of a job again.

It was during this period, in the fall of 1979, that Marvin's wife discovered a lump under her left arm. The doctor said it was just a cyst. But by December it had grown. Ruth Ann went to a specialist, who diagnosed breast cancer. In January 1980, at age thirty-five, she had a mastectomy.

When she returned home from the hospital, Marvin recalled, she was angry. She felt violated. She suffered severe emotional upheaval because of the surgery. But as the months went by and she was told the surgeon had removed all the cancerous growth, her spirits rose, and she went back into the hospital for reconstructive surgery on her breast.

Marvin meanwhile had obtained a job with a Publix supermarket in the bakery department. The routine was so regimented, so different from the work he had done as a bakery manager with the franchise, that he fell out immediately with his manager and other employees. The work atmosphere was difficult, but he hung on, asking to be put on an early shift so that he was home by eleven in the morning to help Ruth Ann, take her for doctor visits when necessary, and spend time with Hilari and Staci, whose schoolwork had been adversely affected by their mother's illness.

Medical bills piled up. Torn between the need to be home and the need for more money, Marvin was forced to take on part-time work selling tools to nearby factories and to garages. He would return home from Publix, grab a quick bite to eat, then drive up and down State Road 7 selling tools.

In August 1981 Ruth Ann took Hilari and Staci on a visit to Canada to visit relatives. While there, several lumps appeared in her neck. She began to feel unwell, with periods of nausea. In a near panic she returned to Florida and was admitted to the hospital. An exploratory operation was performed. The diagnosis was terminal cancer. It had spread throughout her body. She was given three to four months to live.

The doctors first related this to Marvin. The choice of passing this terminal prognosis to his wife was left to him. But Ruth Ann insisted on knowing, and Marvin told her. They did not tell the children, however. "Mommy's very sick," he did say to them, "and we're going to do everything we can to make her better."

Try they did. Soon, however, Ruth Ann began developing severe headaches, and it was revealed that the cancer had spread to her brain. Intense radiation treatments were tried in an effort to destroy these cancer cells. It seemed to slow down her deterioration for a time, but Marvin was told that she was lost. He had known that for some time, had in his heart accepted it, but it did not halt his attempts to keep her alive as long as possible, keep her from pain as long as possible. He fought with the doctors, he fought with the hospital, desperately seeking some new treatment, even experimental, that might, if not save her—for he knew now that was impossible—at least give her years instead of months.

Eventually he was able to gain admission for Ruth Ann at the Biological Research Center in Frederick, Maryland, where, in cooperation with several major pharmaceutical companies, they were experimenting with anti-cancer drugs, including a marijuana derivative to ease the suffering of terminally ill patients. There Ruth Ann was put on the Interferon program. But she began to develop trouble with her arms and legs, found walking difficult. X rays showed that the cancer had spread to her spine. The hospital telephoned Marvin and told him they would have to send her home. There was nothing they could do for her.

Marvin pleaded with them on the phone to keep trying. "This poor woman has been butchered and tortured and put through all kinds of hell," he said to them. "You've got to help her. Save her life! She's got two children! If you send her away, she dies." But they said they were sorry, they had to work with people who had a chance. Ruth Ann had no chance.

Heartbroken, Marvin called his friend Alan Sacharoff, and together they drove to the airport to meet Ruth Ann on her return from Frederick. She could barely walk off the plane. She looked terrible. Marvin could tell that her spirits were at rock bottom.

All he could do for his wife now, he was told, was put her back on a chemotherapy program. Briefly she went back into the local hospital but then was released to Marvin at home. She wanted to be home, with her husband and her children. She knew she was dying, knew her days were numbered now in weeks rather than months.

With all the pressure further affecting his abrasive relationships at work, Marvin had a climactic falling-out with Publix management that resulted in his firing. Fortunately for his shaky financial position at that time, Alan Sacharoff took back, by default, the Cutler Ridge bakery and gave Marvin a job, working an early morning shift starting at six so that he could spend afternoons and evenings at home with his family.

In March, while Ruth Ann was beginning a course in chemotherapy, one of Marvin's brothers died of cancer in Toronto. He flew up to Canada for the funeral, re-

turning as quickly as decently possible to take care of
Ruth. She was in constant, severe pain, requiring injec-
tions of painkilling drugs. One of the Weinsteins'
neighbors, Bookie Rogers, whose daughter Amy was a
close friend of Staci, worked in a doctor's office. She
showed Marvin how to give his wife the required in-
jections.

As a result of the chemotherapy, Ruth Ann's hair
began to fall out—the long blond hair of which she always had been so proud. One day Marvin took her
along with Hilari and Staci to buy a wig. He persuaded
her to buy a red one, trying to make a little joke of it,
saying to his unhappy wife, "I always wanted to be
married to a redhead." The remark brought a small
smile to her lips—a smile, Marvin thought, that was
worth everything he owned. It had been a long time
since his wife had had anything at all to smile about.

Yet again Marvin arranged for Ruth Ann to enter the
hospital for treatment, hoping for some miracle, some
new treatment that might relieve her pain, offer some
possibility of remission. The oncologists there tried
X-ray treatments and radiation. Ruth did not respond.
In fact, she complained to Marvin that she was feeling
worse. Cankers developed in and around her mouth,
and her throat was so sore she could hardly speak.

After two weeks the doctors sent her to a hospice in
North Miami, a last stop for the terminally ill who
needed to be treated with strong painkillers. Marvin
knew exactly what it was from the moment he walked
in the front door. The memory of the stench has never
left him. And yet he remembers, too, with respect and
appreciation, the tender, personal care given to his wife
by the nurses there. They would comb her hair wig, put
on her lipstick for her, tried to make her look good, in-
still some pride in her appearance. Still a woman—
terribly ill, but a woman. A man could look at her and
love her. Want her. If it was an illusion, it was a kind-
ness for all that.

The children reacted differently to their mother's illness. Staci, ten, the more introverted of the two, did not like to linger in her mother's sickroom. She preferred instead to wander through the hallways, chatting with the ambulatory patients. She seemed to enjoy talking to these old people and even had one or two favorites she would seek on her daily visits to the nursing home. Hilari, on the other hand, remained in her mother's room as long as the visit lasted, talking to her—about school, about her success on the school swimming team, about how she was coping at home. Indeed, a very confident young lady who had just turned twelve, Hilari had taken over the housekeeping chores. She cleaned the house, took charge of the laundry, made sure Staci had clean clothes for school and, as best she could, that the family was fed. The latter chore was difficult, because Marvin was so focused on his wife's rapidly fading health that he was feeding himself and his daughters on fast-food dinners. Eating was, in fact, irrelevant to Marvin. What did it matter to him whether he ate or not, or even whether his children ate or not, or if the grass was cut, or the dishes washed, or the house cleaned? He didn't care, and he turned angrily on anybody, friend or neighbor, who dared suggest otherwise. He thought with despair only of his dying wife.

As the days passed in a dreadful monotony of chaos and suffering, and his wife began to drift in and out of a torpid, dreamlike state, comatose at times, Marvin became physically and mentally exhausted. His daily routine began at four-thirty in the morning, when he rose to reach the bakery by six. He returned home at two, dozed for an hour or two until Staci and Hilari returned home from school. Then they all went to the nursing home, stayed there a few hours before going out for a pizza or returning home to open a couple of TV dinners.

He depended on Hilari to see to her own and Staci's

homework, the cleaning up, getting Staci and herself
off to bed, and then he would return to the nursing
home to sit with his wife for another few hours. Rarely
was he home before midnight, falling into bed before
the cycle would start all over again at four-thirty.

One evening at the end of May, while Staci and
Hilari were watching television, Marvin drove to the
hospice to see Ruth Ann. In her hushed room he pulled
a chair to her bedside and sat down beside her. Her
eyes were closed. She looked so pitifully small, her
body so shrunken under those white sheets. Her face
was like parchment, dry, colorless. He could detect her
faint breathing, the very slow, labored movement of
her chest.

Sensing his presence, she opened her eyes. Marvin
reached for her hand. "Do you know who I am?" he
said.

"Marvin." It was an effort for her.

They remained silent for a few moments, hands
touching. She turned her head to look at him, at his
face. Her eyes, painless eyes now, drugged eyes now,
held on his. "Marvin," she said, "you must promise me
to take care of the children."

He nodded, his own eyes misting. He did not want to
cry, to distress her.

"No," she said to him. "Tell me. Say it. You must
say it. You must promise me you'll take care of my little girls."

"I promise," he said to her. "I promise."

Her eyes closed again, and she appeared to fall
asleep. Marvin watched her for a time, watched her
breathe, until a nurse came in and told him she would
probably sleep now through the night.

He drove home. But he did not enter the house. Not
yet. He needed to walk. He needed to be alone for a
few minutes, to relieve the pounding in his head that
had lived with him for these so many weeks. He ven-
tured a few blocks down the road to the edge of one of

the canals that ran through the neighborhood. He had so many questions and no answers. He looked into the darkened waters of the canal. But there were no answers to be found there. He looked up at the sky, at the stars that glittered there on that clear and softly beautiful semitropical evening. Was there an answer there? He was not a religious man, he was not even sure that he believed in God, but as he stood there, looking up at the silent, mysterious, starlit heavens, he spoke aloud: "If there is anybody up there, help me. I need help. Please."

With a deep sigh, he turned and walked slowly home.

Two days later, Ruth Ann died. She was thirty-seven.

The call from the hospice came just before midnight. Marvin was lying on the couch, dozing. Just hours earlier he had been with her, and she had seemed reasonably alert, talking to him. Now she was dead. Was this the answer he had been seeking? Several times in the recent past Ruth Ann had said to him, in her agony, in her hopelessness, that soon he would get what he wanted, that he'd be able to find a younger woman. There had been times when she had accused him of not trying hard enough to save her, not doing all he could to make her well again. When she did this to him he took it numbly. He knew she was just lashing out at him, at the world, for tormenting her, for she knew not what or why. Yet he did wonder at times: could he have done more? Now it was too late. Ruth Ann was gone. And had left him with two young daughters and a legacy of guilt.

As Marvin sat up on the couch after the phone call, he fought to pull himself together. Should he wake the children now or let them sleep? What would he tell them? How do you gently tell your children that their mother has just died?

He telephoned Alan Sacharoff and arranged for Hilari to spend the rest of the night and next day with them. He telephoned his neighbor and friend David Rogers and arranged for Staci to go to them, and for David to drive him to the nursing home, where arrangements would have to be made for the body. The body. As he said those two words to David Rogers, they echoed in his ears. That's what his wife was now. A body.

Marvin went to wake the children. But they had heard the telephone and were wide awake in their beds, fearfully waiting for their father's knock on their doors. He gathered them together in his bedroom and cried with them, rocking them in his arms. Then he helped them dress and gather a few things together to take with them as David Rogers and Alan Sacharoff drove up to the house to take them away. Then, with David, he drove to the nursing home. While David waited in the hallway, he sat with Ruth Ann's body for a time before calling the funeral home.

The funeral itself took place two days later. But Marvin wanted to do one last thing before he put his wife into the ground. He wanted to say good-bye, and he wanted Staci and Hilari to have that opportunity, too. Thus, in the funeral home on the morning of the funeral, he went to the half-open coffin and saw, with approval, that as he had asked, the morticians had touched up Ruth Ann's face to erase the ravages of her cancer. In another room Staci and Hilari were being shown a film on coping with the death of a loved one. Then Marvin led them to the coffin, with just the face and part of the upper body in view. There were some among his friends who had told Marvin it would be cruel of him to let the children see their mother like that, but he ignored them.

The children gazed at their mother and touched her. "How stiff she is, Daddy," Staci remarked. Each in turn then kissed her on the forehead, and the coffin lid was closed. On June 6, 1982, Ruth Ann was buried at Shalom Memorial Gardens in North Miami Beach.

Marvin went back to work in the bakery, the children returned to school. Deeply affected by the death of their mother, their schoolwork suffered, but understanding teachers were tolerant and helpful; both girls had been excellent students previously. During the summer months of school vacation, Marvin was able to get them enrolled in the Jewish Community Center summer camp. On weekends he took a stand at the Thunderbird Flea Market on Sunrise Boulevard in Ft. Lauderdale, where he sold tools. Staci and Hilari went with him and helped. They enjoyed being with him on the stand, enjoyed the hustle and bustle of the busy flea market. They could lunch on pizzas and hamburgers. They were with their father all day long. They felt secure.

All too soon, however, friction developed between Staci and Hilari. They fought as Hilari became in effect a surrogate mother for her younger sister. And Staci didn't like it, wouldn't stand for taking orders from Hilari. "You're not my mother! You can't tell me what to do!" she would shout at her when told to help around the house or do her homework.

Toward the end of that summer, Alan Sacharoff told Marvin that the bakery was going to be sold again. By September Marvin was once more without a job. The weekend earnings at the flea market were a pittance, and Marvin began to scour the classified ads looking for a job. Adding to his problems was the deepening hostility between Staci and Hilari. He couldn't deal with it. They didn't want to come to the flea market with him anymore, and he was forced to stay home with them on the weekends and so lost even that small source of income.

He didn't know what to do. His life was falling apart. It was becoming increasingly difficult for him to function. Friends and neighbors helped with the children, particularly with Staci, who seemed to need help more than Hilari, who was the stronger, more independent. Staci spent many evenings at the home of Bookie and David Rogers, playing at Barbie dolls with their daughter Amy, dining with them, even sleeping over.

Marvin sought help from a psychologist. He thought about taking evening classes at the local university to further his education, which he hoped would help him find a decent job. He even began dating a woman, a divorcee, who had been introduced to him by a mutual friend who thought, justifiably, that Marvin would be interested in remarrying, to regain a mother for Staci and Hilari. The children didn't seem to mind. Staci, in fact, said to him one day, "If you get married again, it can't be to a fatso. [Ruth Ann had been slim.] She has to be thin and very beautiful."

At the beginning of October, Marvin answered an ad for a baker at a nearby Grand Union supermarket. The first interview went well, and he was told he would be called back for a second interview on October 14. Marvin began to think ahead. Staci's eleventh birthday was coming up on the thirtieth. If he got the job he would be able to buy her the bicycle she had been asking for. Maybe things were looking up.

Early on the morning of the fourteenth, Hilari as usual awoke first, showered and dressed and began preparing breakfast. Shortly afterward Staci left her room, wearing her nightdress, and knocked on Marvin's door, calling out to him that she wasn't feeling well. Hilari went to the hallway and told Staci to take a shower and dress for school. Staci ignored her and entered Marvin's bedroom. Hilari finished her breakfast, prepared a lunch to take along to school, and went to Marvin's bedroom at about eight o'clock. She opened the door and told Marvin she was leaving. Staci was in his bed, apparently asleep. "Staci's not going to school today," Marvin said. "She says she's got a headache."

Marvin's appointment at the Grand Union was at eleven, but he had roofers coming to the house about nine to give an estimate on repair work to loose shingles. He got out of bed right after Hilari had gone, showered and dressed. By then Staci was up and about and eating her breakfast cereal. Marvin prepared toast and coffee. Staci went into the den and turned on the TV to watch cartoons. Marvin poured himself a second cup of coffee and took it into the den to watch the cartoons with Staci. He enjoyed Popeye as much as she did. They watched Popeye and laughed together. It was so good, Marvin thought, to laugh together. There had been precious little of that in their lives these many months.

Around nine the roofers arrived, two men in their thirties. Sam Klosky waited outside the front door while Steve Carlucci entered the house to speak to Marvin. Then they went out to look at the area of the roof where some shingles had been damaged by rain and slipped loose. Carlucci gave Marvin an estimate, said he'd telephone next day, and left with Klosky to repair a roof down the block.

An hour later, about ten-thirty, Marvin left Staci watching cartoons to keep his appointment at the Grand Union. He told her he'd be home a little late, since he had some errands to run besides going to the job interview.

Marvin got the baker's job. Elated, he went on to Miami-Dade Junior College to see about taking some courses. Then he went shopping for various items, stopped for a snack at a delicatessen, and later that afternoon—as he did often—visited his wife's grave. His final stop late that afternoon was at a Publix supermarket. Marvin knew he had been neglecting the food situation at home. There wasn't much more in the refrigerator lately than bare necessities. Well, now he had a job and he would see to it that the refrigerator was filled to overflowing. Not just the necessities, but everything Staci and Hilari wanted: cakes, cookies, ice cream—whatever.

He filled the shopping cart from the shelves, piling it over the top in a sudden burst of high spirits. He would get Staci that bike she wanted for her birthday. He would give her a terrific birthday party. And maybe, with a steady job and money coming in regularly, maybe the kids would stop fighting with each other. Get along better. He'd buy them nice clothes, take them to the movies. He looked up at the supermarket clock and noted that it was later than he thought. Six o'clock. He paid for the groceries, got back into the van, and drove home. As he pulled into his driveway some fifteen minutes later he saw, with surprise, that the girls' mixed-breed puppy, April, was tied to the base of the lantern in the front lawn.

Marvin filled his arms with grocery bags and walked to the front door, shouting for the girls to open it for him. . . .

Chapter 3

Even before Officer Higginbotham arrived, Marvin's close friend Alan Sacharoff hurried over from his home just five blocks away. Marvin had telephoned him immediately after the 911 call.

Alan had just been sitting down to dinner with his wife and children when Marvin telephoned and said to him, "Alan, something horrible has happened to Staci. You must come over!" That was all Marvin said. Alan told his wife something was wrong with Staci and he was driving over to see what it was all about. When he got there moments later, he parked across the street. He saw Marvin and Stanley Saul standing in front of the house, Marvin with a gun in his hand. As Alan got out of the car, Marvin ran across the street to him shouting, "Don't tell me anything about guns! Don't tell me anything about guns!" Alan had always voiced his disapproval of Marvin's keeping two handguns around the house.

"What are you talking about, Marvin?" Alan said. "Why are you holding a gun?"

"Staci's dead! Staci's dead!" Marvin shouted at him.

"Dead? What do you mean, dead? What happened?"

"I don't know! Somebody murdered Staci!"

Marvin ran back across the street, expecting Alan to follow him into the house. But Alan would not follow him. He did not want to see Staci. He turned around and threw up on the grass, and remained there across the street, sick to his stomach, until the initial shock had passed. He watched Officer Earl Higginbotham arrive. He watched the Fire/Rescue truck arrive. He watched Hilari arrive, the swarming of the police cars and the crowd. Only then did he return home and tell his wife the sad news.

While Marvin Weinstein sat on the couch in the den, staring into space, the Fire/Rescue unit examined the body of Staci where she lay on her bed. In less than a minute they confirmed Higginbotham's report that Staci was dead—at least two or three hours was their immediate judgment, though a more precise time of death would have to await an official report by the county medical examiner.

As soon as the paramedics concluded their examination, Higginbotham sent them on their way. Their work was finished. Once they ascertain the person is dead, they have no more business on the premises. Higginbotham, conversely, now had a crime scene to preserve. "Okay, out," he said to the rescue unit. And "Out," he said to Marvin, motioning to the front door. Then Higginbotham got on his handheld radio to his dispatcher, and asked her to check out the jurisdiction there. As he had surmised, because of the location of Marvin Weinstein's house, this was a case for Dade County, not for the City of North Miami Beach. Higginbotham realized, in fact, that except for protecting the crime scene, his work was finished, too.

He went outside and stood on the front porch with Marvin to await the Metro-Dade homicide detectives. By now North Miami Beach police cars were beginning to arrive from all directions. With a "32 in progress" broadcast over an open radio channel, anybody who was not otherwise engaged would speed to the scene to back up the first cop there—if needed. But Higginbotham barred everyone from the house. He advised the arriving officers that this was a homicide case, and it was a Dade County jurisdiction. However, the sirens and flashing lights had begun to draw a crowd. Higginbotham told the officers to get ropes out of their cars and cordon off the area.

Suddenly, around the corner, came Hilari on her silver bicycle, fresh from swimming, a damp white towel around her neck. Confused, frightened, she was allowed through the rope as Marvin spotted her and called out to her. Flinging her bike down on the lawn, she ran to him. "Dad! What's going on here?"

What to say? What to tell her? "It's Staci," he said. "She's dead. Somebody killed her."

Hilari screamed. "Oh, no! It can't be true!"

As Marvin hugged her, Hilari broke away. "Let me see her! I want to see my sister!"

"You can't, Hilari," Marvin said gently, his eyes moist. "Nobody can go in there. The police—" His voice broke. He embraced his surviving daughter, and the two of them stood there at the front door of the house, crying in each other's arms until, at Marvin's suggestion, a neighbor in the crowd led Hilari down the street to the home of Bookie and David Rogers. There Hilari would spend the night and every night for some two months before she felt strong enough to return to her own home, to her own bedroom.

After Hilari left, Marvin began to relate to Higginbotham his tragedies of recent months: the loss of his job, the death of his wife, the problems with his two young daughters. All this added to Higginbotham's surprise at Marvin's attitude—and to his increasing suspicion. No excitement, no nervousness, no anger, no despair, and, except for his few moments together with Hilari, no tears. However, since this homicide was outside his jurisdiction, he could not pursue his suspicions. He didn't even touch Marvin's gun—the .25 automatic that still lay on the dining room table—to see if it had been fired. He had been careful to disturb as little as possible from the moment he'd ascertained that Staci had been murdered.

Metro-Dade Homicide arrived in force some ten minutes later: a team headed by Detective Sergeant Art Felton, with Detective Ben Hall as lead investigator, plus detectives John King, Virgil Munn, and Mark Huetter. Right behind them came a crew from a mobile crime-lab unit. There was even an officer from the police information office to handle the media, both newspaper and television, now swarming around the house.

Pure chance sent this particular homicide team to this crime: on average eight teams operate out of the Metro-Dade Homicide Section, on a twenty-four-hour rotation. Each team is run by a sergeant, in this case Art Felton. It fell to his team to be on call when the murder of Staci Weinstein was flashed to Police Headquarters in Miami. Unlike most television cop shows, where homicide detectives are sitting around a squad room, Felton's team had been scattered in their unmarked cars, working on other cases. There is no shortage of homicides in south Florida.

Sergeant Felton turned the scene over to Hall. Higginbotham introduced himself and made his report. This included his observations of what he considered Marvin's odd behavior, and Marvin's account of his recent problems. Hall decided on that basis he would take Marvin down to headquarters and question him. He assigned Detective John King to supervise the "scene and body" portion of the investigation.

Once Marvin had signed a consent form allowing the police to search his house, he was escorted to Hall's car and told to wait there. Puzzled, disoriented, Marvin said to Hall, "Why? What for?" Hall reassured him, "Just routine. We'll want a statement from you about what happened, things like that." King then got his men and the crime-lab crew together and entered Marvin's house.

Guarded by uniformed police officers, Marvin was allowed to talk to no one. But neighbor Rabbi Jean Klein, for whom Hilari and Staci baby-sat, brought him a glass of orange juice. That very afternoon Miriam Klein had telephoned the Weinsteins' house several times to ask if either Staci or Hilari would baby-sit for them that evening. Miriam had wondered why no one answered the phone. "I was thinking," she said, "should I run over to the house and knock on the door? I decided not to. Now I think, who knows what turmoil I might have run into there? Anyway, we got a sitter. But when we left the house to go to the movies, we saw all the police cars and the rope around the house. We knew that when there was a rope around the house that somebody was killed there. Of course, there was no question of our going out after that." The Kleins joined the crowd milling outside Marvin's house. No one seemed to know precisely what had happened, except that Staci Weinstein was dead. Shot. "We thought maybe it was an accident," Miriam said. "We knew Marvin kept guns in the house, and we thought maybe she had been playing around with one and accidentally shot herself. Who could believe it was a murder?"

Sometime before eight o'clock, Ben Hall telephoned Detective Joan Clarke. He filled her in on the crime details and asked her to go over to the Rogers' house, interview Hilari, and get any information she could about her past and about Staci's past. Finally, King having everything organized at the scene, Hall took Marvin down to Metro-Dade Homicide Headquarters in Miami. He put him in an interview room, read him his Miranda rights, and had him sign the appropriate forms. Marvin told Hall he was willing to answer questions without the presence of an attorney, since he didn't have anything to hide. Hall got him a cup of coffee and began to interview him. The time was 9:10.

Back at the Weinstein house, detectives Huetter and Munn told Detective King they were going out to begin an area canvass of the neighborhood to see if they could find anybody who had seen anything of interest that afternoon or had any information at all that might help in the investigation.

According to Clarke's subsequent report, filed next day, Hilari volunteered a substantial amount of background information about the family:

Hilari stated that she and the victim were not close, and the victim did not confide in either herself or her father. Hilari said that whenever she or her father would try to get the victim to talk, she would get very nasty with them and withdraw. The victim had gotten violent in the past and had pulled a knife on Hilari only a few weeks ago. The victim and the father had an argument a few weeks ago, and the victim threw a knife at the father and yelled, "Why don't you kill me!"

Hilari said that when their mother was alive, the mother would always take the victim's side, and now that she is deceased their father was able to see both sides of the arguments and did not "play favorites." Hilari further advised that during their mother's illness the victim never spoke about the mother. Hilari said that the victim was afraid to show her feelings.

Hilari further stated that approximately two years ago their house was burglarized. Since the burglary the victim was afraid to stay alone in the house for more than 10–15 minutes. If her father was going out she usually wanted to go with him. If the victim and herself were home alone the victim would always go to sleep first. . . .

Hilari said the victim liked to sleep with her father and in her father's room. She said that approximately four months ago she spoke to her father about the victim sleeping with him. She told him it wasn't right and that she should sleep in her own room. Hilari said at that time the victim was sleeping in her father's room constantly. Hilari said her father did speak to the victim about it, and he told Hilari that the victim was afraid. For a while the victim slept in her own room, but then she began to go back to her father's room to sleep, but not steadily. Hilari also said that Bookie Rogers also spoke to her father about the victim sleeping with him and in his room. Hilari said she really didn't know why the victim wanted to sleep with her father other than being scared.

Hilari said that her father owned two firearms, a small automatic with a holster and a revolver with a holster. A few weeks ago her father took the guns out and showed them to Hilari and the victim. He unloaded them and the victim handled them and the projectiles. Hilari and the victim both dry-fired the two guns. Hilari said the victim could not pull either trigger without her father pressing on her finger. Hilari said the victim was not strong enough to pull the trigger on either gun by herself. Hilari said she never knew where the guns were kept ... a few weeks ago she found the automatic in the holster in a sock lying on the floor between her father's bed and his nightstand. Last night, however, she noticed it was gone. . . .

Hilari said that the victim had a lot of friends at her school, Sabal Palm Elementary ... girlfriends would come over but she does not recall boys coming to the house. Hilari said that to her knowledge the only sexual acts her sister had were some light kissing ... the victim was beginning to develop, had not begun menstruating and was "boy crazy."

Officer Clarke interviewed Bookie Rogers when she'd finished Hilari's interview. Clarke's report says that Bookie stated, ". . . she spoke to Marvin Weinstein approximately one month ago regarding the victim sleeping with him. She told him it was not right, and he stated the victim was scared. Mrs. Rogers further advised that she called the victim's house at 4:30 p.m., but no one answered the phone."

In the meantime Detective King had got his team underway. The entire house was processed for fingerprints, particularly around doorways and inside Staci's bedroom. One of the questions they hoped to answer was the method of entry to the house by whoever had done the killing. At that point, as far as King was concerned, it needn't have been a forced entry. His investigative method, common to homicide investigations, is to work "from the inside out." That is, the primary suspects initially are always the persons closest to the victim. Marvin, or even Hilari, could have simply walked through the front door and committed the crime. His men did find marks on the jalousie windows of the patio bathroom door, which was locked. The windows were dusted with black fingerprint powder. Apparent arm prints turned up, indicating to King that someone had reached through feeling for locks. All those jalousie windows having marks were removed to be sent to the crime lab.

The lab technicians concentrated on Staci's bedroom, though they did find blood smears on the hall bathroom door and footprints on the toilet seat. Chips including the blood smear were taken out of the door, and the toilet seat was collected for lab examination.

A sketch of the entire house was made and photographs taken of the crime scene. The body of Staci itself was dusted for prints. (Hand swabs had been taken from Marvin to test for gunpowder residue before he had been driven away by Ben Hall.) An extremely careful examination was made of Staci's body. The crime-scene report indicated that the body was clad in pink and white trim terry cloth shorts and yellow panties. The clothing was blood-spattered and the panties and shorts turned over on the right side. Blood was observed on the upper right surface of the panties. Blood was smeared in a circular pattern over the victim's back, appearing as though it had been wiped with an article of clothing. Rigor mortis was complete.

There was a gunshot entry wound to the right-side chest area. Another gunshot wound two and a half inches above the right ear. Three lacerations were observed on her head, a bruise at the cheekbone under the right eye, and an abrasion on the inside of her arm, just above the elbow, with gunpowder residue evident—an indication that Staci had raised her arm to ward off a gunshot she saw coming.

The white headboard and a section of the wall near the headboard were blood-spattered. Near the headboard was a spattered pillowcase. On top of the pillow were a pink nightgown and a white nightgown, both spattered. The sheets under the body were blood-soaked. At the foot of the bed on the carpet was a blue and white pullover shirt and a red and white shirt, both bloody. The two articles of clothing appeared to be rolled together. A *Playboy* magazine dated July 1979 was on the carpet. A blood-spattered piece of paper was on top of the magazine. King and other detectives wondered about that magazine. Had it been left there by whoever did the killing?

Of more than routine interest were four blood-spattered, white plastic fragments of a pistol grip found underneath the pillow and two drops of blood near the feet.

The rest of Staci's room was described as typical of a ten-year-old, with dolls and stuffed toys, school books and papers scattered about on shelves and on the floor.

At 10:13, King called in Dr. Charles Wetli, deputy chief medical examiner for Dade County, who arrived about eleven. He examined the body and estimated time of death at about twelve hours earlier. This estimate was subject to modification, however, pending an autopsy the next day.

Meanwhile, Dr. Wetli examined the gunshot wounds and the head and facial abrasions. He checked Staci's perineal area for signs of sexual abuse but found no contusions or other abnormalities there. He found nothing abnormal around or inside the mouth. Swabs

were taken of what appeared to be saliva from the in-
sides of Staci's thighs, from her neck and back. Other
swabs were taken from inside her mouth and outside
her vagina.

As the hours wore on into the early morning, everything at the scene was collected, carefully boxed, sealed,
and labeled, ready to be delivered to the lab: sheets,
pillowcases, headboard, clothing. The *Playboy* magazine
was taken. Her books and papers, toys, even the contents of her wastepaper basket. The bedroom was thoroughly vacuumed and the bag's contents boxed. Items
were taken from Marvin's bedroom, including a pair of
jeans that appeared to have a bloodstain near the zipper.
His two guns were impounded—they found the second,
a .38 revolver, in a stuffed monkey with a hidden zipper
pouch. From the living room couch copies of the *Miami
Herald* were collected and boxed. Crime-scene procedure dictates taking away everything that might have ev-
idential possibilities.

At Metro-Dade Headquarters, Marvin and Detective
Ben Hall faced each other across a simple wooden table in interview room 2. A slight man in any case, five
six and 135 pounds, Marvin appeared even smaller,
shrunken inside himself. He sat there, blinking nervously behind his wire-rimmed eyeglasses, watching
Hall's face. The detective was in no hurry. He let
Marvin sip his coffee from the paper cup and did nothing. Said nothing. Hall also worked "from the inside
out." He knew that a great many homicides are committed by family members, friends, lovers—persons
known to the victim. He also now knew from Officer
Earl Higginbotham a few things about Marvin's recent
past history of troubles.

After a lengthy silence Hall said to Marvin, "Do you
by any chance have a photograph of Staci with you?"

"As a matter of fact, I do," said Marvin. He ex-
tracted from his wallet a color photo of her and handed

it to the detective. Hall excused himself for a moment and brought back the photo and a photocopy, which he placed on the table, facing Marvin. Hall then began talking to Marvin about his own wife, telling him that she, too, was suffering from breast cancer, and so he expressed his sympathy for what Marvin must have gone through.

Marvin told him about the various treatments the doctors had tried for Ruth Ann, those that helped and those that hadn't, and what new treatments he had read about since her death. Once Hall had his man opening up, he then asked Marvin to account for his movements that day, starting from the moment he woke up. Marvin went through it all, describing the morning at home with the children, how Staci hadn't wanted to go to school, his appointments for the day, and what had happened when finally he returned home.

Hall listened in silence. Then, quietly, he said, "Marvin, there are two people who know what happened in your home today. You and me."

"But there must have been a hundred people outside the house tonight. They all know what happened," said Marvin.

"No, Marvin. Just me and you," Hall said. "Look, you'll feel better when you let it all out. I know you didn't mean to do it."

Marvin stared at him for a moment, transfixed, as the implications of Hall's statement sank in. Then he leaped from his chair and began shouting at the detective. "You must be crazy! You think *I* did it? You think I killed my own daughter? What are you talking about? What's the matter with you!" He began to turn toward the door when Hall said calmly, "Sit down please, Marvin. Don't get excited. Look, I know you're out of work, you just lost your wife, you've had emotional problems and you got a lot of stress. I can understand that."

Hall paused as Marvin sat down again, his face betraying his anger. Hall said, "Marvin, you'll feel better if you let it all out. We know what happened. Okay, you went out, you came back, you maybe had a fight with her about something, you snapped, you killed her. Marvin, we even know she slept with you at night."

It was too much for Marvin. He jumped up and leaned across the table, pointed his finger at Hall. "You're crazy! I'm getting out of here. Either you get somebody else in here to interview me or I'll walk out of this room. Right now!"

Hall shrugged, rose, and left the interview room. Marvin sat down, his head buried in his hands. In came Sergeant Art Felton, Hall's superior. He sat down where Hall had been. "Marvin, you've gotta excuse Ben. You have to understand. It was normal for him to accuse you because you're the one who discovered the body. You have to be cleared. Okay?"

Marvin nodded dumbly.

"Now, to help clear you," Felton continued, "we'll need to do a couple of tests. I'd like to get a lab technician in here. Okay with you?"

"What kind of tests?" Marvin asked suspiciously.

"Hair samples. Take a few pictures."

Marvin agreed. Felton called in a lab technician. He pulled a few hairs from Marvin's head and took scrapings from under his fingernails. He boxed and sealed these samples and sent them off to the chemistry lab. The technician then took mug shots of Marvin. Off they went to the photo lab.

When all that was completed, Hall came back. He asked Marvin if he was ready to make a sworn statement for the record. Marvin agreed. He was again advised of his Constitutional rights, waived the presence of an attorney, and related once again his story of the day's events. A steno-reporter recorded and transcribed Marvin's statement.

By this time it was 2:05. Marvin was washed out. Faint with exhaustion, emotional and physical.

The detectives were finished with him for the moment. Felton came back in and said to him, "Come on, Marvin, we'll take you home now." Felton drove the unmarked car while Marvin sat in the backseat with Detective Greg Smith. But he didn't want to go home. He couldn't go home. To that house. He asked Felton to drop him at the home of Rabbi and Miriam Klein. As they drove past his house, Marvin noticed that all the lights were on and several cars were still parked out front.

"They still working in there?" he asked.

"Yeah, guess so," said Felton. "They've got to get everything, Marvin." The crime-scene crew didn't leave Marvin's house until sometime around four in the morning.

Marvin got out of the detectives' car and watched for a moment as it turned around and drove away, red taillights glowing in the darkness. Only when they had disappeared around a corner did he walk up to the front door and ring the bell.

The lights were on in the Kleins' house, too. Rabbi Klein and his wife were not overly surprised to see Marvin at their front door, though he had not been expected. They ushered him in, embraced him, mumbled embarrassed words of sympathy. Miriam took him into the kitchen and made him a cup of tea and two slices of toast. "What do you do with a man whose daughter has just been murdered?" she would say afterward. Marvin told them of his experience with Ben Hall and Art Felton, how Hall had accused him of Staci's murder. Miriam remembers, "I felt then, in the back of my mind, what if he did do it? Do we have a murderer here? I realized of course that was ridiculous."

They talked together for an hour. It was close to four in the morning before the Kleins retired to their bedroom and invited Marvin to sleep on the couch in the living room. Gratefully, Marvin lay down, fully clothed. And closed his eyes. But sleep did not come. As exhausted as he was, sleep did not come. Too many thoughts, too many vivid images, swirled around inside his head. At last, as sunrise was beginning to gild the eastern sky, he surrendered to sleep. But not before a final thought flashed through his mind:

I promised Staci a bicycle for her birthday. Instead, I'll buy her a casket.

Chapter 4

After three hours of fitful sleep, before the Klein family awoke, Marvin lifted himself off the couch, limbs stiff, back aching, and slipped out of the house. He walked in the morning sunlight to his house on the corner. The police ropes were gone. He walked up to the front door. Stopped. Hesitated. Not yet. He was not quite ready. He turned and looked out onto the streets that converged at his corner house. As usual, traffic was light around his neighborhood, though soon nearby Miami Gardens Drive would be clogged with rush-hour traffic. A normal Friday morning. People going to work, children going to school. Most children. Not Staci. Not this morning.

He entered the house and went straight to Staci's room. It was pretty well stripped clean. The lab boys had done their work well, he observed. Another day, another dollar to them. He wondered how many times in a week they were called upon to sweep up the bloody debris left by some lunatic with a gun.

It appeared the lab crew had taken some of her toys, but they had left behind, he was pleased to notice, her favorite: her stuffed dog, Dougan. It reminded him bitterly of Ben Hall's comment about Staci sleeping in his bed. Yes, she had come to his bed, the scared little kid, and with her, always, came Dougan. He took the dog down from its shelf. He held it in his hands and smiled softly. How she loved that little stuffed dog!

There were some things they couldn't take away, he

noted. The blood on the wall. And, as he examined his daughter's bed, the stains on the mattress they'd left behind, where blood had seeped through the sheets. He shook his head in disbelief. Who could have done such a thing? What kind of person would torture and take the life of a ten-year-old girl? No, not a person. A pervert. A demon. An animal. No, not an animal. Animals killed for food, to protect their young, not to destroy the young of others.

After a time he left the bedroom and went to boil water for coffee. He drank it standing up, opened the refrigerator door, closed it again quickly. The thought of food nauseated him. He took the mug of coffee into the living room and sat on the couch, sipping it slowly. Sighing deeply, he looked up at the ceiling. "Well, Ruth Ann," he said to the ceiling, "promises, promises." He rocked back and forth on the couch, the mug of coffee cupped in both hands, moaning softly to himself. Some father. Some promiser. "I'll take care of the girls, don't worry," he had promised his wife on her deathbed.

As he sat there, fragments of a Hebrew song he had learned long ago, as a child in Toronto, came to him, a song with the words of the 22nd Psalm, a plaintive cry to God born out of centuries of pain and persecution: *Eli, Eli, lamah asaftani.* Father, Father, why hast Thou forsaken me?

Am I a bad person? Have I sinned? Have I done such terrible things that I should be so punished? Maybe in some previous life I was evil and now, only now, God is paying me back? If so, then I was the one who should have been stricken ill and died. Not Ruth Ann. I was the one who should have been murdered! Why punish my wife, that she lived to only thirty-seven and suffered so? Why Staci? What sins of the father were visited upon her that she should be allowed only ten years to live out her life?

He glanced at his watch, remembering something

important. With an inward cry of pain he rose and went to the telephone. He dialed the home of Rabbi Klein.

"Rabbi," Marvin said, "you know I'm not an orthodox person, but you would do me a great favor if you would call the medical examiner and ask that when they do the autopsy this morning that they do it according to our religious tradition." Messianic Jews believe that when the Messiah comes, the dead will rise from their graves and live again. Therefore it is important that they have all their body parts and internal organs.

With a heavy heart Marvin then telephoned Sonny Levitt at the Levitt-Weinstein Funeral Home. Just four months earlier they had arranged for the burial of his wife. Before Marvin could explain the call now, Levitt told him he had heard the news and had been about to call himself. Arrangements already were being made. He had been in touch with Ken Kaye, cemetery director at Shalom Memorial Gardens, where Ruth Ann was buried.

"Marvin, don't worry about a thing," Levitt told him. "Between me and Ken we'll take care of everything. We'll pick up the body from the medical examiner and bring her here. Later today, Marvin, just come down and sign some forms. Paperwork. You know. And . . ." Levitt hesitated, "and you'll pick out a casket." Well aware of Marvin's financial circumstances, Levitt would refuse to accept any payment for the funeral.

Next Marvin had to call Canada to tell his mother and Ruth Ann's father. Again, what to say to these people? So soon after breaking the news to them about the death of his wife—and now this? His mother was eighty and ailing. He was afraid to call her. Staci was the light of her life. But the calls had to be made. His mother screamed and cried, and he cried with her. Then he spoke to his father-in-law, Gord Berman. "I'm on my way," Mr. Berman said. "I'll be there today if I can, if not, then tomorrow."

With the house no longer cordoned off, friends and neighbors came by all morning to express their sympathy and offer help. Whatever he needed, he should but ask. Ask? Marvin thought. What could I ask of these well-meaning people? What I would ask for they could not supply. And actually, at the moment he needed to be alone. He was grateful for their kindliness, but he still had much to do. He called the Rogerses and asked about Hilari. She was fine and resting. He asked David to come with him to the funeral home and lend his support, just as he had when arrangements had been made for the funeral of Ruth Ann. Then he called his lawyer, Stuart Markus, and broke the news. Markus said he must see him that day, as soon as possible.

Marvin told him he'd come over after he'd been to the funeral home. When he got to Levitt-Weinstein, he said to Sonny, "Please fix up Staci so that Hilari and I can see her one last time before she's put in the ground."

David Rogers tried to talk him out of that. "Marvin, why not just remember her the way she was when she was alive? It'll be too emotional for you and especially for Hilari to see her in the casket."

Marvin would not be swayed. "Can you do it?" he asked Sonny Levitt. "Can you fix her up?"

As tactfully as he could, Sonny explained that it was possible but difficult. "You know, Marvin," he said, "because of the way she was killed . . . and the autopsy, I might not be able to do a proper reconstruction."

"I know you'll do the best you can," Marvin said. "I want this. Just like when Ruth Ann died and I wanted to see her and I wanted the kids to see her. It was a good thing." Inside, his guts were churning. He was burning with rage and frustration. What a conversation! he thought. If I could get my hands on whoever did this . . .

Outside, in the parking lot, he broke down and wept. And David Rogers wept with him. "I can't believe it yet, David," Marvin said. "It's like a nightmare. I can't believe Staci is gone, I've lost her forever. It seems like I just left her, a few hours ago, watching Popeye the sailor man on television. And that beautiful, innocent child is gone!"

Rogers shook his fists at the sky. "Who could have done this? I would tear him apart with my bare hands!"

"All I think about, David," Marvin said as they drove back home, "is the terror she went through. Maybe she cried out for me to help her and I wasn't there. She was such a shy little girl. She didn't like to be touched . . . and when I think of what was done . . ." He couldn't say the words.

The entire neighborhood was traumatized by the murder of Staci Weinstein. Such an act of violence had not occurred in that quiet backwater of North Miami Beach in anyone's memory. Crime, certainly. Burglaries, car thefts. Maybe a store robbery. But a murder? Of a ten-year-old child? That same Friday morning after the murder the hardware and building-supplies stores did a brisk business in door locks and chains. Marvin's neighbors began inquiries about burglar alarms, home security systems with twenty-four-hour monitoring. Guard dogs. Parents worried about their children and took new precautions, drove them daily to and from school or walked them to the school bus in the morning, waited for the bus in the afternoon. For many, nothing was ever the same. Two of Staci's close friends needed prolonged counseling after the murder, and to this day, now in their twenties, those two girls cannot bear to be alone in a house or drive their cars without a companion.

Staci's sixth-grade classmates at Sabal Palm Ele-

mentary School were deeply affected. That Friday
morning as they arrived in class some knew of her
murder, some didn't. Those that knew told the others.
Many wept openly as the school's principal, Gertrude
Edelman, came in and addressed the class. "You have
just taken a large step into growing up," she told them.
"Life must go on and you must accept the bitter with
the sweet. It is part of a cycle. Birth, life, death. Some
die sooner than others."

Staci's teacher, Jacqueline Newton, told reporters for
the *Miami Herald,* "Staci was a happy child, good student, pleasing person, a real sweet kid. One you would
want to take home with you. She was a very popular
little girl."

In the days to follow, Staci's classmates collected
money and in her memory planted a small tree in the
school grounds. For all these years Marvin has
watched it grow and cannot help but think, as he drives
by the school: it should be Staci growing tall and
straight and beautiful, not her tree.

According to the newspaper's story, "The Metro-
Dade homicide squad said it had few clues. Maybe
there was a burglar, investigators said. There were no
obvious signs of forced entry. 'The window and door
locks are not the most secure in the world,' said Sgt.
Arthur Felton, head of the team investigating Staci's
death."

Late Friday afternoon Marvin went to see his lawyer,
Stuart Markus. Among the several items discussed was
the attorney's recommendation that Marvin call a press
conference for the next day and get the television media involved. Marvin would make a televised plea for
the killer to surrender, and the publicity might prompt
someone who had information about the killer to come
forward.

The press conference was held the next day at
Markus's office in Coral Gables; Marvin had insisted
that he did not want the press and television crews

marching all over his house and certainly not into Staci's bedroom.

With Hilari at his side, Marvin looked into the TV camera and appealed to Staci's killer: "You are very sick, and it will be very hard to live with yourself after what you have done," he said. "Please, turn yourself in to the police so that you can get some help before you commit another terrible crime."

Later that Saturday Sonny Levitt called Marvin and said he could see Staci before the burial next day. She would need some of her clothes, however. With Hilari, Marvin went through Staci's closets. "Let's find one of her favorite things," he said. Then, with a brittle laugh: "Can you believe it, Hilari? Just a few months ago the three of us were doing the same thing for your mother." Finally they chose a pretty outfit Staci had worn for birthday parties. They picked out underwear and panty hose to go with it. As each garment was chosen, he held it in his arms for a moment, then placed it gently on a clean sheet he'd placed over the blood-stained mattress on her bed. Each garment he touched sent a lance of pain into his chest. He had a sense of being able to feel her inside her clothes still, to smell the child that had worn them so prettily not that long ago. Yet a lifetime ago.

They gathered Staci's clothing together and brought them to Sonny Levitt at the funeral home.

Sunday morning, the day of the funeral, a black limousine from Levitt-Weinstein arrived at Marvin's house. Together with Hilari, his neighbor Stanley Saul, and Ruth Ann's father, he rode to the chapel for the morning's service. There Sonny Levitt took Marvin and Hilari in to see Staci in her casket. Marvin looked down at her. Dead! Dead! What a waste! he thought. He reached out and touched her head, felt a bump. Where the bullet went in? he wondered.

"She looks better from the side," said Hilari.

"Yes, yes, she does," Marvin agreed.

He and Hilari kissed Staci on the forehead and said to her softly, "Good-bye, Staci." Then they cradled in her arms a little blue and white Smurf doll she had loved and often slept with. "So she wouldn't be alone," he said to Sonny Levitt before the casket lid was closed.

Several hundred people attended the service. Then the funeral cortege wound its way through the streets to the Shalom Memorial Gardens.

By bitter irony, on that Sunday, October 17, 1982, Marvin had scheduled the unveiling ceremony for his wife's headstone at the cemetery. But he cancelled it. Instead, he buried his daughter beside her mother.

On Staci's headstone are inscribed these words:

Staci Leigh Weinstein
A beautiful child, deeply loved,
never to be forgotten.

Chapter 5

Ben Hall wasted no time launching his investigation. When Sergeant Felton and Detective Greg Smith returned to the station at two-thirty Friday morning after dropping Marvin at the Klein's house, Hall was waiting for them, and they conducted a strategy meeting. Hall told Smith to check with the burglary sections at Metro-Dade Substation 6 and at the North Miami Beach Police Station and dig out whatever he could find on known and active burglars. Hall, with Huetter and Munn and King, would continue the area canvassing.

Smith managed a few hours' sleep, and by nine-thirty he was making the rounds of the two police stations compiling a list of known burglars and sex offenders. As he was finishing that task at the North Miami Beach station, Hall got him on the radio and told him to get back to Station 6. The roofers, Klosky and Carlucci, had agreed to come in, be interviewed, and have their fingerprints taken. Steve Carlucci, who was the one who actually had spoken to Marvin inside the house, confirmed the account Marvin had given earlier to Hall. Carlucci described Marvin as wearing blue jeans and a shirt. He said he saw a young girl with Marvin, but he didn't remember what she had been wearing. Klosky had little to add, since he hadn't entered the house. Both men were fingerprinted and released.

Smith was not finished for the day. He returned to

Metro-Dade Homicide Headquarters and, as Hall had already arranged, picked up a police diver and drove up to Marvin's house. Marvin was not happy to see them. He was still in a state of shock, hurt and angry that Hall had tried to pin on him the murder of his own daughter. Smith was as tactful as possible under the circumstances. He explained to Marvin that they intended to search his patio pool, where the water was so greenishly murky the bottom couldn't be seen.

"We haven't used it since my wife died," Marvin said. "I haven't taken care of it. So what do you expect to find down there?"

"We don't know," said Smith. "With luck, some physical evidence of some kind. We check out everything." Smith didn't say he was hoping to find the murder weapon. It was a long shot, but you never knew. In any case, the bottom of the pool had to be searched. No lab reports had come through yet on all the items taken from the house, but it had been easy to ascertain immediately that neither of the two guns taken from Marvin had been fired recently. That didn't eliminate Marvin as the prime suspect. It only eliminated those two guns as the possible murder weapon.

Nothing was found in the pool.

Dr. Charles Wetli's autopsy report is not comfortable reading. According to the autopsy notes, Staci had first been pistol-whipped about the head, inflicting a fracture of the skull. Then shot in the chest. Neither the head trauma nor the gunshot wound to the body "would necessarily result in immediate or total loss of consciousness," Dr. Wetli wrote. Staci probably was still conscious when she was shot a second time—the fatal head shot. Both bullets were recovered from the body. They were from a .22.

She had not been raped. But the clear liquid found on her inner thighs and vagina area proved to be saliva.

At a later date, Dr. Wetli would write that Staci "would have survived had she not been shot."

On Monday, the day after Staci's funeral, as practiced by many followers of the Jewish faith, Marvin began the traditional week of sitting shiva—a week of mourning with Hilari and Gord Berman during which time they would be visited daily by dozens of friends and neighbors coming to express their sorrow and sympathy. As was customary, since mourners were not supposed to be troubled by preparing food during that week, gifts of cooked and cold meats and smoked fish would be brought to the house, pots of coffee constantly brewed. Traditionally, too, the mourners were not supposed to leave the house of mourning. However, that Monday afternoon necessity broke that convention.

Ben Hall and Sergeant Art Felton appeared on Marvin's doorstep. With apologies, Hall asked Marvin to telephone his lawyer, Stuart Markus, and ask if he would allow him to take a polygraph test. "This could help eliminate you as a possible suspect," Hall explained. But there was more. Hall wanted Marvin and Hilari to accompany him and Felton to the serology laboratory at headquarters for a blood test. Hall didn't elaborate except to say that this also could help eliminate both of them as suspects.

"Right now?" Marvin asked. "You want us to come with you right now? I have people here!"

Again Hall apologized. Yes, it was necessary. The sooner they could get this done, the better it was for Marvin's own benefit.

Incensed, Marvin called his attorney. Markus told him he should refuse to take a polygraph, but should take the blood test. Marvin conveyed this information to the detectives and agreed that he and Hilari would go down to the lab for the blood tests.

Over the weekend the Serology Unit at Homicide had been busy. The serologist assigned to the case,

Theresa Washam, had diligently tested blood samples taken from everything collected from Marvin's house as possible evidence.

On the Friday morning after Staci's murder she had been given all the pertinent items taken from Staci's bedroom: the bloody sheets from her bed, hair samples found on the sheets, Staci's clothing, swabs from Staci taken for a rape test, and Marvin's trousers with the bloodstain.

At the time, the sophisticated DNA testing of blood samples in vogue today was not yet used at Metro-Dade. Instead, enzyme typing was used. An enzyme is a protein substance found in the blood and, just as some of us have blue eyes and some brown eyes, enzymes are also hereditary. And each one of them has a different number of types. Because homicide-scene evidence of blood samples virtually always comes in the form of dried blood, the techniques for testing that have been developed use what is called anti-sera, made in the laboratory, that are specific to each one of the blood groups, such as an anti-A or anti-B, for example. They will react with whatever blood group is present.

What Theresa found on the bloodied sheets she tested became a key factor in eventually breaking the Staci Weinstein murder case. It was such an important and clever piece of lab work she received a commendation for it.

"The sheets were very interesting," Theresa said. "In a case like this where someone is injured the way [Staci] was, you're going to have a lot of bleed-out. On the bottom sheet, the sheet she was lying on, there were large areas of bleed-out. On the top sheet, which was sort of crumpled up at the foot of the bed when they found her, there was a small smear of blood kind of in the center of the sheet that looked totally out of place with all the other bloodstains. It was a round, very crusty drop. Another part of our job is interpreting bloodstains, and this round stain would have been the result of something dropping straight down at a ninety-degree angle. Not a smear. I don't know why, but the first thing that went through my head was that, gee, it looks like somebody had a nosebleed or something that was just dripping down.

"In the meantime I had found out what blood type Staci was, and what all her enzymes were. She was type AB blood. The rarest. Her particular enzyme profile broke down to one in perhaps ten thousand people.

"When I tested that drop on the sheet it turned out to be type A. I could tell that right off the bat. So I ran all the other enzymes, and a lot of them were different from hers, so I knew it could not have been her blood. It was not her father's blood. It was not the other daughter's blood. So we had this beautiful profile now of someone's blood. We had no idea whose, of course."

Not yet.

This was why Ben Hall had appeared at Marvin's house on Monday. Theresa had called him immediately with news of her discovery. Hall was excited. "I was excited, too," said Theresa. "It's very unusual to find foreign blood in a case like this where there is so much of the victim's blood at the scene." At the minimum it held potential as a real lead, a piece of vitally important evidence in a case where there were no leads at all to follow except for the inside-out pressure on Marvin himself that Hall felt was rapidly leading nowhere.

Until the serology report came in on Monday, Marvin had remained the prime suspect. There were no other immediate leads. The forced-entry possibility by a burglar had been examined and all but discarded. Some forearm prints had been found on the back door louvers that had been taken away, but the door locks had been intact. The front door also showed no sign of a forced entry. The possibility remained that Staci had known her assailant and had let him into the house. Or ... had he used his own key?

Theresa's serology discovery by Monday evening following the blood tests on Marvin and Hilari had all but eliminated Marvin as Hall's prime suspect. Not completely as a suspect, however. He could have been at the scene with somebody else. He might have hired somebody else. Homicide detectives had encountered stranger scenarios in their grim careers. No, Marvin remained very much in Hall's mind.

All through the weekend the detectives had canvassed the area, questioning everybody: who lived in which house; where had they been on the day of the murder; had anyone seen anything or anyone suspicious or different around the Weinstein home that day.

This legwork, monotonous as it is for homicide detectives, often becomes a crucial part of a murder investigation. Homicide cases grow colder day by day, but patience is more than just a virtue in a homicide investigator—it's a necessity.

Most of the neighbors interviewed offered no information whatsoever. Others reported seeing workmen in the neighborhood: roofers, garbage collectors, the mailman, carpet cleaners, gardeners. Two people mentioned seeing a yellow van in front of Marvin's house sometime on the day of the murder—late morning or early afternoon. That stirred the detectives' interest. Marvin owned a yellow van, and men were sent out to recheck Marvin's alibi for the day.

On a telephoned tip, Mark Huetter interviewed one of Marvin's close neighbors who told him that between eleven and eleven-thirty on the day of the murder she had heard a young girl and a man conversing in Marvin's yard. She thought it was Staci's voice, but the man—an older man, she thought—was not Marvin. Even more interesting, her husband said that about an hour later he had heard what sounded like two gunshots coming from the area of Marvin's house. And then he looked out his window and saw a man doing yard work nearby. They hadn't thought anything about all this until they learned of Staci's murder.

On Sunday, Hall interviewed Ted Dipple, a neighbor of Marvin's, who said that a week before the murder he'd noticed two men he didn't know mowing Marvin's lawn. Marvin asked him if he wanted them to cut his grass, too. Mr. Dipple agreed and hired the two men. He described them to Hall as black males, one with glasses, a mustache, and an Afro haircut graying at the sides. The other had braided hair. Dipple said if necessary he would be able to identify the two men. He stated further that on the morning of the murder two workmen had been repairing a leak in his roof. The two men turned out to be Klosky and Carlucci, who had given Marvin an estimate that same morning.

A Mrs. Gold said a telephone repairman had been working in the neighborhood on the day of the murder and had been working at her house in the afternoon hours.

A boy of eleven told Hall that a friend had told him he'd seen a white man with black hair and a black beard running from the Weinstein house on the day of the homicide. The boy said he couldn't remember which friend told him this story.

Two joggers who lived on Marvin's street said they had seen the mailman about one-fifteen. They also had observed an old green car with a white male sitting inside it parked across the street from the Weinstein house. They alleged that the house where the car had been parked had been visited several times by police. They said they didn't know why but suspected that it was a "drug house." An investigation by Hall shortly afterward would disclose that the resident of the house in question had been arrested previously for sexual battery and had a prison record and an FBI rap sheet.

Sergeant Felton contacted the U.S. Postal Service and was told the letter carrier for the area was a man named Scott Fine. Felton got in touch with the man, and Fine was interviewed. He told Felton that at about 12:25 he had delivered the mail to the Weinstein house. He said there had been a small dog tied up to a pole in the garden. He petted the dog for a few moments and was on his way back to his mail truck, parked in front of the house, when a girl he thought was about nine or ten years old came out of the house and told him that the dog wouldn't bite. She was wearing shorts and a sleeveless shirt, Fine said.

Hall and Huetter found a couple, Harry and Lili Morgenthaler, who said two men from the Stanley Steemer Carpet Cleaner Company had cleaned their carpets that day, sometime during the morning hours. Hall contacted Simon Blake at the company, who told him that the two carpet cleaners were John Pierson and Edward Wasko. Hall asked Blake to have them call him to make an appointment for interviews.

On Tuesday, the nineteenth, Hall obtained subpoenas from the Dade County State Attorney's Office for the school records of both Staci and Hilari. He and Virgil Munn took the subpoenas and handed one to the principal at JFK Junior High School, Florence Linden. She gave them copies of Hilari's records and agreed to cooperate with their request to bring Hilari's teachers to her office for interviews.

The consensus among Hilari's teachers was that she was a bright student, had no attitude problems, got along well with her classmates, and had a good attendance record. One of her teachers, in fact, called her "a teacher's delight." Checking out Hilari's movements for October 14, Hall learned that students went to lunch at the school cafeteria between twelve-thirty and one-thirty and were not allowed to leave during that hour.

Joel Goldstein, Hilari's swimming coach, advised Hall that on the day of the homicide Hilari had turned up at the pool for practice about four. The pool actually was not at the school but about a fifteen-minute

bike ride away. On that day, he said, Hilari swam so
well he moved her up from the B team to the A team.
The coach said practice usually let out at six, but since
the team was showing so much improvement he had
kept them practicing a little longer. The detectives
questioned some of the team members about Hilari but
discovered nothing of significance.

It was time now for Hall to take advantage of the foreign blood-type evidence Theresa had given him.
Therefore as he and his team continued to canvass the
area and interview persons who had either worked
there or visited there on the day of the crime, he began
asking interviewees to make appointments with
Theresa Washam for blood tests (they were the simple
finger-stick kind). At the same time he returned to
Marvin and asked him to provide a list of all persons
who might have entered the house in the weeks and
months preceding the crime. He wanted to check out
their fingerprints and their blood.

Marvin was not pleased with this; he felt that he was
being asked to turn in his friends and neighbors. Hall
did convince him, however, that it was important. Re-
luctantly Marvin gave him a list of names, which included Stanley Saul, David Rogers, and Alan Sacharoff
among them. No problems arose with the list. Everybody on it willingly went down to police headquarters,
was fingerprinted, then blood-tested by Theresa
Washam.

Next, Hall contacted several police departments in
north Dade County and asked for names of persons
known to have police records of "lewd and lascivious
behavior." When he got the names he sent Detective
Jim Fraley out to interview every man on the list and
bring him in for questioning, fingerprinting, and a
blood test. Fraley found a bizarre group of men. One
of them admitted to having a sexual preference for

children and had served time in Florida hospitals for treatment.

All the men Fraley interviewed gave him an alibi for the day, which he proceeded to check out, and all submitted voluntarily to fingerprinting and blood tests.

On October 21, Hall picked up a hot lead. A Metro-Dade homicide detective, Jim Ratcliff (not part of his team) said he'd received a call from a City of Miami homicide detective named Rimondi, who said he had got a tip from an informant named Thomas. The man said he knew who had killed the Weinstein girl—and gave him the name George Reece. Rimondi told Ratcliff that Thomas wanted money for the information. According to Thomas, Rimondi said, on the day of Staci's murder he'd had an appointment with Reece for that afternoon, but Reece hadn't shown up until evening and told Thomas that he'd done something bad. He'd just killed a little girl.

Sergeant Felton and Detective Virgil Munn at once drove down to a motel on Washington Avenue in Miami Beach where Thomas said Reece was living. The desk clerk said he was out, but he knew where Reece worked. Felton and Munn drove there and found him. He agreed to appear at Metro-Dade headquarters for questioning, fingerprinting, and a blood test.

Reece told the detectives that he had gone to a neighborhood bar early in the morning and had remained there until he was drunk. He said he went home about eleven-thirty and slept till around five. Then a few friends came over and they all got drunk together. He said they left about seven-thirty or so. At about eight-thirty, Reece said, he had gone to the house of one of those friends and drunk some more. That's all he remembered.

Munn asked him if he had killed Staci Weinstein.

Reece said he had not. And agreed that if requested he would take a polygraph test.

* * *

Theresa Washam was a very busy serologist. A parade of persons sent in by Hall and his team had to be blood-tested and their samples put through her enzyme tests. This was tedious, time-consuming work. Each blood sample might take two or three days for a complete enzyme analysis, and Theresa reckoned she did tests on more than twenty people. There was a continuous stream; as the detectives interviewed new leads, they sent them in to the lab for blood tests.

On October 28, Eddie Wasko, one of the Stanley Steemer carpet cleaners, came in for an interview with Huetter, followed by fingerprinting and a blood sample. He told Huetter that he and his partner, John Pierson, had gone to the Morgenthaler residence about two o'clock on the afternoon of the murder. They finished the job about three-fifteen. As he began reloading his truck, he sent Pierson around the neighborhood to hand out advertising flyers. Pierson was gone for about fifteen or twenty minutes, Wasko stated. Then they both left the area.

Pierson himself didn't come in until November 8. He agreed to have his fingerprints taken, and then Theresa took a blood sample. Pierson's statement to Huetter matched his partner's. He said he hadn't seen anything suspicious in the neighborhood as he was passing out the flyers.

The investigation continued. Hall contacted Bill Garrison of the Metro-Dade Psychological Department and asked if he could put together a possible profile of the type of person who would commit such a crime. Hall also sent to the crime lab at Tallahassee, the state capital, latent prints from the crime scene. Tallahassee had a fingerprint laser there that was better than Metro-Dade's. Hall thought that perhaps they could bring out better prints.

On the same day that Pierson came in for his interview, Hall got word from the North Miami Beach police that one of their units had stopped a young man named Shelby who was seen to be running around the area naked looking in windows. Hall and Munn went to the man's house (he'd been released on bail), but he refused to cooperate with the homicide investigation. His lawyer called Hall the next day and said the same thing: he believed his client had nothing to do with the homicide, and any further contact should be made through him, not his client.

The investigation sputtered to a halt. There were no new leads. The area had been combed for the names of anybody alien to the neighborhood who had been working or visiting on October 14. Men with sex-crimes records had been interviewed. Men with burglary records had been traced and interviewed. Telephoned tips had not panned out. Alibis had been checked and rechecked—including Marvin's. So far—nothing.

Then, on November 19, Theresa Washam telephoned Hall. "Ben, we got lucky," she said. "I've got a name for you. That foreign spot of blood on the sheet? It matches John Pierson."

Chapter 6

His week of formal mourning completed, Marvin went on to his job as a baker at Grand Union, unaware of what progress, if any, was being made by Ben Hall and his team. He knew that many people were being brought in for questioning, for fingerprinting, for blood tests. Whether or not any of this was productive he had no idea. The detectives were not forthcoming. Every day Marvin telephoned Homicide and asked if there was anything new, any leads, any suspects, any progress. He spoke to Hall, to Felton, to Smith, or whoever answered the phone. And every day he received courteous but unenlightening replies.

A routine set in. He would report at the Grand Union store at 5:00 A.M., go through the motions of the mixing and baking, managing somehow to function while he asked himself over and over, Who killed Staci? When he could steal a few moments he would telephone Homicide from the bakery. Otherwise he would telephone as soon as he returned home about two. For hours afterward he would sit alone in the house pondering. Who killed Staci? How can I find out? What are the cops doing? Am I still a suspect?

When his telephone calls availed him nothing, Marvin began turning up at Metro-Dade Headquarters to badger Hall or anybody else in Homicide who would give him an update on progress. Marvin knew no boundaries. He was not intimidated by rank. He railed at the lieutenant and the captain and the police chief himself about the lack of progress.

"Nothing's happening!" he would cry. "Nobody's doing anything! The murderer could be a thousand miles away by now, and all you guys are doing is trying to nail me with this! You still think I killed my own daughter!"

The cops were very patient with Marvin. As toughened as they were to homicides, this one sickened them. They were desperately anxious to solve the murder, and now, following the serology report by Theresa Washam, they had a name, a prime suspect. Marvin was just about a hundred percent cleared, according to Hall. But they could not give what they had to Marvin.

Detective Greg Smith recalls: "I spoke to Marvin many times. I told him, 'Marvin, we're working on it.' Maybe he didn't believe we were. But Marvin wanted to find out everything he could find out. I understood that then. I understand that now. But we are not at liberty to discuss what we're doing. Even with the families. Because if we do, if we go to court and certain information is brought out saying, only the killer knew it . . . bullshit! The defense says the family talked to people, talked to the press, and that's how my client found out about that.

"We try to be sympathetic. We try to keep them informed as much as we can. But we cannot get into the specifics of what we're doing, we can't get into the specifics of our suspects, because it might harm the investigation. In Marvin's case, he kept calling and calling and calling. Well, maybe we were a little short with him."

On many an afternoon and evening Marvin would wander the nearby streets, talking to neighbors, talking to anybody he would happen to meet, retelling his melancholy tale like some latter-day Ancient Mariner. In effect he was retracing the footsteps of the homicide detectives: asking about anything or anybody seen or heard on that day that had been unusual, suspicious. Sometimes well-meaning people would telephone him, or stop him on the street, or ring his doorbell offering what they thought would be useful information. Several claimed to have an "in" with the police and told Marvin they would get some information for him about the progress of the case.

Some nights he would have dinner at the Rogers' home, and saw Hilari. Sometimes he would go over to the Sacharoffs' and dine with them. It made little difference to Marvin where he ate, what he ate, or if he ate. Nothing was important to him but finding Staci's killer. He saw or cared nothing of what was going on around him. As a result, Hilari suffered.

Both needed, and for a time received, psychological counseling. But as far as Hilari was concerned, "my father was dead. Whoever killed Staci killed him, too. After that he was never again the father I once knew."

She couldn't reach him. When she returned home after two months with the Rogerses, it was as though she wasn't there. If she wanted to show him a school paper she'd done, or tell him about her swimming, he brushed her aside. He had no time for her or anybody, or anything that did not bear directly on finding out who had killed Staci. One day Hilari came home from school in tears and told him a girl in her class had said to her, "I heard you killed your sister." Marvin shrugged it off. No hug, no reaching out, no soothing words. He was empty of all that. Who cared what some stupid kid said?

Somewhere in the deep recesses of his mind Marvin knew he was doing wrong. Once upon a time Hilari had been "daddy's little girl." That he still loved her was beside the point. It's quite common that the dead child takes over the parent's heart, mind, and very soul. And the living child is the loser.

He was to discover this for himself when he was introduced to an organization called Parents of Murdered Children. As 1982 was drawing to a close, a member of the south Florida group, a woman named Audrey Sweet, telephoned Marvin and spoke to him about joining them. Her own son had been murdered just two days after the killing of Staci. Marvin turned her down. "My head isn't into it," he told her. "I have no time for things like that now." But she tried him again and again in the new year, until eventually Marvin was ready.

As soon as Theresa Washam gave Ben Hall the name John Pierson, the detective was on his way to the lab. "How sure are you?" he asked her. "Very sure," she said. "I still have a sixth and final enzyme test to run which will add to that certainty, but I wanted to tell you right away what I found."

"When will that be?" Hall asked her.

"Two days. I'll need two more days."

On November 21, Theresa called Hall again and confirmed her findings: not only did the drop of blood on the sheet match John Pierson's enzyme profile, but she'd also tested blood found on Staci's panties. To Theresa the bloodstains were consistent with someone's fingers. Those, too, were consistent with Pierson's blood type.

Well, thought Hall, I'd better get that guy down here.

Late the next afternoon Hall himself picked up Pierson and brought him back to Metro-Dade Homicide for an interview. With Detective Virgil Munn as a witness, Hall read Pierson an Advice of Constitutional Rights Form Before Interview and had him initial each page. Pierson waived the presence of an attorney and at 5:50 Hall began the interview.

Pierson stuck to the same story he'd told when first interviewed: he and Eddie Wasko had arrived at the Morgenthaler house about two and left about four. He said that after Wasko had finished cleaning the carpets, the machine had broken down. While the machine was being fixed, Wasko sent him around the neighborhood to deliver Stanley Steemer flyers. Pierson said he thought he delivered about nine of them.

Hall knocked that story down. He told Pierson his men had done a canvass of the neighborhood, and not one person said they'd received a Stanley Steemer flyer. So if, as he claimed, he had been gone from the truck for fifteen or twenty minutes supposedly handing out flyers—what was he *really* doing during that time?

Pierson said he didn't know. Maybe he blacked out.

Hall asked: "How often have you blacked out in the past?"

It was the first time ever, Pierson said, so he didn't know what happened during that fifteen or twenty minutes.

Hall then confronted him with the serology evidence. He told Pierson that his blood had been found at the scene of the murder. He explained to Pierson in detail how the foreign blood at the scene and his blood had been put through enzyme tests, and they matched. Hall told him how slim the chances were that anybody else at that time and place would have those same blood enzymes.

Pierson protested that he had no idea how his blood could have been left at the scene of the homicide. He insisted that he hadn't killed the girl, and he didn't know of anyone who might have done it.

Hall shook his head slowly. "I think you killed her."

Pierson began to cry uncontrollably. He asked Hall how long somebody would have to spend in prison for committing a crime like that.

"It would be up to the judge and jury," Hall said. "But the maximum penalty would be the electric chair."

Pierson wanted to know if help would be available to somebody who committed such an act. Hall told him psychiatric help might be available. Pierson also wanted to know if it was possible to be married while in jail. Hall said that sort of thing could be looked into later.

Hall said: "I'd like you to draw a diagram of the victim's residence and show on the diagram how a person who would commit this act could possibly enter the house."

Pierson said the easiest way would be through the front door. He began drawing a picture of the living room/dining area that Hall noted was consistent with the Weinstein house. Pierson began drawing Staci's bedroom, then scratched it out and drew the bedrooms on the opposite side of the house. Then, as he began to draw the patio area, he became upset, tore the paper into tiny pieces, and threw it into the wastepaper basket.

Hall looked at him calmly and said, "What would make somebody commit such a crime on a young, innocent victim?"

Pierson lowered his eyes. His hands were in his lap, held as though in prayer. "I can't," he said. "I just can't tell you." Again he began to cry. As Hall continued to talk to him, he placed his hands over his ears as though to block out the sound of the detective's voice. "I didn't do anything!" he cried. "I didn't rape or commit any such acts on such a young girl. Anybody who did such a thing would have to be sick!" Again he asked Hall what kind of help a person could get for committing such acts as Hall had described.

Pierson then began to relate to Hall stories about his childhood. Between the ages of three and six, he had been the victim of child abuse by his mother, who had spent many years in an asylum for the mentally ill. One time his mother had tied him up and locked him in a closet for two or three days without food and water because he had done something wrong. Another time, when his mother's boyfriend was with her, she tied him up and gagged him and placed him in a cabinet, turning it over so that he was left in that position for several days.

Hall listened to all this in astonishment. Pierson went on to relate that when his mother was mad at him she would beat him with a rose bush, causing severe lacerations. One day, to punish him, she forced his hand onto a stove's electric burner. Years ago, Pierson said, when they had been living up north, his mother had gotten mad at him, tied him up, and thrown him out into the snow. He was outside for hours, he said, before an elderly lady saw him and took him to the hospital, where he almost died.

At nine-thirty Pierson again held his hands over his ears and said he didn't want to talk anymore. Hall asked him if he would voluntarily give hair and saliva samples. Pierson agreed, and the samples were taken and sent to serology. Hall also got Pierson to agree to take a polygraph examination the next day.

Hall took him home. When he returned to his desk, he telephoned Pierson's father and related to him everything that had happened during the interview, and that his son had agreed to take a polygraph test.

Donald Pierson agreed that it was a good idea. He, too, would like to clear up the situation.

At 7:35 the next evening, at Slattery's Polygraph Office, polygraph examiner Kent Jurney gave Pierson his test, while Hall waited in another room. Pierson failed it. Jurney told him he'd shown deception in his replies. When Jurney left the examination room to advise Hall of the results, Pierson phoned his father and stepmother and told them to come and get him. He wanted to go home.

Jurney, Hall, and Pierson waited for Pierson's parents in the lobby of the building. When they arrived, Jurney told them of his findings. Pierson's deceptions, he said, meant that either he had committed the homicide himself or quite possibly knew who had committed the crime.

Both father and stepmother demurred. They were not convinced of Jurney's conclusions. They claimed in objection that Pierson had a very bad memory, and though he was nineteen they believed that actually he had the mentality of a ten-year-old child. He was extremely forgetful and had trouble remembering most routine daily activities.

As this conversation continued, Pierson suddenly became belligerent. "I was told to lie!" he said. "Eddie told me to lie about handing out the flyers!" He said Wasko also had told him to lie about being gone from the job they were working on for fifteen or twenty minutes. "I never left the job! It was Eddie. Eddie left for fifteen or twenty minutes!"

"Why would you lie about that?" Hall asked him.

Pierson said he just had gone along with what Wasko told him to say. He repeated the reply when his father asked him the same question.

Suddenly Pierson began yelling at the top of his lungs. "I didn't do it! I didn't kill anybody!" Then, more subdued, he said to Hall that he didn't think he had done it. But as Hall started to question him about that, Pierson stormed from the lobby and sat outside near his father's van.

Pierson's parents were shaken by this performance. Hall told them he was only trying to get at the truth, but he did believe that their son had committed the homicide. Donald Pierson said that he, too, would like to know the truth, and would cooperate any way he could. But he did not believe that his son was guilty of the crime.

Hall turned to the question of Eddie Wasko. Was he involved? Had he told Pierson to lie about the flyers and left the job as Pierson had claimed? If so, why? There was now no question in Hall's mind that Pierson had been at the scene of the homicide. What acts he had actually committed there was still very much a mystery. Following up on Wasko, Hall found out that he had worked for Stanley Steemer in Phoenix, Arizona, as well as in Youngstown, Ohio. He contacted the police departments in both cities and asked them to run a check on Wasko to see whether or not he had a criminal record. Both departments replied that Wasko had no sheet with them.

On December 1, in a bizarre turn of events, Hall got a phone call from a private detective named Barney Long, who said he'd been retained by an attorney named Jeffrey Weiner, acting for John Pierson. Long said they were conducting their own investigation regarding the involvement of John Pierson in the Staci Weinstein homicide. Long told Hall that he had taken Pierson to the University of Miami, where a college professor hypnotized Pierson. Long said he had a tape of the session and Pierson had said he did not commit the homicide. Also, Pierson claimed that Wasko carried a white towel which he used to wrap a handgun in. Finally, Long said that if Hall wanted to contact Pierson again, he should do so through attorney Jeffrey Weiner.

Hall didn't know what to make of all that, except for the fact that Pierson now had a lawyer. He filed the information in the back of his mind. More important to the investigation, later that day he brought Wasko in for another interview. Wasko said he had a good memory and clearly recalled that at the Morgenthalers' house, since Pierson had just been standing around doing nothing while he, Wasko, had to repair the float mechanism in the truck, he gave Pierson some Stanley Steemer flyers to hand out around the neighborhood. Wasko said this generally was something he gave his assistants to do. Pierson was away fifteen to twenty minutes, Wasko said, repeating his earlier story. He did add this time that when Pierson returned from giving out the flyers, he appeared "a little agitated." But not overly so, and he couldn't recall anything else unusual about him that day.

Wasko went on to say that he continually had problems with Pierson and once nearly had a fistfight with him. Pierson was not a hard worker, Wasko said, and once, after he had gotten on him and told him he'd better straighten himself out, Pierson had broken down and cried, complaining that Wasko was working him too hard.

Hall asked him if he owned any guns. Wasko said he had a Winchester rifle, but the gun was in Youngstown, where his family lived. He said he didn't own any handguns; neither had he ever fired one.

What about Pierson's claim Wasko had told him to lie about handing out the flyers and that it was he, Wasko, who had left the truck? Wasko denied it. He also said he'd never left the job, and Hall could verify that with the owner of the house.

He agreed to take a polygraph test.

Two days later, on December 3, detectives King and Huetter interviewed Harry and Lili Morgenthaler to check on the statements made by Pierson and Wasko.

According to Mr. Morgenthaler, Wasko and Pierson had arrived somewhere between nine and nine-thirty in the morning. The older one, who obviously was in charge, was wearing a Stanley Steemer uniform, the other, blue denims and a T-shirt. He said he was certain that the older of the two men was at his residence between nine-thirty and two, when the work was completed. Neither he nor his wife could verify that the younger man had been there the entire time because he had been in and out of their home during the entire course of the carpet cleaning.

Mr. and Mrs. Morgenthaler said they had been given a Stanley Steemer flyer, but they were not aware of any neighbors who had received one.

* * *

On the evening of December 7 Hall took Wasko to the office of polygraph examiner Kent Jurney. Hall gave him further background information about the case and left the room. Shortly afterward, Jurney came out and said that in his opinion Wasko had told the truth both about not being involved in the homicide and not knowing who had committed the homicide.

The focus returned to Pierson. Three days later, Theresa Washam reported to Hall that the liquid swabs Dr. Wetli, the medical examiner, had taken from Staci's groin area, back, and neck had been found to be human saliva. Although such testing could not be used to identify Pierson, it certainly indicated a sexual assault—and thus the motive for the crime.

On the basis of the blood-match evidence, the polygraph examination of Pierson, and this new information from Theresa, Hall went to Samuel Rabin of the Dade County State Attorney's Office and laid it all out for him. Rabin said that in his opinion there was enough probable cause to arrest Pierson. However, he thought that further blood tests would be useful in order to narrow down the margin of another person with the same blood type being in the area at the same time, date, and location.

For the moment, then, Hall could go no further with Pierson. He needed more solid evidence than he had before he could make a case for the prosecution.

Chapter 7

Marvin Weinstein was a man possessed. "He was a crazy man," a close friend and neighbor said. "You couldn't talk to him about anything but the murder, but God forbid you tried to tell him to try to put it behind him, to get on with his life, he had another daughter to worry about. You tried to talk to him about that, he'd bite your head off."

Friends, relatives, advised him to move out of the house, even out of Florida, because everything in that house kept his wounds open and bleeding. Staci's room remained untouched, filled with her clothes, her toys, her schoolwork, her books, the bloodied mattress on her bed. He refused to get rid of it. "It's part of my daughter," he said to everyone who commented on it.

Alan Sacharoff, his closest friend, tried to change the course of Marvin's joyless life.

"Marvin, you've got to do something, you can't go on like this," he said to him one day. "I know it's been a terrible tragedy, one thing after the other, but you can't let this case take over your whole life. It's eating you up alive. You have no other life. You have to try to change it. Get out of this house, find another woman, maybe have another child with her. All you have on your mind is this case, this case!"

"Don't tell me what I should do!" Marvin snapped back at his friend. "Everybody's trying to tell me what to do. Everybody thinks they know better than me what I should do, how I should live. It's nobody's business. How do they know what I feel, what I think? I don't wish on anybody that they should be in my shoes. But unless you or anybody else has something important to tell me about finding out who killed Staci, get out of my way!"

Alan tried another tack. "Okay, Marvin, but how about Hilari? We're so close, Marvin. Until you get this out of your mind, let Hilari come live with us. She will be treated like one of us. If we go on vacation, we'll take her with us. If we buy something for our daughter, we'll buy something for Hilari. We will not adopt her. She will not be ours. Anytime you want to come over the house, come over. But at least she'll have my wife to speak to, another woman. Because Hilari has nobody."

Marvin tried but couldn't suppress his hurt, his anger at Alan's suggestion. He knew his friend meant well, was thinking only of Hilari. But it hurt just the same. "You want to take Hilari from me? It isn't enough I've lost Ruth Ann, I've lost Staci. Now you want to take away from me the only thing I have left in my life! What do you mean Hilari has nobody? Am I dead, too?"

Alan shook his head and sighed. It was useless. There was no arguing with Marvin.

Hilari did not learn of this conversation until years later. By then she was not sure what she would have done if she had known. Gone with Alan and his wife? Remained with her father? Perhaps the latter, because as difficult as the relationship was, she could not be sure, with hindsight, whether she would have been able to leave him. As young as she was, twelve years old, she understood that he needed to know that she was there, in the house with him.

Narrowly focused as he was on the search for Staci's killer, Marvin did, however, manifest his concern for Hilari in one important area: her safety. There were times when he had to be out of the house and she would be alone. He couldn't bear the thought of that.

Strapped as he was for money, he rented out the den to a woman who had a boy of seven in exchange for light housekeeping. Thus there would always be somebody at home for Hilari. But he warned her nevertheless: if ever she walked through the front door and sensed that anything was wrong, she was to turn around and run away, to Bookie Rogers' house or to any neighbor. If for some reason the housekeeper wasn't there, she should leave at once.

Hilari needed no second warning. Actually, she would have preferred that her father sell the house and they move elsewhere. She did not like living there, with Staci's bedroom so close, keeping the fearful memory alive to haunt her. There was no chance of that, she knew. She had heard her father angrily brush off all such suggestions from his well-meaning friends.

For further security Marvin went to the police and asked for his guns back. They had been eliminated as possible murder weapons. There was no longer a reason for them to be held. But Sergeant Felton was reluctant to return them. "We don't want you doing anything foolish," he said to Marvin. "Like if we make an arrest you try to pop this guy in court." Marvin assured him he had nothing like that in mind—although that thought had occurred to him. "No, I want them for the house," he said to Felton. "Maybe the guy that did this, maybe he'll come back, go for Hilari, or me."

Marvin got his guns. Then, a handy sort of man with tools, he rigged up with thin cords a rudimentary security system at the jalousie windows that when disturbed would flip a switch and set off an alarm. Though jerry-built, he felt it would do.

One afternoon, with the housekeeper out somewhere, Hilari was in her bedroom with Alan's daughter Melissa and the housekeeper's son when she heard the alarm go off. Quickly she ran into Marvin's bedroom, pushing the other two in front of her. She closed the door, went to where she knew Marvin kept his .38 revolver, took it out, and telephoned Marvin at the store.

"The alarm's gone off!" she yelled into the phone.

"I'm on my way home!" he shouted. "Where are you?"

"In your bedroom. With Melissa and Joey. I got your gun."

"Good. Now listen to me. You know how to handle it. If you hear anybody at the bedroom door, knocking at the door, saying anything, or turning the knob, shoot right through the door."

"Should I ask who it is?"

"No! Shoot first, shoot twice, twice, you hear me? Then ask who it is."

"Okay. Should I pull the hammer back?"

"No. It's too easy to fire the gun that way. Just hold it tight with both hands and pull the trigger. The first time it'll make a loud noise. The second time it won't sound so loud. Now hang up so I can get out of here. I'll yell when I come in the front door so you'll know it's me."

False alarm. The cat had set off the alarm. They all laughed about it afterward, but the laughter was strained. For a long time Marvin and Hilari were nervous about strangers or workmen in the neighborhood. If they were at home together, a rustle of rain on the rooftop, a sighing wind in the trees, could make both of them jump and send Marvin racing around checking the doors and windows. He didn't like exposing his anxiety to Hilari that way, but he knew he would be jittery until the killer was caught. Until . . . or if. What if they never did catch him?

The fact that John Pierson was the prime suspect in the murder of Staci Weinstein was supposed to be known only within the Homicide Department—unless Pierson himself or his parents exposed it elsewhere. This was in fact what happened. Ben Hall received a phone call on January 25 from a woman named Vera Langhorn, who alleged that about two weeks earlier John Pierson had raped and attempted to murder his girlfriend, Janice, who was her daughter. Hall made an appointment immediately to interview both women the next day. He and Sergeant Felton talked to them both, and after a brief interview, in which Janice repeated the allegation, Hall asked them both to come down to Homicide the following day to make a formal statement and tape an interview.

Janice said in that interview that she and Pierson had gone to his parents' house that evening to watch the house and feed the dogs. His parents were out of town on vacation. She decided to clean the place and wash Pierson's clothing. As she was in the kitchen doing that, he came up behind her and began kissing her roughly. She asked him to stop. He persisted. She began to panic. Although she admitted that they had had sex together before, and as recently as four or five days previously, she did not want to do it that evening. Pierson became so violent and uncontrollable, Janice said, that they fell to the floor together, with Pierson still attempting to kiss her and take her clothes off.

She began to cry and screamed at him to stop. "Get off me, you're hurting me!" She tried to grab the telephone to call the police, but she said he had some kind of device on the telephone that he removed, preventing her from making a call. He then dragged her to the bathroom and began ripping her clothes off. Fearful of being hurt, she said, she stopped fighting him but pleaded with him to stop. She said he had a wild look in his eyes and wouldn't stop. He told her to take her pants off, take all her clothes off. "John, why?" she asked him. He was sitting on the edge of the bathtub and he said, "Do it." She was really scared, she said, so she took her pants off. He then carried her into the bedroom and threw her on the bed. He turned off the lights. She again pleaded with him and asked him not to turn the lights off. He turned the lights back on and undressed. She said the wild look in his eyes as he stared at her frightened her so that she became hysterical and began to scream.

He forced her to have sexual intercourse, Janice said. Fearing now for her life, she gave in. He kept her there on the bed for hours, she said, forcing her to have sex several times, and each time he became more violent. At one time during intercourse he placed his mouth over hers and began sucking the breath from her. She began blacking out and thought she was going to die.

She managed to push him away and tried to talk to him, asking him to let her leave, but he told her she was not going anywhere. After a time, she said, he seemed to withdraw into himself. She took the moment to slip out of bed and get dressed. She then grabbed his car keys, ran to his car, and drove to her mother's house, crying hysterically as she drove. She said it was a short drive, but Pierson had ridden his bicycle and somehow arrived there before her. He was waiting outside. She got out of the car and screamed at him to go away, stay away from her.

Her mother and grandmother, alerted by her screams, ran from the house and asked her what was going on. She told them Pierson had raped her. Her mother confronted Pierson, crying and shouting at him to go home and leave Janice alone. Pierson broke into sobs and asked forgiveness for what he had done. "I'm sorry, I didn't mean to do it," he said. Vera Langhorn tried to help her daughter into the house, but Pierson was hanging onto Janice's arm, still begging to be forgiven. He was kneeling on the ground, moaning, "Oh God, forgive me!"

When she'd completed her narrative, Hall asked her if she knew about the murder of Staci Weinstein. She said she did; it had been in the newspapers and on television. But what shook Hall was that Janice said she also knew that he suspected Pierson of the murder. Astonished, Hall wanted to know why she thought so.

She told him that shortly after the murder Pierson had come to her house and remarked that a little girl had been killed just a few houses away from where he'd been working that day. He said to her that the police would probably contact him as a matter of routine since he had been working in the area.

About that time, she said, late October or early November, Pierson had begun acting very strange. One day, when they were in the backyard of her aunt's house, he blacked out. She couldn't awaken him until she threw ice water over him. When he came to, he began weeping and saying, "Forgive me, God, for what I have done." Janice said she had no idea what he was talking about. When she questioned him, he refused to talk about it.

Janice said she confronted him with the fact that she thought he might have killed the little girl. He became upset at that, but not as upset as she imagined he would be.

Appreciating the significance of all this, Hall contacted Assistant State Attorney David Waksman. He gave Waksman an update on the entire case up to that point and told him of the interview with Janice Langhorn. Waksman listened to the tape of the interview and told Hall that the Metro-Dade Sexual Battery Unit should be brought in. Hall called Detective Harold Ross of that unit and gave him the story. He also told Ross that Pierson was a suspect in a homicide case. Ross came down and listened to the tape, and told Hall that "probable cause" had been established. He wanted to interview Janice and Vera Langhorn himself.

Ross was satisfied after interviewing them that he had a case against Pierson for sexual assault, but told Hall that the women were reluctant to file charges against Pierson "for fear of their lives." They said they wanted to think it over. Janice said that all she really wanted was for Pierson to stay away from her, to stop bothering her. Ross said if Janice wouldn't file charges there was little he could do, but he'd keep an eye on Pierson just the same.

Several days later, Vera Langhorn called Hall and told him she had found fresh writing in the dirt driveway in front of their house saying, "You are dead. You will die." It had to be Pierson's work, she said. Janice told Hall that a day or so earlier, Pierson had called her and, unaware that she had already contacted the police, pleaded with her not to tell them, especially not Hall, about the sexual assault. And he was constantly driving by the house, day and night—she recognized the sound of his very noisy muffler—sometimes stopping in front of the house for a few minutes before driving on.

Hall asked them again if they would agree to file charges against Pierson. Again they refused. They said they were too frightened of Pierson.

It was a stalemate. Hall still lacked the kind of hard evidence needed to indict Pierson on a first-degree murder charge. He had hoped that if they could get Pierson in on a sexual-assault warrant, he had a chance of breaking him down on the homicide case. But as long as Janice and her mother were reluctant to file charges, he had reached another dead end.

Ever since his wife had died in June, Marvin had gone to evening services at a nearby synagogue to say the ritual kaddish, the Hebrew prayer for the dead. Now, as the members of the congregation knew, he was reciting the prayer for two dead, and many a resounding "Amen" was heard from the assembled worshipers at the end of his prayer.

One evening, following the services, he stood in the parking lot of the synagogue chatting with his friend Alan Sacharoff, who now and again went to services to keep Marvin company. As they were standing there

Alan noticed a woman in a car beckoning to Marvin.
As Marvin recalls the incident:

"The woman said to me, 'Don't go home. Something
terrible is going to happen.' And I said, 'It already did.
You know who I am?' She said, 'No, I don't. I picked
it up. I'm a psychic. I pick up these things as though
I have a television set in my head.'

"I said, 'What are you picking up? My little girl was
murdered.' And she began telling me things. She said
she saw a woman with blond hair and with red hair,
and she's carrying on, and she talked about a blue
room. Well that got to me because Ruth Ann was a
blond and we bought her that red wig when she was
getting chemotherapy. And blue ... Staci's room was
blue. She was saying a lot of things, some made no
sense, but a few things like that amazed me. She said
that two men were involved in the murder and they got
in through the back door. Who is Edward, or King
Edward? she asked me. I didn't know. I had no idea.

"She said to me she could go no further, she didn't
want to endanger herself. A lot of what she was saying
didn't sink in, but I thought, at least here is somebody
who is trying to come up with something, and it started
to whet the whistle. I asked her for her name and telephone number and could I call her if I wanted to talk
to her again. She told me her name was Zeta. She
was thirtyish, with dark hair, very gypsy looking.
She was Jewish. Her children went to Hebrew school
at the temple, that's why she was in the parking lot.
She was waiting to pick them up after school."

Alan listened to the conversation and came away
from it as he had entered it—a skeptic. He didn't believe any of it, but he didn't want to sour Marvin's apparent interest. So he tempered his disbelief when
Marvin asked his opinion. In fact, he acted as though
he was astonished at the psychic's references.

Marvin was hooked. Here was an unexplored avenue
that might lead to discovering who had killed Staci. He

called Zeta. She told him she could go no further, but gave him the name and telephone number of a cop with the North Miami Beach police who she said was a clairvoyant, a psychic. And he would help. Marvin called him. The cop said there was nothing he could do for him.

Marvin was only getting started, though.

An auxiliary mounted policeman with the Broward County Sheriff's Office, Arnie Hoffman, son of neighborhood friends, tried to get information about the case for Marvin through the North Miami Beach police department. But the file was closed to them. It was out of their jurisdiction. Often the two would drive around the North Miami Beach area together, talking about the murder, and Arnie encouraged Marvin to keep trying with psychics. "You got nothing to lose, Marvin," he said. "They can help sometimes. I know they work with some police departments around the country to help find missing persons, bodies, giving clues. Stuff like that."

"Well, you know, Arnie," Marvin said to him one day, "somebody gave me an article from a newspaper about this psychic who's worked successfully with the cops in Indiana and Virginia, and she's even been working with the FBI. Maybe I'll give them a call and see what happens."

Marvin telephoned the FBI at Quantico, Virginia, the next day. He spoke to an agent who acknowledged that sometimes they did work with physics, but they could not recommend anyone. Nor would they release to him that particular psychic's address or telephone number. That did not faze Marvin; he did not give up that easily. Working off information in the newspaper article, he tracked her down and called her. But she said she would not work with him, only directly with the police.

He called Sergeant Felton and told him about this psychic, about the admission by the FBI agent that they had worked with her. Felton told him to forget it. He didn't believe in psychics.

Marvin wasn't sure he was a believer, either. But he

was desperate to follow any lead that might help him find the killer. He answered blind ads in newspapers by self-styled clairvoyants, psychics, healers, and readers of Tarot cards. All in vain. One person he communicated with told him to give himself up, he was the murderer. Marvin was discouraged but not disillusioned. He accepted that there were both charlatans and honest persons in this field.

Still searching, like Diogenes the Cynic, for an honest person, Marvin went to a psychic fair that was being held in a nearby shopping mall. Booths had been set up offering readings for $10. Marvin walked over to a reception desk where a woman was assigning psychics to individuals registering and paying the fee. Marvin said to her, "I wonder if you could help me. I'm trying to get information. My daughter was murdered. I understand there are psychics out there who are clairvoyant and could help me. I believe in that stuff. Being as you seem to run this thing, do you know anybody who could help me find the killer of my daughter?"

The woman looked at him curiously. "Why do you want to know?"

"Well, I think that's obvious," Marvin said, and wondered: why is she asking me a dumb question like that? This woman is not going to help me. But the woman then asked him his birth date and the time of day he was born. Dubious as he was at that moment, nevertheless he said, "I'll have to ask my mother," and he actually went to a public phone booth in the mall and called his mother in Canada for the information. "Ma, what time of day was I born?" he asked her.

"What are you talking about, Marvin?" she said. "You're calling me long-distance to know what time of day you were born? Not even a hello, how are you. Only, Ma, what time of the day was I born? What difference does it make? Who needs to know such a thing?"

Marvin explained where he was, what he was doing, and why he was doing it. His mother thought he had departed from his senses, but told him she thought it had been about six o'clock in the morning.

He ran back and told the psychic. "It's apparent you need counseling," she said.

"It's apparent I need to know who did it," replied Marvin. "I don't care what you call it, what words you want to use, I need a psychic who can help me find my daughter's killer."

The woman could offer him no help.

Marvin went back to Zeta once again. Thus far she had been the only person who had told him anything at all that seemed relevant. Zeta was adamant that she personally could go no further, but she gave him the name of another psychic who was a member of the Roundtable in Miami. This was an organization of psychics and clairvoyants that met regularly in Coral Gables.

This psychic in turn referred Marvin to the head of the Roundtable, Morry Cutler. If there was anybody who could help, he told Marvin, it would be Morry, who was himself a psychic and who ran a parapsychology group.

So Marvin did call Cutler, and learned that he was a good friend of Peter Hurkos, the famous Dutch psychic who had helped not only the Dutch police on a number of occasions, but the police in many parts of the United States. Marvin was encouraged, enthusiastic. Cutler said he himself couldn't help, but agreed to try to find a psychic that would.

Weeks went by with telephone conversations back and forth between Cutler and Marvin. Nothing yet, Cutler said. He was looking, but he knew of all the previous disappointments, and he wanted to be very sure before he introduced Marvin to a psychic.

One evening in the spring of 1983, Cutler telephoned. He had something interesting to report. A psychic named Marcía had called him and had seen his advertising for the next meeting of the Roundtable. During the conversation with her, Morry said, "I picked up, psychically, that this lady was the one to help you. She'd mentioned to me that she'd worked with the police on a number of cases. I told her about your case, and she said she would be willing to have an interview with you. Because of what I felt, Marvin, I gave her your telephone number. This is the woman who will help you."

A week later, Marcía called him.

Marvin remembers, "She asked me to send a photo of Staci and something personal, a piece of jewelry, or clothing or something, because sometimes she can pick things up from that. I sent her a photo of Staci and one of her rings. She called me about a week later and asked me about a broken window at the back of the house. I said I didn't have one. She mentioned missing windows. I didn't have any. She also said she'd like to come to the house. I told her that was fine. I was ready for anything. Anything at all that might lead me somewhere."

The appointment was made for a few days later. Marvin asked his friend Arnie to come over as a witness to whatever would happen. Hilari would be on hand, too, though the housekeeper and her son would be out of the house that evening. Marcía arrived about four.

To Marvin's surprise, she was a very attractive young woman with jet black hair.

"The first thing she said," he recalls, "was that I would have to validate her. That she would tell me things that would convince me that she was a true psychic and would be able to reveal things to me, could really help me solve this case. And she said I should take notes because sometimes she goes into like a trance and wouldn't remember what she said.

"She wanted to walk around outside the house. We did that and she pointed to a large crack in the sliding doors to the patio. And she reminded me that I'd told her I didn't have a broken window. She asked about missing windows, and I told her that the detectives had taken some jalousie windows away but they weren't missing now. I had them replaced. She got a little angry. 'I asked you about that,' she said. 'You have to validate me. It's very important.'

"She asked me if the police would work with her. I said sure, why not, why wouldn't the police want to work with you? If you can help at all, why not?

"Then we walked into the house together. She looked around the living room, then walked up the stairs and straight into Staci's room. I didn't tell her which room it was. We all followed her into the room. We had a whole entourage there. She stood in the center of the room, waving her arms around, like she was trying to feel something, and cocking her head as though she was listening for something. It was very eerie. Suddenly she said, 'Oh, my God, the little girl!' And she said, 'You've moved the bed.' Which was true. It had been in the center of the room, now it was up against the wall. She began to rattle off names. Weintraub, David, Edward, Bruce, a bunch of names. Who is Stanley? she asked me. Well, I had a neighbor named Stanley. The name Edward hit me because Zeta, the first psychic I met, also mentioned the name Edward. I was scribbling away on my pad and Marcía was talking, talking. 'Yellow,' she said. 'What's yellow?' Well, my van was yellow. But I never said anything to her. I wasn't supposed to say anything to her, and she did seem to me to be in like a trance. Then she moved her hand around, holding it like a gun and she moved it once, twice, like she was shooting it.

" 'There were two men involved,' she said to me. 'One was dark, the other was light, with blondish hair. He had nosebleeds and his eyes would go funny,' she said. 'And somebody hugged Staci. Whoever did it hugged Staci after he killed her.'

"I was like in a fever by then. A chill came over me. 'I gotta call Hall,' I said. 'I gotta get him down here right away.' "

Chapter 8

Ben Hall had a lot on his mind, and he was in no mood for Marvin Weinstein's song and dance about a psychic. On a personal level, he was in the throes of a very difficult separation from his wife, who at the same time was seriously ill. On a professional level, he was up to his eyes in a very nasty homicide case involving a fellow officer. This was a high-profile, much publicized case involving a robbery detective named Tom Pellechio who had shot and killed an unarmed man during a struggle—the incident taking place on October 6, barely a week before Staci's murder. Pellechio was white. The other man had been black and, as it turned out, a jail guard, a corrections officer who, according to Hall's investigation, had been completely intoxicated at the time. The tension in the community was dangerously close to explosion.

Because of the immediate need to defuse the situation, Hall said he got orders from his superiors to put all his efforts into that case to the exclusion of any others.

Everybody on the force believed Pellechio was innocent of any crime. "It got to the point," Hall recalled, "where Pellechio was advised to testify in a grand jury by Janet Reno. She said if he testified in the grand jury, that even if they brought back a true bill, which is like an indictment, he would not be prosecuted by her office. A true bill came back, and in the end it had to go to a major trial because they did indict him. Pellechio was found not guilty. The prosecution did not present a case if it was manslaughter or a murder or a second-degree murder."

Under orders, while he concentrated on the Pellechio case, everything else went on the back burner, including the Staci Weinstein murder case. So when Marvin called him around eight o'clock that evening all excited about this psychic business and said Hall should jump in his car and come right over to listen to her amazing insights into the murder, he was ready to climb the wall.

No, he said to Marvin, he would not come over and listen to what a psychic had to say about a homicide he had been working on for the better part of five months. With all due respect to psychics in general and the lady in particular, he didn't think it was worth his time. Everything he did in Homicide was scientific and legwork. What a psychic says is not evidence that can be used in court. And Ben Hall needed that kind of evidence if he was to make a case that would stick.

While sympathetic, Hall was losing patience with Marvin, was weary of all these months of his telephoning and barging into headquarters demanding information. Everybody at Homicide was weary of Marvin.

Marvin didn't care if they were fed up with him. He accepted that there could be things going on they couldn't tell him, because then it would become, in effect, public information. Still, nobody down at Homicide had said to him, "Marvin Weinstein, you're off the hook, you're not a murder suspect anymore." He was convinced that the investigation was stalled. "I don't know what the hell is going on down there," he recalled feeling at the time. "So I'll push, and I'll keep pushing, and I'll be a nuisance and if they don't like me, well, that's too bad. My little girl has been murdered, and as far as I can see they're going nowhere with this thing. Whoever did it is still walking the streets. I want him found and if they're going to just sleep on this case, then I'll have to keep sticking pins in them to wake them up."

He scoured the daily Miami newspapers and a local paper called *Neighbors* for stories about local crimes. He saw there had been a shooting in a bowling alley in North Miami Beach, and he called Hall and told him about it. "Is there any way you can find out what kind of gun was used? Maybe it matches the one that killed Staci." Another day he called Hall and said, "Listen, I heard they found a gun near Miami Beach High School. It was a .25 automatic. Maybe that's the gun you're looking for." He read in the papers about a crime called the Bathtub Murders that had taken place in Texas, but the alleged killer lived in the Miami area and had been released from prison just before Staci's murder. He called Hall and asked him to look into it. Maybe this was the guy who had killed Staci. And so it went on, day after day, week after week. He found it hard to believe, in the absence of an arrest, or an encouraging word about a suspect from Homicide, that they had no evidence of any kind, no fingerprints, nothing that would lead them to a prime suspect.

What drove him on and on this way was the suspicion that they had messed up something in the initial crime scene. A cop had told him that the further on down the road it gets, the tougher it becomes to solve a case. He felt that Homicide had missed their best shot at it, and if so, what chance did they have of ever finding anybody? He kept grasping at straws, read every newspaper and watched every television news program in the evenings, looking at every angle, hoping to discover a clue, a name, a similar murder. It was driving him crazy. He hadn't enjoyed a decent night's sleep since the murder, and he knew he could not rest until her killer was found and put away.

Angry with Hall for refusing to meet with the psychic, one afternoon after work he went down to Homicide and confronted him and Sergeant Felton. "How do

I know you guys are really doing anything?" he said to Felton. "In my mind I keep thinking you're looking at me, and I need to know that you're not all asleep down here. I realize you've got lots of other things going on, but I don't give a damn! I want this case solved! Now, what are you doing? At least tell me something, don't leave me here high and dry! You gotta help me!"

Felton put two big boxes on his desk. "I can't show you our files, but you see these two big boxes here? This is all the stuff that has been going on all this time."

Marvin was not satisfied. "How do I know those boxes haven't been sitting under a desk or on a shelf or in a back room somewhere? How do I know you're current and you're working on it now?"

Felton shook his head in exasperation. "I can't tell you very much, but we do have some people we're looking at. There is one young guy we've been questioning. But I can't go any further than that."

This was not enough for Marvin. For all he knew, what was in the boxes Felton showed him had nothing to do with his case. It was all show, just to get him off their backs.

That night he called Hall again, trying to persuade him to meet with Marcía. He said to him, "Bring your file. I know you can't show it to me, but maybe this woman can generate some ideas with you, remind you of things maybe you forgot. She said things to me I don't understand, asked me about names that don't mean anything to me, but maybe they'll mean something to you."

Hall didn't buy it, and he was sick to death of Marvin's nagging about the psychic. "Just don't bother me with this crap," he told him finally. Marvin was furious. As Hall recalled, "He was gonna call the governor, he was gonna call the director, he was calling the president. I didn't care. But he just kept bugging us three or four times a day. Finally, Arty Felton got fed up with him and told me, 'Go down and talk to him with this psychic.' I ended up going down."

Marvin organized the meeting at his home, with a precaution from Marcía that if she worked with the police, she could not tell him anything further about her part in the investigation.

When Hall was introduced to Marcía, his skepticism was obvious to her. Hall recalled: "First of all she said, 'I don't think you're gonna be a believer unless I do something of a personal nature with you. So I'll have to make you a believer so you understand me.' She said, 'You're having marital problems.' Well, everybody's got marital problems. That didn't mean shit. She said then, and she was right, 'You've got two little kids, a boy and a girl. Your wife has been sick.' She then went into some background about me, that only I knew. I'm starting to watch her a little closer now. Then she said, 'You're going to be out of Homicide in two weeks.' I said, 'What? I'm not ready to leave Homicide.' I laughed that one off.

"We started going over stuff then. She took me into the bedroom and she started showing me things and she said, 'This is where the bed was, and this is the way Staci was laying.' Which I figured she could have got that from Marvin. She said she was shot twice. I didn't think Marvin would know about that. She pointed and she said, 'In the head, and in the side.' Then she said, 'Does the number 22 mean anything?' Staci was shot with a .22. And she said, 'Let me draw you a picture of the gun.' She drew a picture of a revolver, instead of an automatic, by showing me the cylinder. That was true. Staci was shot with a revolver.

"We went into the kitchen after a while, and she said to me, 'There are two people involved in this murder. One's name is John and one's name is Ed.' And I'm like . . . Jeez! I knew that already, but then she said, 'There's a color yellow involved.' And that was the yellow Stanley Steemer van."

It will be recalled that during the area canvass right after the murder investigation began, two neighborhood people had reported seeing a yellow van at Marvin's house that afternoon, and since Marvin owned a yellow van, this had added to Ben Hall's initial suspicions about his possible guilt. Neither of the two people mentioned seeing writing on the side of the yellow van. Marvin's had none. The yellow Stanley Steemer vans have the company name imprinted.

"Then she said, 'The guys had boots on and were clomping through the house.' Nobody knew that. And that they broke in through the back door. Well, we thought there was a break-in. And she said one of them went into the refrigerator and drank milk. Which was unusual. She said there was no sexual assault, which there wasn't, though there was a lot of saliva on her body."

There was more at that meeting, enough for Hall to go back to Sergeant Felton and tell him about it. But Felton did not want to know.

Hall remembers, "Felton was from the old school. Basically, I'm from the old school, too, except I'm open-minded about a lot of things, and that's probably why I did do well in Homicide. When I explained to Felton later what I'd learned, he said I was not to go around there anymore, stay away from her, I don't want you getting involved. I told him she's been calling me. He said I don't care, hang up on her. He started taking her phone calls to me, taking messages.

"It was difficult to work because the things she gave me I knew were true, and some of the things she predicted actually came true. So in other words she saw the past and the future. I had a hard time—even today I have a hard time—stomaching some of the stuff she said, because they came true. And I don't understand these kinds of powers.

"I think she's legit. I didn't think so in the beginning because I didn't know for sure. Anybody could have told her anything. But the things she predicted started coming true . . . and in my opinion she should be used in other cases. But I think if you're gonna use something like that in a homicide case—and this would be just a warning to other detectives—use it as a last resort. You can't use a psychic in court, but what they can do for you is lead you in the right direction."

Hall did not see Marcía again during the investigation, but despite Sergeant Felton's warning he did have several telephone conversations with her that continued to startle him. "She told me how the case was going to be closed. She said there was going to be a sexual-battery warrant issued on one of the subjects. Well, I just shook my head. I couldn't believe that would happen. In another phone call she said to me to go over numbers. Wherever you have numbers involved in this case you have a discrepancy, she said. You need to review it. Whatever it is, I don't know what it is, she said. But numbers."

Two weeks after that first meeting with her, he was given a third murder case to handle. He was overloaded, and he went to Sergeant Felton and asked to use an extra detective to help him find the suspect in that third murder case.

"Obviously Arty was having a bad day," said Hall. "He got real uptight. He exploded. I said, 'Don't be mad at me, Arty, I'm just trying to resolve this thing.' Arty and I always got along well together and I wanted to make things easy for him, so I said, 'Look, Arty, you want me to transfer to another squad or something?' And he said, 'Instead of you finding a new squad, why don't you find a new job?'

"I said, 'Why are you doing this to me, Arty?' And he said, 'Well, I'm just tired of all this stuff.'

"So I said, 'Fine, I'll go,' and I went out and I tried to find the suspect. I couldn't find him, so I came back about five hours later figuring Arty had cooled off, but he said, 'I'm not gonna change my mind. Find a new job.' "

This decision by Sergeant Felton stirred a heated argument in the department, said Hall, because they didn't want him out. "They brought in Captain Matthews from his vacation and Assistant Chief Willie Morrison. They said that since the sergeant wanted me to leave and he was the supervisor, they would agree to it. But they didn't want me to go."

Hall was transferred to Transit, a detective working embezzlement cases and such. Strangely, however, he kept working the Staci Weinstein case. How could this have happened? Who told him to keep working the case?

"Captain Matthews," said Hall. "He knew I was so close to closing the case, he told me to keep working it."

Hall was convinced he was close to cracking the case because of what the psychic Marcía had told him about checking discrepancies in numbers. It was not lost on him, too, that she had predicted his sudden departure from Homicide. So he reviewed the entire case file, looking for discrepancies. And eventually he found something. "I noticed that the times had been changed on Ed Wasko's work sheets. They were scratched over. So I started looking at things differently, and I got together with Captain Matthews and told him, 'I got the guy now. I know I can work the case.' I showed him. I said this is what I got, this is what I need. I can close the case. And he said, 'Well, we're gonna give it to the Cold Case Squad.' "

Hall's mention of the alterations he had discovered on Ed Wasko's work sheet prompted me to ask him a question that had been on my mind since I had first reviewed the Homicide case file many months earlier. This was not the well-known twenty-twenty vision of hindsight; that file, which began with the day of Staci's murder and contained all the investigation reports of all the detectives on the case, would of course been seen by Hall—and presumably by Felton, for that matter. I asked Hall:

"Hadn't anybody noticed or brought to your attention that during the second canvass of the neighborhood in December, the Morgenthalers had stated that the Stanley Steemer men had arrived in the morning and left sometime before two o'clock, but Pierson and Wasko had claimed they arrived there at two and left at about three-fifteen? Once they both said three-fifteen, the second time they both said four. Pierson failed his polygraph. Wasko passed his. Polygraphs are not necessarily totally reliable. But obviously both were lying about when they were working just down the block from the Weinstein house. How come nobody picked up that they were lying about the times?"

Hall said, "That was an oversight on my part. I gotta admit that. When I think back on it, how I could have done it differently, I was so strapped between the Pellechio case and this case, I should have given the case to another person during the time I was investigating Pellechio."

Hall believes to this day that he was treated unfairly, and that part of Felton's decision was due to his association with the psychic. "I took a lot of personal hits, bad. And I'll tell you something, I was good in Homicide. And I was kicked out because of a sergeant who was upset at me and I feel it was unwarranted. However, he was a sergeant and he called the shots. Now I'm a sergeant and now I call the shots. That's one of the reasons I decided to become a sergeant."

Captain Don Matthews (who retired recently with the rank of major) has a slightly different account of events. At the time of the investigation into the murder of Staci Weinstein, he was commander of Homicide.

He was at pains to point out that he has always liked Ben Hall. "Ben is a very nice person. He worked for me in the Southwest District. I transferred Ben into

Homicide. However, I'll say this on the record. I removed Ben Hall from the case because it was over his head and Mr. Weinstein was directing the investigation through Ben, and we would never have solved it."

He did not take Ben off the Weinstein case immediately after the rift with Felton. "We moved Ben off Felton's team. He took the Weinstein case with him at the time. Which meant that even though he was working for another sergeant he was still supposed to maintain and work on this case. He was still with Homicide, but Felton didn't want him working for him anymore. Because he wouldn't listen to Felton. It was one of Ben's problems. He had difficulty with a sergeant telling him what to do."

To Matthews and Felton it appeared that Hall was working too closely with Marvin, allowing Marvin to influence him, lead him off on wild goose chases.

"We told Ben that Marvin Weinstein had the right to go off on tangents because he's the father of this girl. He can act like a complete idiot. . . . In dealing with the man we found him to be totally irrational . . . but I'm not saying if my daughter was killed that I wouldn't be in the same mental state. But Ben was following every direction of Mr. Weinstein.

"Felton told me—and Felton's dead, so you can't interview him—that Ben was actually taking the case file and letting Mr. Weinstein read everything that was in the file, showing him pictures, showing him everything. It was a very irritating case. I was getting calls from the governor's office, I was getting calls from senators' aides, I was getting calls from anyone who would listen to Marvin. I guess he felt it's the squeaking wheel that gets the grease. Which in our society in the United States, it's a true statement."

Matthews said Hall did do a lot of work on the Pellechio case. But that case was a very technical case, because it involved a police shooting, and, Matthews felt, Ben did not have the technical knowledge to handle it though he was lead investigator, so he was assigned to Sergeant Felton, who was a more experienced homicide detective.

"The Pellechio case did not get out of hand till after the grand jury. Probably before the Staci Weinstein case Ben had that one completed. Written up, signed off, and presented to the State Attorney's office. We have in the state of Florida what we call an inquest. That's where the state attorney reviews the facts and circumstances of a shooting, which is generally a police shooting but can also be you as a home owner when someone breaks into your house and you shoot that person. They can render a decision, but generally it goes before a judge and he hears all the facts and circumstances. That's called an inquest. And then he renders a decision that it's not going to be bound over to the grand jury if he finds the home owner acted properly or in the case of a police officer that he acted properly. And he'll rule that the shooting was either justifiable, excusable, or it was murder. Then we've got to bind this guy over to the grand jury.

"Well, in this particular instance Janet [Reno] sat on this case. She was being pulled by the black community in one area, and the facts were presented to her. Over a month or two period—this is where she and I had a difficult relationship working—I would say no less than ten times, maybe as many as thirteen or fourteen times we had telephone calls or personal conversations where she assured me she was going to write a memo stating that the Pellechio shooting was justifiable." However, as events turned out, that decision was changed, a grand jury was enpaneled and it returned a true bill.

"And it was at that point I would have to say Ben got a little busy, because basically we reinvestigated. We reinterviewed every witness in the case . . . so Ben had to do more work after the true bill was returned than he did before . . . probably from about December

1982 to February 1983. But the Pellechio case did not dominate all of his time."

Matthews mentioned that his problems with then State Attorney Janet Reno ran through his entire stint in Homicide. When, for example, Hall confronted John Pierson with the facts about his blood being found on the sheets of Staci's bed and accused him of the murder, there was no chance of getting a warrant for his arrest. While it was true that the evidence of the blood and Pierson's failure of the polygraph possibly were not enough for a "probable cause" warrant, Matthews stated that it was extremely difficult to obtain a warrant on any homicide from the state attorney.

"At that time to get a warrant for someone's arrest out of the Dade County State Attorney's office you needed a videotape of the murder. It got so bad that [Janet Reno] was making complaints weekly about me to Director Jones because I would go over and demand arrest warrants on murders. We got into knock-down, drag-out fights over this. She's a very honorable person. But at the time and the way she ran this office, we had to fight for everything. You would have to have five confessions and a videotape of the murder before she would want to prosecute."

Matthews feels that Felton "probably should have been more on top of the Staci Weinstein murder investigation. He may have been . . . but he was fed up with Mr. Weinstein and fed up with Ben. And I remember the day we were sitting in the office and Ben comes in and says he wants to bring this psychic in. I said absolutely not. Felton almost chopped his head off. We didn't find out till later that Ben and Mr. Weinstein had already met this psychic."

Matthews completely discounts any contribution by Marcía in the solving of the case. When she arrived on the scene in early April 1983, Matthews felt there was enough in the file for Hall to work with: John Pierson was a prime suspect, and while they had nothing con-

crete on Ed Wasko, and he had passed his polygraph
test, he had been, after all, Pierson's partner and indeed
senior on the day of the murder. So when Hall came to
him with his new evidence of the alterations on
Wasko's worksheet, it was too late. Matthews had already made his decision.

"Ben later worked for me in Miami Lakes. I have
nothing personal against Ben. He's a good law enforcement officer. But not for Homicide. I'm not criticizing
Ben. Listen, I couldn't be a brain surgeon. And not everybody can be a good homicide investigator. If you
look in the files you'll see how many go through here.
A lot of them last ten years, fifteen years. Some last
three months, or six months, a year, or three years.
And the reason they're not here anymore is that they
didn't do their jobs correctly. Homicide is the epitome
of investigative work. And not everybody can do it."

Early in May 1983, Sergeant Jim Ratcliff and detectives Greg Smith and Steve Sessler—an entirely new
team—took over the investigation.

Chapter 9

In the weeks preceding Ben Hall's dismissal from Homicide, Marvin sensed that the momentum in the investigation was changing. There was forward movement after months of what he considered to be stagnation. He didn't know exactly what Hall was doing, but to Marvin there appeared to be a new excitement in the detective's voice, a new aggressiveness in manner. As he had hoped, bringing the psychic and Ben Hall together had somehow stimulated the detective's thinking. All the things that to Marvin had meant nothing when Marcía pronounced them the night they met must have meant something to Hall.

Marvin was therefore profoundly shocked when he learned from Marcía that Hall had been taken off the case. Why would they do this just when Hall appeared to be on the verge of closing it out? Politics, he fumed. All of them, worried about their careers, massaging their egos. Even Hall, it turned out, had never passed on to his superiors the information Marcía had given him. At least that's what Marcía had said when she'd given him the news.

Why not? Who knows, thought Marvin. Maybe he was afraid they'd think less of him for needing the help of a psychic to solve his case, and what would that do to his career? He was a dedicated cop, no question about that, and maybe he figured he could close the case and Felton might never need to know about the psychic.

To Marvin it looked like a typical CYA operation: cover your ass.

A bitter sadness overwhelmed him, a sadness mixed with anger. So, what's going to happen now? Back to square one?

He did not dwell morbidly on this crisis for long. At work the next morning he fidgeted and fumed, straining at the leash, waiting for the workday to be over. And early in the afternoon, he charged down to Metro-Dade Headquarters. He asked to see Director Bobby Jones. The director was "unavailable," but Chief Willie Morrison came downstairs and brought Marvin back to his office.

"What are you guys doing!" Marvin stormed at Morrison. "Hall is finally on the verge of cracking this case after all these months and now you throw him off? If you didn't think he was doing his job, why didn't you do it months ago?"

Morrison calmed him down and brought in Captain Matthews. Marvin continued the tirade. "I don't care what you guys think about the psychic. I know you don't believe her, but I do, and at least she got something moving here. Nothing was happening till she came in and gave Hall some stuff. And all of a sudden Hall's got some hot leads."

They told him not to worry, not to get excited, that things were moving along and that they were putting a new sergeant on and several new detectives who would be working full-time on the case.

"And they're going to start all over again? Waste all these months? You'll never close this case! I know you're looking at somebody, I know you got a suspect, why don't you arrest him? Why don't you tell me what you're doing?"

"Where are you getting your information from?" Matthews wanted to know.

"It doesn't matter where I get it. You don't tell me everything. I don't have to tell you everything."

Matthews glared at him. "Marvin, you got a big mouth. Get out of this office and don't come back. Just stay out of the investigation and we'll solve this case."

Marvin stomped out, half mollified, half frustrated. He'd had his say. At least they were putting some new guys on the case right away. That was something. Who they were and where they were starting he had no idea. They wouldn't tell him that. But somewhere out there, smugly sure that he'd gotten away with murder, was Staci's killer, and Marvin's deepest fear was that as the investigation dragged on, the trail would get colder and colder, eventually freeze over completely and be put on ice forever.

He did not then know that the new detectives taking over were aptly called the Cold Case Squad.

Captain Matthews had created Florida's first Cold Case Squad in 1981. It was one of those ideas whose time had come.

Until 1978 his command's closure rate on homicides had been between 95 to 100 percent. They had been extremely successful using the team concept of a captain commander, an investigative road lieutenant, an investigative administrator lieutenant, and underneath them three teams working around the clock in three shifts, composed of a sergeant and four or five detectives. In 1978 the serious drug wars began in Dade County. As a result the closure rate dropped to between 40 and 50 percent. Homicide was having a difficult time even identifying victims. The Whodunit? became the Whoisit? There are victims to this day who have never been identified: illegal aliens mostly, involved in the drug wars. Nameless bodies that nobody claimed as kin or friend, filling the chill drawers of the morgue until buried in unmarked county paupers' graves.

By 1981 the entire country had focused on south Florida because of the sheer onslaught of violence. The homicides were coming in so rapidly the investigation teams were being swamped: they'd be given a case to work, then given another two weeks later and yet another after that. Inevitably the first case took a backseat. Maybe even the second case took a backseat. Matthews saw it and hated it. Thus he created the Cold Case Squad. A sergeant and several detectives were given a case directly by Matthews where there were workable leads. The job of the squad was to concentrate on that case and close it out quickly.

The South Florida Cold Case Squad as conceived by Matthews was one of the first of many now operating in cities all around the country.

When the Cold Case Squad took over in May, the three detectives got together to review the complete case file. Greg Smith was the only one of the three familiar with the case, since he had worked on it for several days at the beginning before switching to the investigation of a different homicide. There was general agreement that as the prime suspect, the focus of their investigation would be John Pierson. There was no doubt in the minds of the detectives that he had been at the scene and more than likely was guilty; that the motive was of a sexual nature. However, they too, as had the investigators before them, understood immediately that the blood-enzyme evidence against Pierson, what he had said to Ben Hall under interrogation, the rape accusation against him—all these things did not give them a PC, a probable cause, to procure an indictment for murder. Not enough for an arrest. The blood evidence was not definitive. All in all, after reviewing the file, the detectives agreed that what they had, as Smith said, "did not give us the right to take his freedom, put handcuffs on him, and put him in jail on a charge of murder."

They knew they needed further evidence. They had no fingerprints. They had no gun. They had no eyewitness. Therefore what they needed was people, or other sources of information that would corroborate that

Pierson had been involved. Accordingly, they agreed that a complete new background check on him was in order. And since Eddie Wasko had been with him on the day of the murder, they decided to do a complete background check on him, too, before they talked to him.

On May 11, Sergeant Ratcliff assigned the case to Steve Sessler as lead investigator. Sessler, thirty-three years old, a former schoolteacher, had a solid background in law enforcement: general investigative detective, member of a special response (SWAT) team, hostage negotiator, and three years in Homicide.

The next day he and Ratcliff held a meeting with Sergeant Felton. He gave them his overview of the case to date, including the parts played by Marvin, by Marcía, and of course Ben Hall. The consensus on the participation of a psychic was that while they had to keep an open mind, they did not want Marcía involved. They had enough leads to go on. They had a suspect. They could not use a psychic in a trial, and indeed did not want to be in a position where a defense attorney could bring to the attention of a jury that a psychic had helped them in their case against his client. Sessler telephoned Marcía at Marvin's request and explained all that to her politely, and said if they felt she could be of some use to them in their investigation, he would call her.

After seeing Felton, Sessler and Ratcliff went to see Ben Hall at the Metro-Dade Transit Division, where he had been assigned.

Hall showed up with his sergeant, Jimmy Martin. Sessler realized the discussion could get touchy. Put in Hall's place, he, too, would deeply resent it. He hoped all would go smoothly.

It didn't. Hall soon felt that this was not a discussion among fellow officers but an interrogation. He showed them the altered time sheets. He told them he'd found out Wasko was now working for Stanley Steemer in

Ohio. The reaction he was getting troubled him. Finally, angrily he said to Ratcliff and Sessler, "Look, you guys want to close this case? Okay. This is what needs to be done. Wasko was polygraphed by Kent Jurney. Jurney passed him. You need to go up there, up to Ohio, you need to reinterview him, and I don't care if it takes five days, interview the man and if you can get a polygraph, repolygraph him, because this guy is involved in this totally."

The squad had already decided to talk to Wasko, but not yet. They wanted to develop a book on him. They wanted to know enough to be able to question him thoroughly and in depth. Maybe he knew something, maybe he didn't. They knew very little about him compared with all they had on Pierson. And they wanted to learn more about Pierson, too. Talk to some of his friends, people he'd worked with. Maybe he'd made a slip somewhere, talked too much, even confessed to the crime to somebody who was protecting him.

The focus was on putting together a case against Pierson strong enough to take to the state attorney's office and obtain an arrest warrant for murder in the first degree. There was much to do, much ground to cover, and the detectives set out to do it quickly.

Following the meeting with Hall, Sergeant Ratcliff got an update from Detective Harold Ross of the Sexual Battery Unit. Ross said Janice Langhorn and her mother were still too frightened of Pierson to file rape charges against him. Ratcliff went around to see them, hoping to change their minds. Nobody was home, but he made a note that either he or Sessler or Smith would follow up and talk to them.

Sessler went to the Firearms Section to get details on the murder weapon. Ray Freeman, the technician expert, told him the weapon used to shoot Staci Weinstein had been a .22 revolver. The projectiles had been short golden bullets. The broken bits of white grip from the gun used to assault Staci, found on her bed, indicated the gun was a Rosco; these Rosco grips had the name on the right-hand side of the grip and the words VEST POCKET on the left-hand side. The partial pieces the lab held showed them to be part of the left-side grip. Freeman said it was possible that the gun's identification disc, which was attached to the grips, might have been left at the scene with the other broken pieces. Now at least Sessler knew exactly the gun they were looking for. He didn't need to find it, invaluable as that would be. But if he could trace the ownership of such a gun to Pierson, it could prove to be an important piece of evidence, though in itself not absolute proof that he'd used it on Staci Weinstein.

The next afternoon he and Ratcliff interviewed two secretaries at Stanley Steemer, Marilyn Allyn and Betty Owen, who was related to Donald Pierson. They told how the carpet-cleaning trucks worked, assigned to specific districts within Dade County. Marilyn told them Wasko was working for the company now in Columbus, Ohio. He had been fired by the company manager after an argument with him following an incident in which Wasko was accused of deliberately ramming his truck into a motorcycle owned by another employee, Bob Green. Wasko had been rehired at the headquarters branch of Stanley Steemer in Columbus because, Marilyn said, he was well liked and had a relative high up in the company.

Marilyn said that before he left, he had been living with a coworker named Jack Straw, with whom he had arrived in Miami in the fall of 1982. Both women said Wasko was known for making up stories and often had told them that he'd had sexual encounters with various women who were having their carpets cleaned by him. They didn't believe him. Then both girls mentioned that Wasko always had carried with him a small, racquetball type of bag; he was particularly protective of this bag and always kept it within his sight. The bag was blue and gray. They had no idea what was inside it.

They gave Sessler the work log for October 14, 1982, and told him that Wasko had called in that something was wrong with the machine on the Morgenthaler job. They thought it odd since the machine was fairly new. According to Betty Owen, the Morgenthaler job should have taken about an hour. The work log showing that the Morgenthaler house was the fourth job of the day indicated that the machine had run for nine-tenths of an hour.

Sessler decided to interview the Morgenthalers the next day. He got there about six in the evening. Their granddaughter Barbara, who was living with them while she attended Broward Community College, also was there. She said that on the day of the murder, she had returned home from school before two o'clock. The Stanley Steemer truck was gone and the carpets were still wet from the cleaning job. The Morgenthalers agreed that the men had left before two. They were fairly sure that workers had arrived in the morning and left about one-thirty. They said the man who appeared to be the boss had never left the house, but his assistant walked in and out of the house carrying equipment. When the job was done, they said, the workers told them the machine was broken and had to be repaired before they went on to the next job. They were seen to be working on the machine, but the Morgenthalers couldn't say whether or not either of the men had walked away from the area during that time.

While Sessler was reinterviewing the Morgenthalers, Ratcliff and Smith were back at headquarters going over the old paperwork and making telephone calls, trying to trace people connected to Pierson and/or Wasko. Ratcliff telephoned the police department in Aurora, Ohio, and learned that Wasko had a current Ohio driving license with an address in Youngstown, Ohio, was five eleven, 175 pounds. He had no criminal record with the Ohio police but a long sheet of traffic violations.

On Thursday morning, May 19, Sessler sent a tele-type message out to all agencies of Dade County asking for any information on burglaries or suspicious incidents of any kind involving Stanley Steemer carpet-cleaning trucks. Then he and Ratcliff went out to talk to Marvin Weinstein.

Marvin understood that he had long since been eliminated as a suspect, but he was a bit taken aback to be interviewed again by two new detectives. Suspicious, still burning over Hall's dismissal, he did not warm to Sessler and Ratcliff. But he had to admit he was impressed with their confidence and by the questions they asked him. He was impressed, too, with the concept of the Cold Case Squad. By the time the detectives left some four hours later, he was feeling better about them and by what seemed to be their rapid progress in the investigation. For the moment he would give them the benefit of the doubt.

Sessler told Marvin they had eight latent fingerprints from the lab, unidentified. He wanted the names of all the children who had been friends of Staci or Hilari and who had ever been to the house so their fingerprints could be compared with the eight latents. Sessler said fingerprints of Marvin's late wife, Ruth, had been taken when she died and already checked against those found in the house.

The detectives moved all the furniture around in Staci's bedroom, hoping to find more pieces of the murder weapon's broken grip, particularly a piece with the identification disc on it. No luck there. They asked Marvin if the front door had been locked when he got home. Marvin said he used his key to get in, but that didn't mean positively that the door had been locked. He didn't know. Sessler asked him about pets: had he had any in the house during October 1982? Marvin said he'd had a pit bull that was tied up outside the house, but the dog was now at a farm. He'd also had a black cat. But it had disappeared.

Sessler said he'd like Marvin to try to find that cat because animal hairs that appeared to be from a cat had been found on a jacket left by John Pierson at a friend's house. That jacket was being held in the Metro-Dade property room. The cat, however, was never found.

By fortunate circumstance, Sessler and Ratcliff lived nearby, and every morning and evening they had time in Ratcliff's car to toss ideas back and forth about the case. They had worked together before; Ratcliff had been Sessler's sergeant when they'd been tagged for the Cold Case Squad. Ratcliff lived in Broward County, Sessler south of him, in Dade County's Miami Lakes. In the past when they had worked on a case together, Ratcliff, in a "take home" unmarked squad car, would pick up Sessler in the morning on his way south to the Metro-Dade headquarters building, and sometimes drop Sessler off in the evenings on his way home. That routine continued on the Staci Weinstein case.

They used the evening ride home to review the day's work, and talked about the case again in the mornings after each had had the time to think about it overnight. Homicide detectives tend to take their cases home with them at night, an occupational hazard that causes many a rift between them and their loved ones. So in the car Sessler and Ratcliff would toss ideas at each other as new evidence was gathered, new lines were opened, new leads followed. There were a lot of "what ifs" and "buts" bounced off each other, then tried on Greg Smith for his reaction. It was a useful exercise that helped shape their approach to the case.

On May 24, Sessler and Ratcliff went looking for Wasko's former roommate, Jack Straw. He was not home, but the detectives decided to interview Straw's current roommate, Louis Fasani, who said he also worked for Stanley Steemer. Fasani said he'd never roomed with Wasko but had worked with him for about a month and a half. He said Wasko had always carried a tote bag, a kind of gym bag, holding a change of clothes. As far as he knew, Wasko didn't own a gun.

Sessler asked him if he knew John Pierson. Fasani said he didn't because by the time he'd started work for Stanley Steemer in November 1982, Pierson already had been fired. He didn't know where Pierson or Wasko lived now. But he said he was pretty sure he'd met Pierson one day while out working with Wasko. A young guy had walked up to their truck and said hello to Wasko. As a conversation began, Fasani said he noticed that Wasko was angry at the other man for accusing him of keeping a gun under the seat. Fasani said Wasko told the other man that there was no need to tell the police that he was in possession of a gun during October 1982. The other man left, said Fasani, then Wasko told him the man had been working with him on October 14, 1982, when a killing had taken place in the neighborhood where they were working. And the man had tried to get him into trouble with the Metro police.

While Fasani was talking to the detectives, Straw telephoned. Sessler spoke to him. Straw said he had no idea where Wasko was.

The next day Sessler got a phone subpoena asking for a list of all long-distance calls made from the apartment of Straw and Fasani to see whether or not they had been or were now in touch with Wasko in Ohio. The results were negative.

Greg Smith now began his share of the extensive legwork undertaken by the Cold Case Squad. Early in June he interviewed Angela May, her son Gary King and daughter Melanie King, and Angela's mother, Peggy. Pierson had lived with this family on two separate occasions, between August and November 1982 and in January and February 1983. And they knew Janice Langhorn, who had accused Pierson of rape.

Angela said that they had met Pierson briefly while he had been working at Lum's Restaurant. He said he had no place to stay, and Angela's mother said he could stay with them. Soon afterward he went to work for Stanley Steemer. While working for that company, she told Smith, he appeared to have suffered some kind of injury to his left hand; it was bandaged from forearm to his fingers. She never asked him about the injury.

Pierson had told her in January about the murder of a little girl that had occurred while he was working for Stanley Steemer, and said that the police were trying to blame the crime on him. He told her that during the time he had been cleaning carpets nearby with Eddie Wasko, he couldn't account for his time for about two hours, and that's why they suspected him. He said to Angela that the girl had been about ten years old and that after the murder, whoever did it had hugged her as if they were sorry for committing the murder. But Pierson never admitted committing the murder himself or knowing anything about it, Angela said.

Significantly, she told Smith that Pierson had claimed Wasko carried a paper bag in the truck, and inside that bag was a gun. It was for protection, he said, when they had to go into bad neighborhoods. Pierson didn't tell her what kind of gun it was, but the bag was always kept on the front seat. He told her that on the day of the murder the bag as usual was on the front seat, but when he returned to the truck after those two hours when he said he went missing, the bag was no longer there. As far as she knew, Pierson himself did not own a gun.

Pierson had a bad temper, Angela said. Often he mistreated her children. He became wide-eyed when he was angry, and his nose would start bleeding during his fits of anger.

Angela's son Gary, ten years old, said Pierson had gone to work for McDonald's after leaving Stanley Steemer but didn't know if he was still there. He remembered the bandage on Pierson's hand, and that he spoke about the murder of a little girl. Gary said Pierson told him he was in the wrong place at the wrong time and the cops were blaming him for the murder.

Melanie King, eight years old, also remembered the bandage on Pierson's hand. When she had asked him about it, she said he told her, "It's none of your business." He never spoke to her about a murder or a gun. She never saw him with a gun.

The three detectives decided it was time to interview the Stanley Steemer attorney, Dennis Potter. At his office in Coral Gables, the attorney told them he was well aware of the investigation into the murder and was concerned that it was being directed toward John Pierson, a former employee of the company. He would of course cooperate fully with the police.

He said he'd never spoken to Pierson, but he and Wasko had talked about the events of October 14, 1982. Potter said Wasko told him he and Pierson had arrived at the Morgenthaler house between one and two and remained there for about an hour and a half. Following the completion of the job, Wasko said something had gone wrong with the machinery. He called the assistant manager for instructions. While repairing the machinery, he gave Pierson door hanger flyers to pass out in the neighborhood. Pierson was gone for about fifteen or twenty minutes. When he returned, he looked battered, according to Wasko, had his shirt out, and there appeared to be blood and scratches on his hand. Potter said Pierson had not made out an injury report. He confirmed that Wasko was still working with the company based out of the office located at Dublin, Ohio.

Before they left Potter's office, the detectives obtained a list of all employees of the Stanley Steemer

Company, with their addresses and telephone numbers. All three detectives then began the task of tracking them all down and taking statements from anyone knowing John Pierson or Edward Wasko.

A second trip back to the apartment shared by Louis Fasani and Jack Straw found Straw at home. He told Sessler that Wasko had confided to him the story of what he and Pierson were doing on October 14. Wasko's version to Straw was almost identical to the stories he'd told various people except that he told Straw, too, that when Pierson returned to the truck after handing out flyers he had blood on his hands. That piece of information was important enough for the detectives to get Straw down to the office of Assistant State Attorney David Waksman, where he repeated it in a formal statement with a steno-reporter on hand.

On a tip from Angela May, Sessler and Ratcliff looked up a young man named Mike O'Malley, who had worked with Pierson at Lum's Restaurant. O'Malley didn't volunteer very much, and the detectives felt he was hiding something. They got him to come down to headquarters for another talk. This time he said that in the fall of 1982 he had borrowed a .22 revolver from a man named Virgil. He said he had it for only a week, and though he showed it to Pierson, he never gave it to him but returned it to Virgil a week later. O'Malley said he'd be willing to take a polygraph to the effect that he never let Pierson have the gun.

Sessler and Ratcliff thought they might be on to something here. The source of the gun that killed Staci Weinstein had thus far been frustratingly elusive. They found this Virgil, who admitted to owning the .22 revolver with white grips. He said he had found it. He loaned the gun to O'Malley in October 1982, but O'Malley never returned it. He said O'Malley had told him he'd left the gun in a green car that was towed away to a Broward County facility following a traffic arrest. Then he said, well, maybe he loaned O'Malley the gun in 1981. He also admitted currently owning a .22 revolver. He agreed to surrender the gun for a ballistics comparison and take a polygraph test. He failed it. The polygrapher said Virgil was showing deception about whether or not he ever got the gun back from O'Malley and where that gun might be now.

O'Malley also was given a polygraph, and he appeared that he, too, was lying about what had happened to the gun. He then admitted that he'd never given the gun back to Virgil but claimed he didn't know where it was.

From Ballistics came back the report that Virgil's gun was not the one used to kill Staci Weinstein. A dead end, in a case that seemed to be plagued with dead ends.

However, a rough picture was beginning to emerge out of these weeks of patient legwork. A scenario that just might play. As June was coming to an end, the detectives began to firm up an opinion that Eddie Wasko was the key to closing the case against Pierson. He was a witness—exactly to what they didn't know. But there were too many differences in the stories he and Pierson were telling. There was the blood on Pierson's hands. There was that racquetball bag Wasko seemed to guard so closely. There was Pierson's claim that Wasko kept a gun in a bag on the front seat of the van. There was that angry conversation Wasko allegedly had with Pierson telling him to keep quiet about the gun.

The detectives' scenario went along these lines: suppose Pierson never did own a gun. But Wasko did have a gun in that gym bag on or under the seat. Suppose Pierson took it that day without Wasko's knowledge and used it to kill Staci Weinstein after sexually assaulting her. Now, Wasko, being from Ohio, might think he was in serious trouble for carrying a concealed weapon in the van, and if it was used even without his knowledge to kill the girl, he could be considered an accomplice. Further possibility: known to be a loyal company man, a top performer, maybe he was concerned about the consequences for Stanley Steemer if it came out that one of its employees had killed a ten-year-old girl while on a nearby job. And what about his own feelings of responsibility if Pierson had stolen his gun from the van and used it on her?

Wasko had passed his polygraph, but Sessler recalled that at the company they called him "Electric Eddie," the smoothest talker in town. He could have beaten it. Neither Sessler nor Ratcliff believed polygraphs to be infallible. They were useful for developing leads but not necessarily conclusive evidence. And as time passed, maybe Eddie had realized that by not telling the truth initially, he now could be considered an accessory after the fact. So he was reluctant to talk.

Now Wasko was in Ohio, transferred after an argument with the manager, after running his truck into another man's motorcycle. Had he done it deliberately to get transferred to Ohio, away from the heat of the investigation? He'd known he wouldn't be fired. He was too good, and he had a contact at the company's headquarters in Ohio. Finally, was he the kind of person who would cover up such a crime just to protect his company and a man he barely knew and probably didn't like?

These hypothetical questions kicked around by the detectives led to a conclusion about what had to be done to close out the Weinstein case. Jim Ratcliff, as the squad's sergeant, decided that Greg Smith would remain at headquarters as their liaison man while he and Sessler flew up to Ohio to interview Wasko as the prime witness against John Pierson. Somehow they had to extract from him the truth of what he knew about the sexual assault and murder of Staci Weinstein.

Just before the long Fourth of July weekend Marvin Weinstein entered his bank to make a deposit. The teller knew him well; he'd banked there for years, and the bank held his mortgage. She knew all about the murder of Staci from the newspapers and Marvin's appearances on television. Marvin also had discussed the case with her often, as he had discussed the case with everyone interested enough or polite enough to listen.

The teller asked about his health, she asked about Hilari, then asked him how the case was going. Anything new?

"Well, I think they may have some suspects," said Marvin, "but they don't really tell you very much."

"What about those two Stanley Steemer guys?" she asked.

Stunned—what Stanley Steemer guys?—Marvin quickly regained his composure, acting as though he knew exactly what she was talking about. He said to the teller: "Oh, I haven't heard anything new. I know they were talking to some people . . . but what did you hear?"

"Well, you know Sophie, one of the other tellers, she was across the street at the chiropractor the other day and she's sitting there in the waiting room and she overhears these two women talking, and one of them is saying to the other that the detectives have been around to her house again, maybe the third time already, she says, asking her and her husband about the two men from Stanley Steemer who were cleaning her carpets on the day that little girl was murdered."

"What were they asking, did she say?"

"Sophie didn't say. But she said the woman had a foreign accent."

A foreign accent, thought Marvin. That could cover more than half the population of south Florida.

"Yeah, thanks, Gertie," he said to the teller. "That's very interesting."

"Gee, Mr. Weinstein," she said, "maybe I shouldn't have told you that."

"No, no, that's okay, I knew about those guys anyway," he said, his mind spinning.

He got back into his van and sat there for a few minutes, thinking. Stanley Steemer. Two guys. Marcía! She'd mentioned the name Stanley. I thought maybe it was Stanley Saul, my neighbor. And didn't she say that two guys had done it? And names. She mentioned a lot of names ... Edward! Zeta, that psychic I met at the temple, she mentioned an Edward or King Edward, and Edward was one of the names Marcía had mentioned, too!

Excited now, he drove home, his mind racing. He had to call Steve Sessler about this. Never mind that he didn't want to get involved with a psychic, this was too good to ignore. Cruising along Miami Gardens Drive in the right-hand lane, suddenly he noticed a truck beginning to pass him. As it went by him, he couldn't believe his eyes. A Stanley Steemer truck! There it was, a yellow truck, the words in large black letters stenciled on its side. And two guys in the front seat. The coincidence almost sent him careening off the road. "There's got to be something in this psychic business," he thought. "What a coincidence! I'll bet I've seen these trucks a hundred times on the road and paid no attention. But to pass me just now! And of course—it's yellow! Didn't Marcía mention the color yellow, and didn't two people say they saw a yellow van at my house on the day Staci was killed, and didn't Hall think it was my van?"

He realized that this was not necessarily the solution to the crime. Nevertheless, the Stanley Steemer guys must be important or the detectives wouldn't be asking questions about them in the neighborhood again this late in the game.

As soon as he got home he called Steve Sessler. He wasn't in. He wouldn't be back until after the holiday weekend. Marvin fretted impatiently, pacing the living room floor. He couldn't wait that long. He strode from the house and began his own private canvass of the neighborhood. He'd made the rounds before, right after the murder, asking a few of his neighbors whether they'd seen or heard anything unusual that day. But this was different. He had something specific to ask: were two guys from Stanley Steemer cleaning your carpets the day Staci was murdered? Sophie at the bank had said the woman had a foreign accent. Okay, he could eliminate a few people that way. But this was a tough weekend for talking to people; some went away over the holiday, others would resent being disturbed. Well, Marvin concluded, they'd just have to be disturbed.

His first try around the neighborhood availed him nothing. On Sunday, on his second try, he tried the Morgenthaler house. A lovely older couple, they certainly had a German accent. Yes, the Morgenthalers told him, two men from Stanley Steemer had cleaned their carpets that day. Two or three times already they had told the detectives the same story. The men had come in the morning and left early in the afternoon. The older one seemed to be the boss, the younger one his helper. There was some trouble with the machinery. As they had told the detectives, they didn't know anything else.

Marvin roamed the house, couldn't sleep, impatiently waiting for Tuesday, the first workday after the holiday weekend. Early that morning he called Sessler. Detective Sessler, he was told, was out of town. They couldn't say when he'd be back.

Out of town? mused Marvin. Where's he gone to? There's no way in the middle of this investigation he's gone off fishing somewhere for two weeks. Not Sessler. Unless ... yes ... yes, that could be the answer. That's got to be the answer. Sessler's gone after somebody.

Chapter 10

On Tuesday, July 5, after making the necessary arrangements with the police department in Dublin, Ohio, Sergeant Ratcliff and Detective Sessler flew up there to interview Eddie Wasko. They had return tickets for a five o'clock flight on Friday, July 8, and reservations at a motel near the airport at Columbus with a Friday evening departure date. They reckoned that two or three days with Wasko should be enough to hear what he had to say. If he told them what they hoped to hear, they would get a sworn statement from him, a deposition, and ask him to return voluntarily to Miami if and when they needed him to testify against Pierson. If he was for any reason reluctant to testify, they were prepared to subpoena him as a witness. A great deal depended on his cooperation and honesty.

Because they arrived late on Tuesday they didn't get to the offices of Stanley Steemer in nearby Dublin until noon the next day. As the first order of business, they met with the firm's legal consultant, Phil Ryser, who told the detectives that Wasko had discussed with him his movements on October 14, 1982. He related that Wasko had said Pierson had left the area of the Morganthaler residence for about forty-five minutes, and when he returned he saw scratches on various parts of Pierson's body. Wasko described Pierson as "looking like he'd been through the mill." Wasko said Pierson claimed a dog had chased him, causing the scratches.

Following this discussion, Sessler and Ratcliff met with the vice president of the company, Wes Bates. He said Wasko had discussed the case with him, too, saying Pierson had disappeared for about thirty minutes, returning with his shirttail hanging out and breathing hard. Wasko had told him, too, that Pierson claimed a dog had chased him.

The detectives noted that these stories did not jibe with Wasko's statements to Ben Hall and others in Miami. It was significant as well that he had thought it important to tell these two Stanley Steemer executives anything at all about his movements on the day of the murder. To Sessler and Ratcliff it meant nothing less than that Wasko was expecting visitors from Miami to come up and question him again.

At 5:45, when he'd finished his day's work, Wasko returned to the office in Dublin and was introduced to the detectives. They explained why they were there. Wasko said he'd be glad to cooperate. He agreed to accompany them to the Dublin Police Department, where a private interview room had been arranged.

Wasko told the detectives he remembered going to the Morgenthaler house sometime after noon. He was definite about leaving there before three. A few moments later he said that in fact he remembered arriving at the house at one and spent about forty-five minutes cleaning the carpets. When the job was done he began fixing the float in the truck's dump tank, and as he was doing that he sent Pierson out with some advertising flyers to distribute at nearby houses. Pierson was gone about fifteen to thirty minutes. When he returned, Wasko said, he looked as though he'd been running. Pierson said he had been chased by a dog. Wasko said he didn't see any cuts on Pierson; neither had he seen a dog.

The detectives did not let him off the hook with that story. They asked him to tell them the story again in further detail, and to think about whether or not he'd left anything out. Wasko now said he did remember seeing what might have been blood marks on Pierson's red Stanley Steemer shirt. He indicated the lower right abdominal area. He recalled asking Pierson if he wanted to go to a hospital but Pierson refused.

Sessler asked him about the time he had been working with Louis Fasani and Pierson came over to talk to him. Wasko said he was traveling in the van when he stopped for a red light at 95th Street in Bal Harbour. All of a sudden Pierson ran out from somewhere and began talking to him, saying he was no longer a suspect and the cops weren't looking for him. Wasko admitted being mad at Pierson for telling people he'd had a gun but denied talking about a gun at that time, with Fasani in the van.

At nine-thirty they drove him back to the Stanley Steemer headquarters, where he was then living. During the drive Wasko asked Sessler if the gun used was a .22-caliber revolver. Sessler said he couldn't release that information. Wasko then asked him if the girl had been beaten. Sessler again said he couldn't talk about that. When they dropped him off, Wasko agreed to meet with the detectives the following morning and take a polygraph test to prove that he had been telling the truth.

At the motel that night Sessler and Ratcliff discussed the questions Wasko had asked in the car about the gun and the beating of Staci Weinstein. "Too close to the mark," Sessler commented. "He knows more than he's saying right now. Let's see what he says tomorrow."

Early the next morning, the detectives brought Wasko to the Columbus Police Department, where civilian polygrapher Randy Walker would give him the test. Walker, a former police officer in Columbus, had been hit in the spine during a shoot-out and was paralyzed from the waist down. He was in a wheelchair.

Before the interview began, Wasko was given a urine test to affirm that no alcohol was in his blood.

Just before entering the interview room with Walker, Wasko admitted to the detectives that the entire story he'd told them the night before was false: in particular, he didn't remember seeing any blood on Pierson's shirt.

Walker gave Wasko a Miranda form and the standard Columbus Police polygraph form to read and sign. Following the polygraph examination, Walker told Sessler and Ratcliff that he believed Wasko was trying intentionally to distort the polygraph recordings. He told the detectives Wasko kept changing his story slightly every time he told it. With several short breaks in between, interviews between Walker and Wasko lasted throughout the day and into the evening before they stopped about nine o'clock. Wasko agreed to return the next day for another interview with Walker.

Again as the detectives drove him back to the Stanley Steemer building, Wasko began talking to them about the case. He said Pierson probably thought he had a gun because once he told him he carried a gun for protection. But he never did own one, though at one time he had had a .22-caliber rifle that previously belonged to his father.

That night back at the motel Sessler and Ratcliff conferred again. Wasko, they agreed, was lying. He was telling too many different stories. He was perhaps more involved than they'd believed at first.

Friday morning, July 8, before they checked out of their motel to meet Wasko, Sessler and Ratcliff called Greg Smith in Miami and asked him to go over to Assistant State Attorney David Waksman's office and fill out a perjury warrant on Wasko. A warrant was obtained, signed by Judge A. Sepe, and Smith called Sessler to confirm it. The detectives didn't tell Wasko about the perjury warrant; had they done so it would have altered the entire complexion of the situation. At the moment Wasko was being questioned as a potential witness, advised continually by the detectives and by

Walker that he did not have to talk to them, he did not have to answer questions, he did not have to take a polygraph, and he was free to leave at any time. For legal reasons it had to be patently clear that whatever he might say, he was doing it voluntarily without threat or coercion of any kind.

Sessler went over that voluntary position again with Wasko before the second Walker–Wasko interview took place at noon. Sessler asked Wasko to get his story straight this time. All he and Ratcliff wanted from him was the truth of what he knew and what he had observed on the afternoon of October 14, 1982.

Wasko again was given a Miranda and polygraph form to sign. During the pre-test interview, Wasko said to Walker, "I'm really worried about what my mother is going to think. . . . This last eight months have been hell. . . . My whole life changed that day." To Walker this was an obvious reference to the day Staci Weinstein had been killed.

Wasko began changing his previous story as the polygraph test got under way. He said that on their way to the Morgenthalers' house he and Pierson had seen an "attractive lady" standing in front of a house just down the street. Wasko described her as wearing pink shorts and a blue top. He stopped the truck and greeted her. Wasko said that at this point he was interested in "getting John laid" because John had complained that his girlfriend would not let him have sex with her. He told the girl that either he or Pierson would be back to give the girl an estimate for carpet cleaning.

While Wasko was working at the Morgenthalers', Pierson went back to the girl's house, said Wasko. When Pierson returned, Wasko asked him, "Well, did you score?" Pierson said no. So Wasko told him to go back to the girl's house and wait for him; he would join him when the job was completed. At the girl's house, he tried to "sweeten her up for John" by kissing the girl's neck. He then grabbed her and pulled off her top. Wasko said the girl got mad and threatened to call the police.

The girl then resisted Pierson's advances. Wasko said to him, "Be a man and go up there and do it." The girl said no, and Pierson hit her in the head with his fist, grabbed her by the wrist, and pulled her upstairs. Wasko said he helped, and that once upstairs, "things got out of hand."

At one point in this interview Wasko said he might have been downstairs on the couch while Pierson was upstairs, when he heard a shot, ran upstairs, and saw Pierson standing over the girl, a gun in his hand. He left the house and waited for Pierson, who came out about fifteen minutes later. Wasko was very descriptive of Staci being beaten, saying to Walker, "She was beaten really bad ... it was bad, Randy." Wasko said she was moaning and groaning and saying repeatedly, "You're hurting me!"

The story Wasko was telling did not always emerge in chronological order. At times it jumped backward and forward, and at times it appeared contradictory. He said at one point that when Pierson went upstairs with the girl he waited in the truck to "keep an eye out," then went to the door, opened it, and called out to Pierson, "Hurry up." Pierson came out and said he'd beaten the girl. Wasko said he then reached into his brown bag and removed a towel with his .22 in it. He said he gave it to Pierson and told him, "Go finish her off and put her out of her misery."

He went on to say that the girl was "gasping, and then sighed as she took her last breath and died."

Walker related all this to the detectives about three o'clock, when he took a coffee break with Sessler. Ratcliff then went into the interview room, closed the door behind him, and began interviewing Wasko. A half hour later he came out of the room and told Sessler to cancel their plane reservations.

Unexpectedly the situation had changed dramatically. Eddie Wasko was no longer an important witness to the murder of Staci Weinstein. Wasko's admissions were tantamount to a confession of complicity in the homicide.

Ratcliff said Wasko was now claiming he had seen Pierson running from between two houses as he picked him up in the van after fixing the machinery. Among other information Wasko was now providing, said Ratcliff, was the allegation that Pierson told him he'd hurt a girl really bad and that she was unconscious.

Before proceeding further, Sessler thought it a good idea to call the company's legal adviser, Phil Ryser, and tell him that Wasko was giving them new information about the Staci Weinstein homicide and they would be continuing the interview before returning him to the Stanley Steemer headquarters.

As the afternoon stretched into evening, Walker informed the detectives that Wasko was opening up more and more, describing the interior of the Weinstein home and adding details to his earlier story, though some of them were inconsistent with that account.

Sometime after seven Walker and Wasko became emotionally overcome by their conversation about the crime's details. They actually broke down in tears.

Walker said to Wasko that he was free to end the conversation and leave the room, but, as Walker later told the detectives, Wasko said he wanted to keep talking about the case, to get things "straightened out." The more he talked, the less weight he felt on his shoulders. Walker said Wasko told him he was amazed how much better he felt about telling all this after he had held it in for the past eight months.

At 9:45 Sessler sat in on the conversation between Walker and Wasko. And heard more or less the same story repeated.

On the afternoon of the fourteenth, said Wasko, Pierson had left him at the Morgenthaler job and went to the Weinstein house in an attempt to have sex with the young girl there. He would get into the house on the pretext of offering the girl a free carpet-cleaning estimate. On completing the Morgenthaler job and fixing the float valve on the truck, Wasko said he drove into the driveway of the Weinstein house to wait for Pierson to come out. Shortly afterward Pierson came running out of the house and said he had just hurt the girl badly by beating her, that things hadn't happened the way they were supposed to. Wasko then said he opened his brown zipper bag and removed his .22-caliber pistol. He gave it to Pierson and told him to finish off the girl. Pierson went back into the house. When he returned they made plans to hide the gun.

When Wasko finished this declaration, Sessler took him outside to the hallway and told him something was wrong with that story he'd just related. Something he'd said about the gun didn't fit. Wasko admitted Sessler was right; the story couldn't be true because the gun had a broken grip on the left side, and it had a broken grip because it was used to beat the girl.

Sessler said to Wasko that maybe he'd like to rest for a while and think about the truth and asked him if he wanted to continue the conversation. Wasko said he was willing to keep talking. They returned to the interview room, just the two of them, and for more than an hour Sessler deliberately did not talk about the case but, in an attempt to put the other man at ease and establish some kind of rapport, he chatted about sports, about travel, about family background, about work, about anything but the case.

Shortly after midnight, Sessler asked Wasko if he still wanted to talk about events on the day of the murder. When Wasko said he did, Sessler produced another Miranda form and gave it to Wasko to read. As was necessary, he read aloud to Sessler each of his Constitutional rights. After each was read, Sessler reread them back to him, then Wasko initialed each right, stating he understood it. Wasko further indicated both verbally and via his initials and signature that he was willing to talk to Sessler without the presence of an attorney. Sessler signed as a witness to Wasko's signature and began a fresh interview about a quarter past midnight.

A more detailed story emerged:

Wasko said on their way to the Morgenthaler house he had seen a girl walking south of their job location. He pulled off to the side of the road and casually greeted the girl, who, he said, looked to be about seventeen. She was wearing a blue top and light, possibly pink shorts. He told the girl he and his partner, John, were on the way to clean the carpets of a house a bit north of there. After arriving at the Morgenthaler house and while he was setting up the machinery on the truck, this same girl walked up to him. She told him where she lived, and arrangements were made to give her a free estimate for carpet cleaning.

After the job was done and he was fixing the machinery, Wasko said he sent Pierson over to the girl's house, using the ploy of a free estimate but actually so that Pierson could have sexual intercourse with her, his own girlfriend being uncooperative at the time. When he finished the repair job on the truck, Wasko said he drove to the girl's house. She greeted him at the door. He entered and saw Pierson sitting on the couch. He said the young girl began to make verbal and physical sexual advances to him, rubbing her body against his and asking if there was anything she could do to get a lower price on the carpet cleaning.

Wasko said it was obvious to him that the girl wanted to have sex with him, but since the idea was that Pierson was to have sex with the girl, he told her to go to her bedroom with him. Pierson then took the girl by the hand and started to lead her up the stairs to the left of the living room. The girl began to resist and Pierson hit her in the face. She deserved it, Wasko said, since it was she who had made the sexual advances. Pierson then forced the girl into the first bedroom on the left.

Moments later, Wasko stated, he walked up the stairs and looked into the bedroom. Pierson was lying on top of the girl, who was on her back. It appeared that Pierson was trying to have intercourse with the girl while wearing his pants. The girl was pushing Pierson away. Pierson then, according to Wasko, dropped his pants and underwear on the floor, leaving on only his red Stanley Steemer shirt. The girl began to laugh at Pierson because he had such a small penis. Pierson became angry and tried to remove the girl's shorts and panties and have sexual intercourse. However, he couldn't penetrate because he failed to get an erection. Wasko said that as far as he was concerned, it was an attempted rape. He repeated that the girl deserved to be hit.

Wasko continued, stating that Pierson was kissing the girl all over her body, on her neck, breasts, stomach, and thighs. By this time the girl was struggling violently, resisting him. Pierson began beating her about the face and head with his fists. Wasko admitted that he, too, hit her to stop her resistance to Pierson.

Wasko said that he had his .22-caliber revolver with him while Pierson was attempting to rape the girl. He described the gun as having a dark finish and white grips. The gun had a short barrel. He'd bought it before leaving for Miami in 1982, paying a friend of his named Cal Gossie twenty dollars for it.

Wasko said that as the girl continued to resist Pierson, he told him to hit her with the gun. Pierson hit her with it until the girl appeared to be semiconscious. That scared him, Wasko said, because the girl could get him in trouble by calling the police. So he told Pierson to stop beating her and shoot her. He told Pierson to be a man and shoot her. Pierson then shot her in the chest.

Wasko said he then left the room. As he was walking

back down the stairs to the living room he heard a second shot. He left the house and got back into his truck. There was no blood on him, but when Pierson returned he had blood on the lower front portion of his shirt. He gave Pierson a fresh shirt, yellow, with a Stanley Steemer logo on it. Pierson wrapped the gun in the stained shirt and they went on to the next job. Wasko said he didn't remember where they threw the shirt and the gun.

Sessler now needed a formal confession on the record. And it had to be absolutely legal.

Sessler stopped the questioning and gave Wasko a bathroom break. At 1:27 Sessler asked him if he was willing voluntarily to give a taped interview. Wasko agreed. On the tape, Sessler began by again reviewing with Wasko the Constitutional Rights Form he'd signed. The Miranda spells out such things as the right to remain silent and not answer questions, but should the interviewee answer the questions, then anything he or she says "can and will be introduced as evidence in court against you." Wasko's confession, which eventually ran to twenty-seven transcript pages, is quoted here in part.

The initial questions and answers more or less gave background to the events of October 14, 1982. Then Sessler asked him what happened after Pierson had gone to the girl's house pretending to give her a carpet-cleaning estimate and Wasko followed on later.

Sessler: "And when you drove your truck to that house, where did you park?"

Wasko: "In the driveway."

"What did you do next?"

"Got out, went to the door."

"Did anybody answer the door?"

"When I knocked on the door it was answered by the girl."

"Was it the same girl that you had two conversations

with previously? Once as you were arriving at the Morgenthalers' and once at the Morgenthalers' house?"

"Yes."

"And what did she say to you?"

"She said, 'Stan, it's about time you got here.' "

"By 'Stan,' what did you take that to mean?"

"It was like she was waiting for me to come."

"Do you know why she used the name Stan since your name is Eddie?"

"Because it was on our shirts."

"Is that in reference to the word Stanley, for Stanley Cleaner . . . Stanley Steemer?"

"Yes."

Sessler asked him about his conversation with the girl.

Wasko: ". . . I asked her about . . . 'Did John give you a good price?' "

"And what did she say?"

"She said the price wasn't low enough."

"And what did you say?"

"I said, 'Well, we can do better than that.' "

"And what else was said?"

"She asked me what she had to do to get a better price."

"And what did you say in response to that?"

"Said, 'Anything you want.' "

"What did she say then?"

"She didn't say, she kinda like leaned on me."

"In what way did she lean on you?"

"Kinda like a kitten."

"Like a kitten?"

"Cuddling up to you . . . you know . . . snuggling up to you."

"How did you interpret this action that she took?"

"I took it to be very . . . very aggressive."

"I see. What was John doing while this was taking place?"

"Sitting on the couch."

"What happened next?"

"I told her that she'd have to take care of us in order to get a better price on the job."

"And what were you implicating when you said that?"

"She'd have to give us some . . . happiness."

"By happiness . . . can you define that a little better?"

"Perhaps sexual . . . release, or sexual happiness."

"Did she know what you meant when you said to her, 'she'd have to take care of us'?"

"Yes."

"Did she appear to be cooperative at that time?"

"Well, she knew what I was leading on to."

"Then what happened?"

"She wanted to go upstairs with me."

"Did you escort her upstairs?"

"No, I didn't."

"What did you say?"

"I told her that my helper was a cherry."

"By cherry, what'd you mean by that?"

"Very inexperienced in this."

"And what did she do when you said that?"

"She laughed."

"And then what happened?"

"She invited him to come upstairs."

"Did John accept her invitation?"

"At first he was kinda shy, but I kinda told him . . . I said, 'Go ahead, John.' "

"At this time did she and John go upstairs?"

"Yes."

"Did her attitude change at any time?"

"Yes."

"And what was her attitude as she started going upstairs?"

"She kinda like started pulling back."

"And what was John's attitude as she started pulling back?"

"He started pulling her up."

"Were they kidding or was she serious about not going upstairs at this time?"

"She was very serious."

"How did John get her upstairs?"

"By hitting her."

"How did he hit her? Can you explain that?"

"He backhanded her."

"In what part of the body did he strike her?"

"In the face."

"What happened then?"

"She went upstairs with him."

"At this time, did you feel that this young girl was trying to tease or seduce either you or John?"

"No."

"By the previous action of rubbing up against you like a kitten, or, you know, teasing John, did you feel like she might have been ... trying to seduce either you or John?"

"Yes."

"When John struck her in the face, how'd you feel then?"

"That he was taking control of the situation."

"Did you feel that she deserved this?"

"Yes."

"Do you know if when you entered the front door walking in, if these stairs are to the right or the left?"

"To the left."

"And upon John taking this girl upstairs, do you know where he then took her?"

"To the bedroom down the left hall."

"Is that down to the left on the hall?"

"Yes."

"Where were you at this time?"

"I was waiting until I thought that it was enough time to go upstairs and watch everything that was going to proceed."

"When you went upstairs, did you at that time enter the bedroom?"

"No."

"What did you do?"

"I opened the door just enough so that I could see in and visibly watch what was occurring."

"And did you observe John and this girl in the room?"

"Yes."

"What was taking place?"

"John already had her on the bed. He was on top of her."

"Was she clothed at that time?"

"Yes."

"Was John wearing his clothes at this time?"

"Yes."

"Was she . . . resisting John or was she being passive or cooperative with John's advances?"

"She was trying to push him off."

"What happened then?"

"John started getting more aggressive."

"By more aggressive, what did he do?"

"He started proceeding to take her clothes off."

"What portions of her clothes did you see John Pierson take off Staci Weinstein?"

"Her top."

"Was John still clothed at this time?"

"Yes."

"At this time was she still resisting?"

"Yes."

"What happened next?"

"Proceeded to kiss her."

"Where did he kiss her."

"On her face . . . on her neck . . . on her chest . . . on her breasts."

"At this time was she . . . on the bed, or standing, or what position was she in?"

"She was laying on her back."

"What happened after that?"

"She . . . she laughed at him."

"Why did Staci laugh at John Pierson?"

"Because he was attempting to make love to her with his pants on."

"Was there anything said between her and John at this time?"

"Yes."

"What was said?"

"She said, 'Asshole, if you're going to fuck me, take your pants off.' "

"She said that to John Pierson?"

"Yes."

"And what was John's reaction to that?"

"He was mad."

"Was she more passive at this time rather than being resistant?"

"More passive."

"What happened after John got mad?"

"He began to pull his pants down."

"After he pulled his pants down—does that include . . . his trousers and his underwear?"

"Yes."

"What did he do then?"

"Proceeded to lay on top of her and try to make love to her."

"Was she wearing her bottoms at this time or did she have 'em off?"

"She was still wearing her bottoms."

"Didn't that strike you as rather funny, due to the fact that he was naked from the waist down and she was clothed from the waist down?"

"Yes."

"What happened next?"

"I heard her laughing."

"Do you recall why Staci was laughing?"

"Yes."

"Why was that?"

"She was laughing at the size of his penis."

"What was John Pierson's attitude at that time?"

"Very bad."

"What did he do then?"

"He hit her."

"How did he hit her?"

"With a closed fist."

"On what portions of her body did he strike her?"

"Upper part."

"Did you ever see John Pierson make penetration into any of the orifices of Staci Weinstein?"

"No."

"Were you still at the door at this time looking in?"

"Yes."

"And about how far open was the door that you were looking in?"

"About an inch."

"Was Staci still fighting at this time?"

"Yes."

"Do you recall what happened after John had taken his pants off and Staci had started laughing at him? And I believe you stated that he struck her. Then what proceeded to happen?"

(No answer)

"Were you still at the door?"

"No."

"Did you enter the room?"

"Yes."

"What was your attitude toward the female at this time?"

"I was mad."

"Why were you mad at her?"

" 'Cause she wasn't cooperating with John."

"Did you feel at all like she was teasing the two of you and then changed her mind?"

"Yes."

"And did you strike her in any manner?"

"Yes."

"Where did you strike her?"

"In the face."

"What did you use to strike her?"

"My fist."

"What was John doing at this time while you struck Staci?"

"He was watching."

"At this time was Staci still protesting or resisting?"

"No."

"Why not?"

"She was hurt."

"You said she was hurt. Was she conscious or unconscious?"

"She was semiconscious."

"What did you or John Pierson do or say next?"

(No answer)

"To the best of your memory what happened at this point after you struck her?"

"I got away, and I went downstairs."

"Prior to going downstairs, did you see any weapons on that day, October fourteenth, inside the Weinstein house?"

"Yes."

"And who had possession of a weapon?"

"John Pierson."

"Where did John get this weapon?"

"From my truck."

"Are you saying that John Pierson took the weapon from the truck, or is this the weapon that he kept in the truck?"

"This is the weapon that he kept in the truck."

"And which one of the two of you, John or yourself, had the weapon when you first went into the house?"

"I did."

"How did John get the weapon?"

"I gave it to him."

"Was there any reason why you gave him the weapon?"

"So that he could scare her even further."

"How did you expect him to scare her even further?"

"I just felt that the gun would make her cooperate with John."

"Did you tell John to hit her again . . . or shoot her?"

"No."

"Did you previously tell me during an interview that we had prior to this formal statement that you told John to go ahead and shoot her, to give him the courage to shoot her?"

"Yes."

"Why did you say that to John? In other words, do you feel that John may have been too weak to shoot?"

"Yes."

"Do you feel that you have control over John at all?"

"Yes."

"How's that, Eddie?"

"I felt he looked up to me like a big brother. I felt he respected me. I felt he'd obey me."

"Did he obey you?"

"Yes."

"Did he in fact shoot her?"

"First he hit her with the pistol . . . several times."

"And following hitting her with the pistol several times, what did he do?"

"I told him to do it right . . . shoot her."

Side one of the tape ended there. Sessler turned it to side two and wanted Wasko to repeat that last statement, so he asked: "What did John Pierson do after repeatedly striking Staci Weinstein with the pistol?"

"He looked at me, and I told him to shoot her."

"Why did you tell him to shoot her?"

"Because he had hit her hard enough to hurt her badly, it appeared."

"Did you ever think about the fact that since you had a marked van outside with the name of the company, and the fact that she had seen both you and John . . . did you ever feel that she would come back to get you in trouble someday?"

"Yes."

"Could this be one of the reasons why you instructed John to shoot her?"

"Yes."

"And do you feel it was necessary to tell John to shoot her?"

"Yes."

"Did you feel like you could control John Pierson?"

"Yes, I did control . . ."

"How many times did you observe John Pierson shoot the girl?"

"Once."

"And do you recall to what portion of the body you observed her shot?"

"The upper chest area."

As the confession continued, Wasko claimed the gun was Pierson's, and, contrary to what he had told Sessler in the interview before this formal statement, he did not mention hearing a second shot as he walked down the stairs and out of the house. Responding to the detective's questions, Wasko said Pierson had blood on his shirt when he came out of the house and was given a clean one. Wasko said he never saw what Pierson did with the bloodied shirt. He didn't recall where they got rid of the gun, except that it was in "some abandoned field area."

Sessler: "Do you think if we had a chance to, you could show me the area where the gun was taken to?"

Wasko: "Maybe."

Wasko said Pierson was very nervous after the incident, but he himself was calm, that he had the situation under control as far as getting rid of the evidence was concerned.

Sessler: "Did you feel sorry for the girl at all, or did you think she deserved what happened to her."

"Feel she deserved what happened to her."

"Going back one second to the time when John was forcing himself on the girl, would you consider this just being sexually aggressive or do you actually consider it a sexual battery or a rape that was taking place in your presence? In other words, was this just John pushing himself on the girl? Did it appear that it was what we would call a rape? In other words, he's forcibly pushing himself on the girl attempting to have sexual intercourse?"

"Yes."

"Did you have intercourse with her in any way?"

"No."

"Besides striking her that one time that you mentioned, did you kiss her or pet her in any way? In other words, did you kiss her or touch other parts of her body?"

"Ah . . . no."

Sessler asked Wasko if he'd ever given Pierson advice about talking to the police about anything. Wasko replied that he'd told Pierson to lie about passing out advertisements because he felt it would link both of them to the crime.

An experienced homicide detective and interrogator, Sessler was satisfied with the details that had been confessed on the tape. He drew the interview to its conclusion.

"Has your treatment during this interview with me been fair? In other words, have I been kind to you and listened to everything you had to say?"

"Very fair."

"Have you been given beverage, such as Pepsi-Cola, as the cans are in front of you now, prior to giving this formal . . . or this taped interview?"

"Yes."

"Have you been given some food, some of which was in the form of potato chips, to eat?"

"Yes."

"How about cigarettes? Were you given cigarettes?"

"Yes."

"Has everything you stated to me been true and correct to the best of your knowledge?"

"Yes."

"Has anybody threatened you or coerced you to give this statement?"

"No."

"Have you given this statement freely and voluntarily?"

"Yes, to the best of my knowledge."

"Okay, Eddie, this statement that we have just given on the formal tape recorder on the ninth of July 1983 is now concluding at 2:24 a.m. During the course of this taped interview, besides the fact that we ran out of tape on the first side, do you recall the tape being stopped to edit or change anything you said?"

"No."

"Thank you very much."

Between 2:28 and 3:03, while Randy Walker and Sergeant Jim Ratcliff stood witness, Wasko was given the opportunity to listen to a replay of the tape. At 3:20 the detectives gave the tape to clerk-typist Barbara Robinson for a transcript. Wasko was offered pizza, a Pepsi, and cigarettes, but he said he wasn't hungry. A few moments later Wasko was asleep in Randy Walker's office, his head cradled in his arms on the desk.

At 3:40 Sessler telephoned Metro-Dade Homicide. He spoke to the midnight shift steno-reporter Joan Batt and gave her the details for the preparation of an arrest affidavit. Sessler then called Detective William Venturi, explained the circumstances, and asked him to witness the affidavit.

Wasko awoke around six, said he was hungry, and ate several slices of pizza that had been ordered from a local shop. About an hour later Barbara Robinson came in with the transcribed pages of the taped interview. Sessler read the transcript aloud to Wasko, who then read the statement, made several minor corrections, then initialed each of the twenty-seven pages at the bottom. At the bottom of the last page, in capital letters, he printed: I HAVE REVIEWED THIS STATEMENT AND MADE CORRECTIONS. THIS STATEMENT IS CORRECT.

He dated it and signed it, and it was witnessed by Barbara Robinson and Steve Sessler.

At 7:45 a teletyped copy of the arrest warrant was forwarded to the Columbus Police Department, charging Eddie Wasko with first-degree murder.

Chapter 11

Strange but true, during the three days of Wasko's questioning and polygraphs a "bonding" developed, first between Wasko and polygrapher Randy Walker, and then between Wasko and the detectives. It's an experience well known to psychologists, criminologists, and in particular by the FBI and other law enforcement agencies specializing in kidnap and hostage situations, wherein a kidnap victim or a group of hostages develops this "bonding," manifested by an empathy with the kidnapper or bank robber or terrorists or whatever.

In this case it was demonstrated by the mutual breakdown in tears by Wasko and Walker, an emotional empathy built up between them as Wasko related his terrible tale and, as he said to Walker, felt a surge of relief for getting it off his chest. Walker, himself a father of young twin girls, could feel and even express to Wasko his fear of anything similar happening to them.

The calm and patient method of questioning used by Sessler to gain Wasko's confidence, to establish the rapport he sought, the atmosphere he wanted that would enable Wasko to relieve himself of his burden without being intimidated, formed that "bonding." This emerged as Sessler and Ratcliff, along with a Columbus detective, Rick Sheasby, prepared to take Wasko down to the Columbus Jail in Franklin County later that morning. Before they left for the jail, Wasko agreed to having his picture taken with the detectives and Randy Walker. In the photo there is the bearded Walker in his wheelchair holding aloft the pizza they'd ordered in, and behind him Wasko, Ratcliff, and Sessler. It could have been the boys snapped after an all-night poker game.

Further, at nine o'clock, when Wasko was escorted to the jail, he said to Sessler and Ratcliff, "I like you guys. You're still my friends. When I get out I'll do your carpets."

A half hour later the three appeared in Franklin County Municipal Court before Judge George C. Smith for an extradition hearing. Michael Miller, a Franklin County prosecutor, was there for the state, and Dane Chavers, a public defender, had been called in to defend Wasko. Technically, Wasko was charged with being a fugitive from justice. He was advised that he could fight extradition or sign a waiver and return immediately to Miami. Wasko said, "I want to go with you guys." He waived extradition. That afternoon he was flown back on an ordinary commercial Delta flight.

That "bonding" continued as the three flew back together. The case was not discussed. As they had done earlier during the questioning process, Sessler and Ratcliff talked to Wasko about his work, about their work, about sports, girls, and everyday chitchat. Interestingly enough, due to FAA regulations, Wasko could not be handcuffed during the flight, so the two detectives and their prisoner sat as any other three men on a business trip. Wasko sat between them. They read magazines; Sessler, who was reading a *Sports Illustrated,* glanced at what Wasko was reading, a *People* magazine, when Wasko flipped a page and stared, transfixed, at a picture of an electric chair. Instantly Sessler grabbed the magazine away and said, "I want to read that article. Here, you read my *Sports Illustrated.*" There wasn't much more light conversation for the rest of the flight.

Perhaps that flash of the electric chair did it, but by the time the detectives picked up an arrest affidavit at headquarters that evening and took Wasko to the Dade County Jail, the "bonding" appeared to be broken. Wasko was now sullen and cold. He stared at Ratcliff and Sessler as though his two "friends" were abandoning him into the hands of strangers. It was as though suddenly the "game" was over and this was for real. Jail. Jailers. A cell.

The following evening, Sessler telephoned Marvin Weinstein. "Marvin, I'd like to come by with my wife," he said. Marvin said he was more than welcome. He turned to his daughter, Hilari, and told her Sessler was coming over. "This is no social call," he said to her. "Sessler's been out of town. If he's coming here on a Sunday night it's because something's up. And it's gotta be real important. Like they got the guy who did it. Sessler is not coming to our house for coffee and cake."

Since the previous Tuesday, when he'd learned Sessler was "out of town," Marvin had been waiting for that call. He had felt it in his bones. Things were coming to a head.

Marvin ran upstairs to change his clothes. He didn't know why he was bothering to change, but he was excited, flustered, thinking of Sessler: what is he gonna tell us, what is he gonna say? Marvin scurried about the house, straightening up papers, plumping cushions, opening and closing the refrigerator door. Hilari stared at her father in astonishment; normally he couldn't care less about the state of the house or the contents of the refrigerator. "Why have you put on that awful pink shirt?" she asked him. "You hate that shirt."

Marvin looked down. "I don't know. Why are you bothering me about the shirt? What's so important about the shirt? But you're right. I always hated it. It's one of the shirts Dave Rogers gave me." Marvin sat on the couch and held his head in his hands. His heart pounded in his chest. Could it be? Could we be coming to an end of the nightmare here? After all these months . . . nine months and no killer . . . his head throbbed with it all as he waited for Sessler . . . the daily phone calls to the cops, the runs downtown to fight with them . . . Ben Hall . . . the psychic . . . waiting, waiting for something to happen . . . the worry, the frustration . . . fighting the system . . . breaking out in hives, nerves constantly on knife edge . . . cops suspecting me . . . he began to feel ill with the flood of memories, physically sick to his stomach until he was brought around by the ringing of the doorbell. Sessler!

The four of them—Marvin and Hilari, Sessler and his wife—sat around a table in the dining room and talked. As usual Marvin wanted to know everything. Nervously he bounced up and down in his chair. "You went out of town to make an arrest, didn't you?"

Sessler explained to Marvin that, yes, an arrest had been made. However, he said, he and Sergeant Ratcliff had gone to Ohio to interview a potential witness. As it turned out over three days of questioning, the probable witness confessed to being involved in the homicide itself.

"He's a Stanley Steemer guy, right?" said Marvin. "They drive yellow vans, like mine, only theirs is a brighter yellow. Remember Hall suspected me because I had a yellow van? What's the guy's name?"

Sessler told him it was Eddie Wasko. No harm in that; the name would soon be announced in all the media.

"Okay," said Marvin, "but if you went up there to question a witness, that means there's another guy maybe involved, another guy you were looking at, right? Two guys sit in that van."

Sessler said yes, there was another suspect they were looking at, but he couldn't go into any detail on that with Marvin.

"How did you feel, sitting there talking to a murderer?" asked Marvin. "A child killer, a baby raper?"

"You have to remain professionally under control," Sessler said. "You can't show any emotion. You have to let him talk, encourage him to talk, and listen carefully to what he has to say."

Marvin wanted to know if Wasko had given him details of what had happened to Staci. Sessler replied that Wasko had, but he couldn't disclose them to Marvin for legal reasons. There were, of course, merciful reasons also for keeping the grim details from Marvin. He might hear them later in court, or even from the media, but Sessler would not reveal them. Certainly not here, certainly not now.

"Who's the other guy you're looking at?" asked Marvin. "This Wasko's partner? What's his name?"

"You know I can't tell you that, Marvin," said Sessler. "But look, I'll be in touch and I'll let you know what's happening as best I can."

"So what happens now with this Wasko killer? He in jail down here?"

"Yes, he's here. Without bond, of course." Sessler explained that there would be all the usual legal niceties to go through: a grand jury indictment, depositions, motions, a trial.

"A trial," Marvin said bitterly. "Did he give my little girl a trial before he killed her?"

On Monday Wasko agreed voluntarily to leave the jail and help Sessler and Ratcliff find the .22 revolver Wasko said had been discarded by Pierson. He led them to a large field located west of NE 24th Avenue and 204th Terrace, about a hundred yards from the last carpet-cleaning call made on that October 14. The field had already been checked by detectives. Still, Sessler and Ratcliff combed the area again but found nothing.

On Wednesday the Dade County grand jury brought in a true bill for the indictment of Wasko. Only then was the arrest story given to the media. Thursday morning's *Miami Herald* broke the story with a banner six-column headline: "Workman's arrest may end mystery in girl's killing." Head shots of Wasko and Staci were included. Sessler and Marvin were interviewed. Sessler explained how he and Ratcliff had gone up to Ohio to interview Wasko as a possible witness. As they questioned him, Sessler said, "we found out he was more than a witness. He played an active part, he was directly involved in the homicide.

"It appears that sexual advances were the motive," said Sessler. He acknowledged to the media that the investigation was continuing, that a second man was either a participant or a witness.

Marvin had just returned from work and was still in his baker's uniform when a horde of journalists descended on his house. A television crew appeared from the local ABC affiliate, Channel 10, in addition to newspaper reporters.

"It's not over yet," Marvin told them. "They should have a proper trial for him—and then fry him."

Somehow—the detectives never learned how—a TV newscaster that night revealed the name of John Pierson as the second suspect in the case. Immediately the TV station and all the newspapers were warned that a repeat of Pierson's name could lead to a prosecution for interfering with the course of the investigation.

Marvin saw that newscast. Now he knew who the second man was, the other man in the truck with Wasko, the other man who had participated in the killing of Staci. Marvin made up his mind to go out and try to find this John Pierson—before Sessler and Ratcliff did. But he did wonder why they didn't just arrest him and charge him. Or at least bring him in for rigorous questioning.

The fact of the matter was that there was nothing they could hang on Pierson. Janice and Vera Langhorn were still resisting Detective Harold Ross's requests to file charges of sexual assault. As for a charge of murder based on Wasko's confession, that was not a legal option.

Assistant State Attorney Abraham Laeser, deputy chief of the Major Crimes Division of the State Attorney's Office, who was monitoring and supervising the prosecution stages of the case at the time, explained:

"In essence, what a prosecutor is looking for and what we would recommend to the police is to have some type of evidence to corroborate a claim. Pierson could have said, 'There's a man from Arkansas named Bill Clinton who really did it.' That's not going to ever be the basis for an arrest unless we have exhausted all avenues of attempting to corroborate, because the statement alone is not going to be admissible. Somebody's claim that another person committed a crime is not admissible against that other person."

So John Pierson remained at large while Ratcliff and Sessler pondered their next move. They discussed the possibility of arresting him on the sexual-assault charge. Janice Langhorn and her mother were resisting, but both would now know, as Pierson did as well, that he was the second murder suspect. In effect, the State Attorney's Office had advised Ross that due to Pierson's possible complicity in a felony murder, the rape victim really no longer had a choice. An arrest warrant for Pierson on a sexual-assault charge could be issued and served at any time.

Ratcliff and Sessler could use a tactic frequently used by detectives when stymied on a serious felony investigation such as a homicide: try to bring the suspect in on a lesser charge, give the perpetrator all the time he wants to talk, and see what happens. Often enough, handled cleverly, he will open up on the more serious charge. Sessler and Ratcliff discussed that option with Ross and decided to put it on the shelf for the moment while they scouted for anything else they could get on Pierson to support a murder charge.

After he'd been fired by Stanley Steemer the previous fall, Pierson had drifted around North Miami from job to job and from residence to residence. Sessler and Hall did a circuit of all those places, talking to everyone who knew Pierson, or worked with him and who might have heard him speak of the murder. No one had anything to offer. One of the restaurants where Pierson had worked briefly before being fired for incompetence was called the Triple Three, a popular spot with the younger set.

While Sessler and Ratcliff were making the rounds, Marvin Weinstein was also prowling about, looking for Pierson. After all these months he had become streetwise about the ways of the police. So he learned that Pierson was working the late shift at the Triple Three as an assistant cook. Late one night he stuck a revolver in his belt under his shirt and drove to the restaurant. He had a permit to keep the gun in his house and his van—but he did not have a permit to carry a concealed weapon.

Marvin didn't really know what he was going to do if he found Pierson at the restaurant. One side of him wanted to kill him. The other side thought that it might not be such a good idea. What if the man was not guilty? Maybe he had been there, in the house, maybe he had done something, helped Wasko, even hit Staci. But what if he hadn't shot her himself or played an important part in killing her? Who knew the truth? Killing Pierson without knowing the truth was more than unjust: it was crazy. And what would be the consequences? He would go to jail. And Hilari would be alone.

With his thoughts in turmoil, Marvin entered the restaurant. "Pierson around?" he casually asked the first employee he ran into. "Nope. His night off," came the reply.

Marvin breathed a sigh of relief. Decision postponed. There would be another night.

The next afternoon, however, Sergeant Jim Ratcliff telephoned and said he was coming by the house. What's up now? wondered Marvin.

Ratcliff came straight to the point. "Marvin, we've had an eye on a restaurant called the Triple Three. We've told the manager there that if anybody calls asking about John Pierson, he's to call us. I know that you know we're looking at him. So last night somebody telephoned the place asking for Pierson. Was that you, Marvin? Did you call the restaurant asking about Pierson?"

"Not me," said Marvin. "I didn't make the call."

"You'd better not," warned Ratcliff. "Because if you do I'll have you arrested for interfering in the investigation. Got it?"

"Got it."

Marvin's personal vendetta was overtaken by events, in any case. The decision to charge Pierson with sexual battery was taken off the shelf and put into play. Harold Ross contacted Janice and Vera Langhorn and explained to them that the situation had become far too serious to delay any longer. They knew Pierson was the focus of the continuing homicide investigation. They'd known for months that he was a suspect. Pierson had talked to them about the murder, admitted to them he was a suspect. They must now file charges against Pierson so he could be brought in for questioning. If he was put behind bars for a long time, they'd be safe from him. Janice and her mother agreed.

Ross knew Pierson was living in a trailer park in Dade County, on 119th Street. On the morning of Tuesday, August 30, armed with a warrant for Pierson's arrest, the detective set up a surveillance at the park in a position from where he could see Pierson's front door and his car. Ross did not want to get into a possible siege situation, so he decided to wait until Pierson came out of the house. About two o'clock he emerged with a young girl. They got into Pierson's car and drove off. Ross followed the car for a few blocks, then, aware that Pierson had a reputation for violence, called in two squad cars for assistance, and they forced Pierson to a stop. Ross had him get out of the car, read him his rights and told him he was under arrest for sexual battery. He let the girl go after she'd identified herself. He put Pierson into his car with one of the uniformed cops and drove him back to the Sexual Battery Office. He allowed Pierson to use the rest room, gave him a cup of coffee, then put him into an interview room. With Detective Alan Kaplan of the Sexual Battery Unit on hand as a witness, Ross gave him the Miranda form, scrupulously reviewed it with him, and had him sign and date it.

Ross asked him, however, if he wanted to speak to his attorney before answering any questions.

"I have no attorney at this time," said Pierson. "My attorney was Mr. Weiner, but I got rid of him and now I'm going to get a public defender."

Ross wanted to confirm that. "Is Mr. Weiner in fact still representing you or isn't he?"

"No, he wanted too much money."

Ross told him he had an arrest warrant for sexual battery with the victim, Janice Langhorn, who claimed he had sexually assaulted her at his mother's house on December 30, 1982. Pierson said he knew that's what it was when his car was stopped, but stated he had not raped her. He said they had gone to his mother's house, she had said she wanted to have sex and took off her clothes. Then she changed her mind and began screaming. He put his hand over her mouth to keep her quiet. She began breathing hard, Pierson said, hyperventilating. She was scared. She grabbed a pair of his shorts and his car keys and took off.

"Did you in fact have sex with her that night?" asked Ross.

"No, no sex," said Pierson.

"If you didn't have sex with her, why is she stating you raped her?"

Agitated, Pierson said angrily, "I don't know why she's trying to put this on me. She knows I didn't rape her. We were planning on getting married. She has been acting weird since then, and we stopped seeing each other. I'm now dating the girl you stopped me with. We're getting married and I think she's pregnant. I'm trying to straighten out my life. And then Ed Wasko told police that I was involved in killing Staci."

Ross felt that little frisson well known to investigators. This is what he wanted: Pierson to start talking. He feigned ignorance. "Who? What did he say?"

"Ed Wasko told police that I killed a girl last year. You probably read that or heard it on the news."

"Well, I seem to remember vaguely hearing something about that," Ross said. "What happened?"

"I was working with Ed Wasko at Stanley Steemer when that happened. Ed Wasko told police I murdered the girl, but they have no evidence on me. Ed Wasko told the police I took a gun and killed Staci. Ed Wasko, by his temper, is the type who would do that. Before he was picked up in Ohio, he was arrested for pinching a girl on the behind."

"And then what happened?" Ross asked.

"We were working as partners for Stanley Steemer, and we were cleaning carpets at this old Jewish couple's house. We went inside, and Ed Wasko had me measuring the carpet, getting the solution line, the vacuum hose and the carpet wand and the chip box. He told me to start vacuuming, and then he disappeared for thirty, forty minutes."

Pierson said he looked around for him but couldn't find him. When Wasko returned eventually, Pierson said, Wasko seemed very nervous and said to him, "Hurry up, let's leave."

Ross said he'd never heard of this guy Wasko and had heard only bits and pieces about the homicide, was not familiar with it. "But if you say you had nothing to do with it," said Ross, "you shouldn't go to jail for something you didn't do. Why don't we get the Homicide guys down here who are working on the case? Maybe you can be of assistance to them. You willing to talk to them?"

"Yeah, I want to clear my conscience," said Pierson. "I didn't do nothing. I have nothing to hide."

The time was 3:45. Pierson asked to go to the rest room. When he got back, Ross gave him another cup of coffee and telephoned Homicide. He asked for a detective who was working on the Staci Weinstein case and got Greg Smith of the Cold Case Squad. Ross explained what was happening and asked for Smith or some other detective familiar with the case to come to the Sexual Battery Office to interview Pierson.

Thirty minutes later Sessler and Ratcliff turned up at Ross's office. Ross briefed them, advised them that Pierson had said he was willing freely and voluntarily to talk to them. Introductions were made, and the detectives took Pierson into an interview room.

At five-thirty Greg Smith went to Ross's office and found Assistant State Attorney David Waksman there, monitoring the investigation. A few minutes later Assistant State Attorney Jayne Weintraub arrived. Both these attorneys by now had been assigned to prosecute the state's case against Wasko as soon as a trial date could be set on the crowded court calendar. Their presence here indicated that what was happening in that interview room was of supreme importance to them, no matter which way it went with Pierson.

The four of them—Waksman, Weintraub, Smith, and Ross—pulled up hard chairs in Ross's office and settled in as comfortably as possible. Plastic cups of hot coffee were brought in.

Nobody bothered to state the obvious. It was going to be a long night.

Chapter 12

The first thing Sessler and Ratcliff did when they were alone in the interview room with John Pierson was review with him the Constitutional rights form he'd signed when questioned by Detective Harold Ross. To reinforce that Sessler asked him if he wanted to talk about the Weinstein case without the presence of an attorney. Pierson said he'd fired attorney Jeffrey Weiner weeks earlier and would willingly talk to them about the case without an attorney present.

Pierson began his account of what happened on the day of the murder by denying he had ever been in the Weinstein house. He said while he was busy cleaning carpets at the home of the "old Jewish couple," Wasko disappeared for a time, and when he returned he appeared to be "very shaky." He said he'd noticed that Wasko always carried with him a dark-colored gym bag. That day, Pierson said, was the first day he'd worn his new red Stanley Steemer shirt identical to the one worn by Wasko.

Sessler said to him, "John, it's very important that you tell the truth now. It's been ten months since it happened, and I've got to remind you that it was you who asked to talk to us. You told Detective Ross you'd like to talk to us and clear things up. So tell us again, what happened on that day, on October 14?"

"Okay, I wasn't telling the whole truth," Pierson admitted. "I did go inside that house."

"Tell us about it," Sessler said.

As Pierson began his story, Sessler called for more coffee and cold drinks. Ross brought them in, and cigarettes, a routine developing that included escorting Pierson to the men's room several times through the passing hours. In Ross's office styrofoam coffee cups and soft drink cans accumulated on his desk and filled the wastepaper baskets. In time he ordered from a nearby shop the inevitable pizza for everybody.

Pierson told the detectives that after finishing the carpet-cleaning job, Wasko had driven the truck to a corner house nearby and said they were going to give an estimate to the girl who lived there. At the house, Wasko asked the girl, who appeared to be nine or ten years old, if her parents were home. She said no, and Wasko told her that her father had asked for an estimate on carpet cleaning, and she let them in. She was wearing short pants and a short-sleeve shirt, with no shoes.

He waited in the living room, Pierson said, while Wasko and the girl went upstairs to her bedroom. Shortly afterward he heard her screaming. He ran upstairs and saw Wasko with his pants half off. The girl was lying on the bed with her shirt pulled up above her breasts. Pierson said Wasko was attempting to rape the girl. He jumped on him and tried to stop him, but Wasko punched him in the nose, which began bleeding. He then left the house, and as he got back into the van he heard two shots. Wasko then came out of the house carrying a small black revolver. He appeared to have blood on his red shirt and blue work pants. He got back in the van and put the gun in the gym bag he carried. Pierson said he asked Wasko if he'd shot the girl but received no answer.

They drove away toward the next job. On the way they stopped at a convenience store that had a Dumpster along the side. Wasko went into the store to buy apple juice for the two of them. When he came out, said Pierson, he was now wearing a yellow Stanley

Steemer shirt and a different pair of pants. What he'd done with the red shirt, blue pants, and the gun, Pierson said he had no idea.

Sessler asked him if he remembered an incident in the spring of that year when Wasko and another man had stopped their Stanley Steemer truck at a red light and he'd run up to it to talk to Wasko.

Pierson said he did remember. He had gone up to Wasko to sort of say hello, and Wasko had asked him if he'd mentioned anything about the gun to the cops. Pierson said he'd told Wasko that "everything was cool" and he hadn't told the cops anything about the gun. Then the light turned green and they drove away. Sessler and Ratcliff looked at each other with a slight nod. That tied in exactly with what Louis Fasani had told them.

"You ever get nosebleeds that seem to start for no good reason?" asked Sessler.

Pierson said he never had nosebleeds. The only time was when Wasko punched him in the nose. That did not tally with information the detectives had received from various people who had told them Pierson suffered nosebleeds whenever he became angry.

At eight o'clock Pierson said he'd left some things out of his earlier stories. Now he said that as they were driving to the Jewish couple's house, a girl whistled at them. Wasko stopped the truck, got out, and began talking to the girl. She began giggling and Wasko was hugging her. Back in the truck, Wasko said to him that later they were going back to the girl's house to do an estimate "and get some pussy." Pierson told the detectives that his intention was not to have sex with the girl but just watch. Pierson then repeated more or less the same story he'd related earlier.

When Pierson finished this story, the detectives called a break. Pizzas, coffee, cold drinks, and cigarettes were brought in by Ross. He made another trip to the men's room with Pierson.

The break lasted about an hour. Sessler then asked Pierson if he would voluntarily make a formal statement to them that would be taken down by a steno-reporter. Pierson agreed.

Sessler left the room for a moment and announced this to Waksman, Weintraub, and Ross. Steno-reporter Carole Green was called in to take down the statement. Pierson started talking at 9:32. The more significant parts of his statement are directly quoted below.

As Pierson began, the telephone in Ross's office rang. The caller was Captain Coogan, who was commander of the Detective Bureau Shift. Coogan told Ross that he'd been contacted by attorney Jeffrey Weiner, who wanted to know where John Pierson was. He gave Ross Weiner's number. A quick conference was held in the office among Ross, Smith, Waksman, and Weintraub. All were aware of Pierson's assertion that he had fired Weiner several weeks earlier and no longer wanted to be represented by him. Neither had he requested an attorney now. He had signed a waiver to that effect. Nevertheless, the attorneys thought it best that Detective Smith call Weiner and advise him of current circumstances.

Smith called at 10:09. He told Weiner that Pierson was in police custody and at that very moment was being interviewed. Furthermore, he told Weiner, according to Pierson he was no longer his attorney. Weiner said he wanted to talk to Pierson. Smith said Pierson was being interviewed by Sergeant Ratcliff and Detective Sessler, and that the interview would not be interrupted.

"Are you saying you're not going to allow me to speak with my client?" demanded Weiner.

"I'm saying, Mr. Weiner, that John Pierson says he's no longer your client," said Smith.

Weiner repeated his question, and again Smith told him what Pierson had said.

"Fine!" Weiner said and hung up the phone.

A half hour later, the phone rang again. This time it was a Sergeant Hebding of the Northeast District, who told Smith that he had been contacted by a Major Heller. He had asked him to call Smith to find out what was going on with John Pierson and would Smith, as a courtesy, please get in touch with Pierson's parents and tell them what was going on.

Smith telephoned Pierson's mother at 11:05. He explained the situation to her and said that John was being interviewed at that time by detectives Sessler and Ratcliff. Mrs. Pierson told Smith that her son had specific instructions not to speak to the police without first contacting his attorney, Jeffrey Weiner.

"According to your son," said Smith, "Jeffrey Weiner is no longer his attorney."

Mrs. Pierson retorted that her son was retarded and was unable to make a decision for himself, and that as far as she was concerned, Jeffrey Weiner was still his attorney.

Patiently, Smith reiterated the position: her son had said Weiner was once his attorney but no longer represented him. Further, John appeared to be in good health, he had been given food and drink, was allowed to use the rest room when needed and had been advised of his Constitutional rights, at which time he had waived his right of an attorney's presence during the interview.

Mrs. Pierson replied that her son had no rights as he was mentally retarded, and he was not in good health.

Smith advised her that her son did in fact have Constitutional rights. Under Florida law, he was an adult and could decide for himself whether or not he wished to invoke them.

Mrs. Pierson then demanded to speak to her son. Smith told her that the interview was still going on and could not be interrupted. When she persisted, Smith told her that at the conclusion of the interview John would contact her if he so wished.

Indignant, she accused the police of mistreating her son. She said he was probably sick to his stomach and had acquired pneumonia as the result of his treatment by the police. She added that John's father was extremely upset and physically sick as a result of what was now going on. She warned Smith that she was going to notify Jeffrey Weiner about the physical maladies afflicting her son and her husband at the hands of the police. What the detective inferred from this diatribe was that Mrs. Pierson might be planning a civil action.

Meanwhile, in the interview room John Pierson was making his formal statement to Detective Sessler, witnessed by Sergeant Ratcliff. That concluded at 9:55. From 10:00 to 12:40 A.M., steno-reporter Carole Green transcribed the statement. It begins with another review with Pierson of the Constitutional rights form he'd signed previously. The most consequential portions of Pierson's confession following that review are given here verbatim:

Sessler: "Going back to the afternoon, the early afternoon of October 14, 1982, do you recall responding with Eddie Wasko in the Stanley Steemer carpet cleaner van to North Miami Beach?"

Pierson: "Yes."

"Can you describe the couple that had asked for this job to be done?"

"Some old Jewish couple."

"Approximately what time did you arrive in the area of the old Jewish couple's house?"

"At approximately twelve, twelve-thirty."

"Who was driving the van at that time?"

"Eddie Wasko."

"While en route, just prior to arriving at the old Jewish couple's house, did you observe a young lady near the roadway?"

"I didn't, Ed Wasko did."

"Approximately how old did this girl look to you?"

"Nine, ten."

"Did you see Eddie conversing with this little girl?"

"Yes."

"How did the conversation start?"

"Eddie Wasko was looking toward her direction and she whistled at him. He stopped the truck, got out, and started to talk to the girl."

"Do you recall what the girl was wearing?"

"Yes. She was wearing a white shirt and some kind of—wearing a pair of shorts."

"Did you hear any of this conversation between Eddie and the girl?"

"No. The girl was giggling and Eddie Wasko walked back to the truck and he told her he'd be right back."

"Upon Eddie Wasko returning to the truck, what did he say took place during the conversation?"

"He told me that he could have a chance to have sex with the girl."

"Do you recall what his exact words were?"

"He wanted to—he wanted to get her pussy. And he kept on teasing me about being a virgin and stuff like that, and he wanted me to have sex with the girl also and I told him no."

"After the conversation between Eddie and the girl, where did you and Eddie next go?"

"After that we went to the Jewish house."

"Approximately how long did it take you to clean the carpet at the Jewish couple's house?"

"A good hour."

Pierson then talked about the repair job Wasko had done on the truck while he himself passed out four advertising flyers at nearby houses.

"And then where did you and Eddie go?"

"We went around the block and stopped over to the little girl's house."

"While en route to the girl's house, what did Eddie talk to you about?"

"He was telling me he had a chance to have sex with this girl, and he told me I could have a chance to have sex with this girl too, and I told him I already had a girlfriend at the time and I wasn't interested in anything like that."

"Did he tease you about not having sex often?"

"Many times."

"What would he say to you?"

"He said I was a virgin and that I needed to get my cherry popped and stuff like that."

"What happened when Eddie arrived at the house at that time?"

"We arrived at the house and Eddie knocked on the door and he started talking to the girl, and the girl said she wanted the couch estimate."

"Who had spoken to the girl about this?"

"Eddie."

"What was the real reason why Eddie went to that house?"

"Because he said he thinks he could get some pussy."

"Did the girl let you and Eddie into the house?"

"Yes."

"While you and Eddie were inside the house, what did the girl say to either you or Eddie?"

"The girl didn't really talk to me. Eddie Wasko told me to measure off the couch, and Eddie Wasko talked to the girl. The girl was giving him signs and stuff like that."

"Can you describe better the type of signs she was giving Eddie?"

"She was winking at him and smiling and just tongue movements on her lips."

"Did you interpret these as friendly or promiscuous signs?"

"Promiscuous."

"Did it appear that the girl was flirting with you and Eddie?"

"She was—the girl wasn't flirting with me. She was flirting with Eddie."

"When you saw her inside the house, was she wearing the same clothes that you had previously seen her in outside the house?"

"Yes."

"Was anything mentioned in reference to her parents being home by anyone?"

"Eddie asked her was her mother and father home."

"What did she say?"

"She said no."

"Then what happened?"

"Then after that her and Ed Wasko—Eddie asked her to show him around the house. And then after that Eddie was inside her bedroom."

"Did she voluntarily go with Eddie?"

"Yes."

"At that time did you think that Eddie was going to have sex with her?"

"Probably. Yeah."

"What happened after they got to the bedroom?"

"Well, I went back to the truck and put my book back inside the truck and came back in and asked Eddie if he was ready or not, and all of a sudden I heard the girl screaming."

"When you came to the house and heard the girl screaming, what did you do?"

"I ran into the girl's room and kicked the door, and I saw the girl having her panties off halfway and Eddie Wasko, his clothes were, he had his pants down part of the way and the girl had her shirt up and I was jumping on Ed Wasko and then Ed Wasko, he hit me in my face."

"When the girl was screaming, could you interpret what she was saying or what she was screaming?"

"She told him to 'Stop, stop,' to leave her alone, just screaming out loud."

"Did you think the girl was being raped at this time in your presence?"

"Yes."

"When the girl was screaming, pleading with Eddie to stop, what was Eddie doing?"

"Well, when I walked in—I just—he was just—I jumped on him, okay, and tried to avoid him hitting the girl or anything like that."

"You were trying to stop Eddie from hitting the girl, okay. Did you observe Eddie hit the girl?"

"No, I didn't, no, sir."

"Was there any indication by looking at the girl that showed you that the girl was hit?"

"Yes. She had red marks on her face and her head was bleeding."

"Did you ever observe Eddie Wasko trying to have sex with the girl?"

"No, I didn't."

"What about the rest of her clothing? Was she wearing a shirt?"

"She was wearing a shirt. At the time the shirt was like over, like up over her bra, training bra."

"You stated you tried to stop Eddie from attacking the girl?"

"Yes."

"And how did you do that? What did you do?"

"I jumped on top of him, trying to avoid him hitting the girl. I'd seen marks on the girl. So I jumped on top of him, and then he slapped me in the face, took his fist and hit me in the face and around the nose."

"When he hit you in the face with his fist, did your nose start to bleed at this time?"

"The first time, no."

"Did he hit you again at a later time?"

"Yes, he did."

"What part of the body did he hit you in?"

"In the nose."

"When he hit you in the nose, where were you standing?"

"By the bedroom door."

"After your nose started bleeding, did you ever go back to the girl again?"

"No, I didn't."

"Approximately how far were you from the girl when Eddie punched you in the nose and your nose started bleeding?"

"Eight or ten feet."

"What did you do after that?"

"After Eddie hit me and it started bleeding, I put my hand over my nose and ran outside and went to the truck and sat down and put a rag over my nose and tilted my head backwards."

"Prior to leaving the bedroom did you ever assist Eddie in attempting to attack the girl?"

"Never."

"Did you ever kiss or lick the girl in any manner?"

"Never, never."

"Was there anything in the room that you recall which would indicate that the room belonged to a little girl?"

"There was a brown stuffed animal there."

"Do you recall what kind of stuffed animal it was?"

"A dog."

"After you were punched in the nose and ran to the truck, what did you see or hear next?"

"I heard two shots from a gun."

"Were these two shots rapid?"

"They were one after another, bang, bang."

(Sessler: "Let the record indicate within one second.")

"What happened then?"

"What happened after that was Eddie Wasko came running outside and came to the truck and we drove off."

"After Eddie Wasko left the house, did you notice anything unusual about him? Did he look different from when he entered the house?"

"He had blood on his shirt and pants."

"What type of clothing was he wearing?"

"He had a red Stanley Steemer shirt and navy blue, baggy pants."

"Had you observed Eddie Wasko with a gun prior to the shooting or before the shooting?"

"No."

"When he returned to the truck, did he ever show you a gun?"

"Yes."

"What type of gun did he show you?"

"It was a pistol—revolver."

"Was it a large or a small gun?"

"Small gun."

"What color was the gun itself?"

"The gun was black."

"With a pistol you refer to an automatic, with a revolver you refer to a gun which has chambers that rotate. What type of gun do you think he had?"

"He had the chambers."

"Indicating a revolver?"

"Yes."

"Who drove the truck away from the house?"

"Ed Wasko."

"Did you ask Eddie Wasko any questions as to what took place inside the house, if he had shot the girl or not?"

"I did, and got no reply."

"What did you and Eddie do next?"

"We went—Eddie Wasko drove—he drove around and stopped at a small store, there's a gas station right there. And he went inside and got some apple juice."

"When he came out of the store, did you notice anything different again in reference to his clothing? Was he wearing the same clothes when he came out?"

"When he came out he was wearing a different shirt and he had another pair of navy pants and a yellow T-shirt with Stanley Steemer on it."

"Did you ever actually see Eddie dispose of these clothes?"

"No."

"Did you ever see what Eddie did with the gun?"

"No."

Sessler concluded the questioning and the statement by verifying with Pierson that he had been fed, talked freely and voluntarily, had not been threatened or coerced, was treated fairly and was not currently represented by Jeffrey Weiner.

At 12:50 A.M. Pierson read out loud the entire statement, then initialed each page of it with a few minor corrections. After that he asked to talk to his parents. He was given permission, telephoned, and spoke to his father. Sessler then spoke to both Mr. and Mrs. Pierson and explained to them the facts concerning the arrest of their son.

That completed, the detectives picked up an arrest form and warrant for John Pierson on a charge of sexual battery from Detective Harold Ross and took Pierson downtown to the Metro-Dade Homicide office. On the way down in Ratcliff's car, Pierson told them that he felt much better having discussed with them the Staci Weinstein case and cleared his conscience. He said he realized that since he knew that sex was going to take place at the house with the girl, he never should have gone there with Eddie Wasko.

At Homicide, Pierson was photographed and fingerprinted. At 2:40 he was then taken by Sessler and Ratcliff to the Dade County Jail and formally charged with first-degree murder and attempted sexual battery. He was also charged under Ross's warrant with sexual battery.

As the arrest report read, "On July 9, co-defendant

Edward Wasko gave a statement to homicide investigators implicating the defendant. The defendant, after receiving his rights per Miranda, admitted in a formal statement that he entered the victim's residence with knowledge that the sexual battery was to be committed upon the victim. During the attempt to commit the act, the victim was beaten and shot."

Later that day, Wednesday, August 31, Pierson appeared in court for a bond hearing, wearing blue cutoff shorts and a polka-dot short-sleeve sports shirt. Judge Oppenborn ordered him held without bond. In addition, the judge ordered a psychiatric examination.

Pierson's statement was not entirely to the satisfaction of the detectives, or to Waksman and Weintraub. They were convinced he was lying, that he had not been an innocent bystander to Wasko's assault on Staci Weinstein, that he had not suffered a nosebleed from Wasko's fist. There was enough evidence to the contrary. However, his admission that he knew the reason for entering the Weinstein house was to commit a sexual act on a ten-year-old girl who then was shot and killed was enough to make him guilty of a felony murder. For the moment at least, this indictment had to suffice.

Marvin Weinstein was ecstatic. He was well aware that if Pierson and Wasko were convicted on the charges, both faced the electric chair.

"That won't bring Staci back," he said. "Nothing will. But at least I'll have the satisfaction of seeing her murderers pay for it. Maybe then I can sleep in peace. Maybe then Staci can sleep in peace."

It is interesting to recall Ben Hall's statement that Marcía told him the case would be closed by a sexual-battery warrant issued on one of the subjects.

Chapter 13

The *Miami Herald* and *Miami News* blazed John Pierson's arrest across their pages: "SECOND MAN ARRESTED IN SLAYING OF GIRL, 10." "NEW ARREST IN LAST YEAR'S KILLING OF 10-YEAR-OLD GIRL." Head shots of Staci and Pierson accompanied the articles. Both papers quoted Sessler saying that Pierson had been arrested initially on an unrelated sexual-battery charge by Detective Harold Ross. Then, "while he was talking to Ross," Sessler said, "Pierson said he wanted to talk to the homicide guys to straighten everything out."

The newspapers said that if convicted, both Pierson and Wasko faced the death penalty.

Once again reporters from both the print and television media descended upon Marvin's house. With Hilari at his side, Marvin told them how gratified he was at Pierson's arrest, how he hoped that his ten-month nightmare was over at last. "But now we have to wait and see what they do with these two killers. They deserve to burn for what they did to my little girl."

That night as he watched himself on the TV news, Marvin was horrified at the image that flashed back from the screen. He looked terrible! He'd never really noticed his appearance before, but now he saw that his body, which always had been slim and wiry, was now scrawny, positively skeletal. "My God," he remarked to Hilari, "I look like I just got out of Dachau! Skin and bones! Like I haven't had a decent meal for a year!"

"Well, you haven't," Hilari said. "You've been eating garbage when you've eaten at all."

Marvin stared at her, noticing, perhaps for the first time in a long time, that actually he had a very pretty thirteen-year-old for a daughter. "So how come you look so good? You look terrific on the TV."

"I take care of myself," Hilari said. "I eat out a lot. Like at Bookie's or Alan's."

Marvin nodded. "That's good. That's good," he said to her, but the exchange had pained him. One day, when all this is over, I must find her again, try to be a real father to her, he thought. But he didn't know how to express that to her. Hilari was, at least superficially, a self-sufficient, self-contained young lady. He knew that vaguely, and therefore he wasn't overly concerned about her daily life. What he failed to appreciate was while she dined well, she was emotionally starved.

Knowing that the self-confessed killers of his little girl were behind bars at the Dade County Jail was not enough for Marvin Weinsten. He was suspicious enough of the justice system to worry how their trials would come out. Vengeful thoughts filled his days and nights. Florida's electric chair was too good for them.

In his agitated state he turned to the Parents of Murdered Children group seeking some kind of therapy. Testing the waters, he went one night to a meeting.

A loosely knit organization, POMC is not a club anyone would want to join. As the late Charles Whited wrote in his column, "God forbid that anyone should qualify for membership."

The local meeting of POMC Marvin attended had a dozen members, holding their monthly sessions in the back room of Ann Land's real estate office in Coral Gables. Ann Land and her husband, Jack, were among the founding members of the local POMC chapter. Their son Jimmy, twenty-two, had been shot dead in

California—the killer had wanted his car. It is a grim fact that today the local membership is several times the original number and continues to grow, with meetings now held in a Coral Gables church.

Equally chilling is the fact that from its founding in Cincinnati in 1978 by Lutheran pastor Robert Hullinger and his wife, Charlotte, after their daughter, Lisa, was murdered, POMC now has some 300 chapters nationwide and provides support for nearly 40,000 survivors.

Marvin liked what he heard at his first meeting. What impressed him most of all was not the therapeutic value of support that members gave one another in their mutual grief—it was the anger in some of them. These were people to whom he could relate. He'd found confederates, others like himself who were unhappy with the system as they had found it and wanted to fight it.

At the end of that first evening, Marvin knew that this was for him. He told Nelan and Audrey Sweet, who were also founding members of the Dade County chapter, that he would be back, and he intended to be an active member. He would help people, not only with his knowledge gained from personal experience, but would become a source of controlled, directed anger for victims and their survivors such as himself and Hilari.

But first he had to concentrate on justice for the murderers of Staci.

Once John Pierson and Eddie Wasko had been interred in the Dade County Jail, the investigators rapidly proceeded to fill out their cases. The same afternoon Pierson was booked, Detective Harold Ross collected state attorney investigator Mary Myerscough, and a steno-reporter, and drove out to interview Peggy May, her daughter Angela, and her thirteen-year-old son, Jimmy. For a time Pierson had lived with them, and all three had previously stated in interviews that Pierson admitted to them that he'd raped Janice Langhorn. He had also admitted to them that he'd attempted to strangle her and had prevented her from leaving the house.

What Ross wanted now was formal statements from them.

He interviewed them carefully, and separately, as witnesses in a trial, so that none was able to listen to the statements made by the others. First was Peggy May. She started by saying she had allowed Pierson to live with them for a while. She knew Janice, but had never known her surname.

Ross: "Referring to Janice, did [Pierson] tell you anything unusual about what he had done to her?"

Peggy: "Yes. He said he had raped her and kept her in the room for an hour or so afterward, and then he let her go."

"How many occasions did he tell you he had raped her on that night?"

"He told me at least twice and probably more than that. He discussed it several times."

"During the time that he told you he raped her, was he joking about it, or was he very serious and remorseful?"

"He was very serious and remorseful. In fact, at times he cried when he talked about it."

"Did he give you any reason for raping her if he was, in fact, in love with her?"

"He said he was in love with her. He said they had been having sex regularly, and he raped her because she didn't want anything to do with him because she had heard he was in trouble."

Next was Angela May. She told virtually the same story, that Pierson had told her he'd raped Janice Langhorn.

Ross: "Did he use the word *rape*?"

Janice: "Yes."

"What did he say happened?"

"He said that she had found out he was being investigated for the murder of the little girl, and she didn't want anything to do with him, and he did. He thought it would straighten things out, and she didn't want to, so he forced her to."

"During the time he said he raped Janice, did he state that he used any violence, or did he hurt her or use a weapon?"

"No. If he did, I don't recall."

"He did say he held her there against her will?"

"He told me he raped her. She didn't want to, and he forced her to, and he wouldn't let her leave, like, for an hour and a half afterward."

"Did he state anything about not allowing her to use the phone or to leave?"

"He ripped it out of the wall."

"Did he indicate on more than one occasion to you that he had raped Janice?"

"He talked about it a lot. I know it was over five times."

Finally, Ross interviewed Jimmy May, who said that Pierson had been dating Janice, but "he had gotten into a fight with her and it was over."

Ross: "Did he tell you what happened during the course of the fight?"

Jimmy: "He said he raped her."

"When you say the word *rape*, do you know what the word *rape* means?"

"Yes, sir."

"What?"

"Unwillingly for someone to be forced to have sex."

"And when he said rape you understood what he meant?"

"Yes, sir."

"And what did he tell you about raping Janice?"

"He said she came over to his—where he was at and said that he started arguing, and then he didn't say nothing about their clothes or anything like that. He said she started screaming and he put a pillow over her face and she went for the phone and he jerked the phone out of her hand and wouldn't let her go near it."

"And did he state during this incident or occasion that he forced Janice to have sex with him?"

"Yes."

"Did he tell you he used any violence on Janice when he raped her? Did he hurt her, hit her, or use a weapon or anything?"

"No, he didn't, but on the phone, she did—she said he was very violent and like he went nuts."

"Did he use anything to harm her?"

"The pillow that he put over her face."

That was it; the three interviews took a total of ten minutes, but Ross had now three strong sworn statements to help buttress his sexual-assault case against Pierson.

Both Wasko and Pierson pleaded poverty, were declared indigent and entitled to public defenders. It was the responsibility of the sitting judge on the case to appoint an assistant public defender from the 125 on the Dade County Public Defender's list at any one time.

Major-crime cases are assigned to various court divisions. In this case, it fell into the division of Judge Ellen Morphonios. A flamboyant, high-profile judge whose reputation extended beyond Florida's borders, she had won the sobriquet "Maximum Morphonios" for the stiff sentences she handed down in her courtroom. She had given one killer 1,698 years, another 1,197. If a fair share of those sentences never survived the appeals courts, Morphonios had at least made her point. In twenty-one years she had handed down eight death sentences; all were reversed.

To defend John Pierson, Judge Morphonios chose Bruce Lehr, formerly a chief prosecutor of the Dade County Courts and senior trial attorney of the Narcotics Division who only recently had switched to defense

Marvin and Ruth Weinstein cutting their wedding cake, May 2, 1965. (PHOTO BY HARVEY WEINSTEIN)

Below: Staci Weinstein in October 1982, just days before she was murdered. (PHOTO BY MARTY GOLDAPPLE)

Above: Hilari Weinstein, age 9. (PHOTO BY MARTY GOLDAPPLE)

From left to right: Staci, Ruth Ann, cousin Jana Blue (*front*), and Hilari in 1980. Ruth Ann died two years later of cancer. (PHOTO BY MARVIN WEINSTEIN)

Staci opening gifts at her seventh birthday party.
(PHOTO BY MARVIN WEINSTEIN)

Staci in 1979. She was
seven years old. (PHOTO BY
MARVIN WEINSTEIN)

Staci in 1981. (PHOTO BY
MARVIN WEINSTEIN)

Ruth Ann and Staci in 1978.
(PHOTO BY MARVIN WEINSTEIN)

Marvin's mug shot October 14, 1982,
the day Staci was killed. At first, Marvin
was the prime suspect in his daughter's death.

Marvin and Hilari on television, October 16, 1982, pleaded with Staci's murderers to turn themselves in. (PHOTO COURTESY *THE MIAMI HERALD*)

Marvin Weinstein spoke to Staci's grieving classmates at a memorial at her school in June 1984. (PHOTO BY MYRA GOLDAPPLE)

Marvin and Hilari Weinstein display a memorial plaque at Sabal Palm Elementary School where an olive tree was planted in Staci's memory. (PHOTO BY MYRA GOLDAPPLE)

Eddie Wasko's mug shot from the night he was arrested for the murder of Staci Weinstein, July 10, 1983.

John Pierson in January 1984.

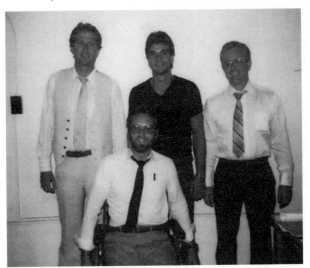

Eddie Wasko admitted to investigators in Ohio that he had been present at Staci's murder. The mood of the interview was strangely friendly. *From left to right, top row*: Detective Steve Sessler, Eddie Wasko, Detective Jim Ratcliff. *Front:* polygrapher Randy Walker.

Detective Steve Sessler took over
the Weinstein case in 1983. The
arrests of John Pierson and
Eddie Wasko soon followed.
(PHOTO BY ALFONSO BLANCO)

Marvin Weinstein
testifies at Eddie
Wasko's pre-
sentencing hearing.
He argues for the
death penalty.
(PHOTO COURTESY
THE MIAMI HERALD)

Marvin Weinstein, barred from the courtroom during
the trial of Eddie Wasko, waits in the pressroom.
(PHOTO COURTESY THE MIAMI HERALD)

Miami Prosecuting Attorney
Jayne Weintraub.

Judge Arthur Snyder presided
over the trial and sentenced
Eddie Wasko to death. This
sentence would be overturned
by the Florida Supreme Court
and reduced to a life sentence.

Left to right: Florida Prosecutor David Waksman,
Marvin Weinstein, and Detective Jim Ratcliff
at a celebration after the trial. (PHOTO BY SARA ARNWINE)

Hilari Weinstein,
age 24. (PHOTO COURTESY
GLAMOUR SHOTS)

Hilari Weinstein at her June
1993 college graduation.
(PHOTO BY MARVIN WEINSTEIN)

David Waksman receives a plaque from then
State Attorney Janet Reno for his work
as a prosecuting attorney.
(PHOTO COURTESY SARA ARNWINE)

as a major-crimes attorney. For Eddie Wasko she appointed Peter Ferrero, a career public defender, also a major-crimes attorney. Ferrero realized almost at once that this was the kind of case that would need two people, so he asked another major-crimes attorney and career assistant public defender Brian McDonald to assist him.

McDonald and Ferrero divided their work in what in a capital crime such as the Staci Weinstein murder is the normal, if rather macabre, fashion. McDonald would be responsible for what was known as the "guilt phase"; Ferrero would take responsibility for the "death phase." In the state of Florida, a trial takes place in two parts. The first part is: is the defendant guilty of first-degree murder? If the answer is yes, the trial then goes into a second phase, the sentencing phase. Almost always the same jury decides on both phases. At the second phase, which in a first-degree murder would be the death-penalty phase, the state is allowed to introduce more evidence that they feel establishes certain statutory aggravating factors, which are listed in the death-penalty statute book.

The defense is allowed to introduce evidence concerning various mitigating factors. There are now eleven aggravating factors on the statute books, and the state is not allowed to deviate from that list. There are eight statutory mitigating factors. The last one is, "any other aspect of the defendant's character or record or any other circumstance of the case." That pretty well opens it up to anything that might be appropriate.

At the close of the death-penalty part of the trial the jury returns an advisory verdict, either death by electrocution or life with a minimum mandatory twenty-five years to be served. Recommendation must be by majority vote. A tie goes in favor of the defendant, that is, life rather than the death penalty.

In certain circumstances the judge can override the jury's recommendation, but he must give it great weight. A death-penalty sentence would automatically go on appeal.

As the weeks went by, there was quiet maneuvering by all sides. Lehr and McDonald/Ferrero did not communicate in a common defense strategy because they were in fact on opposite sides of the fence. What was good for Wasko was bad for Pierson, and vice versa, since each was fingering the other for the sexual assault and shooting. What they did have in common, however, was the need for background search. This meant that within a comparatively brief time frame they had to reexamine potential witnesses, search out the homicide records, to which they were entitled, and anything else the state planned to use as evidence under the discovery rule. This entitles the defense to see, in effect, all the cards the prosecution is holding.

Keeping in mind mitigating factors should their clients be found guilty, the defense lawyers researched personal backgrounds: family situations, schooling, teachers, friends, relatives, coworkers, previous criminal records if any.

On October 31, depositions were taken once again from Peggy, Angela, and Jimmy May about the rape of Janice Langhorn. This time Janice herself also was deposed. However, this was background to the homicide charges conducted by Bruce Lehr and Peter Ferrero, with Waksman there to witness all four depositions.

The questioning of Janice was unusually extensive and detailed and at times deeply embarrassing to her—with apologies from the attorneys—but she was frank and forthright throughout. What her deposition revealed this time was a latent streak of violence in Pierson, an inherent flaw in his character that extended to his sexual proclivity.

Janice described her fear of Pierson after the rape, how the fear of his violence had stopped her from reporting it at once to the police and when finally she had, she refused to prosecute because she feared his revenge. "I was afraid," she told Lehr, "I was afraid nothing would happen, and I was afraid that he would get mad and try to come and hurt me again."

Ferrero: "When did the point come when you decided you did want to prosecute?"

Janice: "I never wanted to prosecute."

"Do you want to prosecute now?"

"No, I don't."

"So in other words you are still sticking with the story that the rape happened but you don't want to testify in court?"

"Yes."

"At any time did any law enforcement officer tell you anything to the effect of, 'You won't have to testify but we want this rape to help us in the murder case'?"

"Yes."

"Who told you that?"

"They didn't say that I wouldn't have to testify. At first, they said, it probably wouldn't get to that."

"Tell me exactly who that was, first."

"Ben Hall, wait a minute, not Ben Hall, it was Ross, Detective Ross."

"Exactly what did he tell you?"

"He told me I would be giving my statement which would probably be able to be used in court, but I probably would never get around to my ever having to go to court and testify."

"Did anybody tell you any relationship about your going forward on the rape charge and the murder of Staci Weinstein?"

"No, they never told me it would be mixed together."

"Did they tell you that giving this statement would help them in the Staci Weinstein case?"

"Let me think. I can't recall. I really can't remember."

"If you are subpoenaed to testify in court in the sexual-battery case, are you going to testify?"

"I would have to."

"But if you do it, it would be purely because the state is making you testify?"

"Yes."

Janice related then her relationship with Pierson, how they had had sex together on several occasions, but she hadn't wanted to on this particular night, which made him turn violent. She described how she began crying and asking him to stop, repeating more or less what she had said to Hall in her recorded statement with him. She described how he told her to go to his sister's bedroom, where he proceeded to rape her.

Fererro: "Now, I realize this is personal and it is difficult for you to talk about, but I am afraid I have to know the details to compare it to statements that you have made in the past, so you can tell me everything that happened from the time that he took you in the bedroom.

"If you feel you need a break or water or you need to talk to the prosecutor or need to talk to your mother or anything else that would make you more comfortable in explaining this, please just say so, and you are welcome to do any of those things."

"I am trying to use words."

"Use any words that you are comfortable with, as long as you get the idea across."

"He proceeded to have sexual intercourse with me."

"Did you scratch him?"

"No, I didn't."

"Did you sustain any injuries that night?"

"I got scratches on my face."

"How did you get the scratches?"

"Well, this was toward the end, the very end. He was putting his hands over my nose and mouth and I couldn't breathe, and I am fighting him and while he is doing that, he had his hands like this, [indicating] trying to hold on, and he scratched my face."

"Did you do any screaming that night?"

"Yes, I did a lot of it."

"Was there anything that struck you as strange or what you might call kinky about John Pierson in any of the sex that you had had in the past?"

"No, not really."

"How about that night, anything strange or kinky?"

"Yes."

"What?"

"He tried to choke me with his penis."

"He tried to choke you with his penis?"

"Choke me, yes."

"What else?"

"Oh, man, he rolls over and he says, 'Do anything disgusting right now. I want you to do something really perverted and disgusting to me. Prove to me that you love me.' "

"Did you try to talk your way out of the room and out of the situation?"

"Yes, I did."

"Did it help?"

"No, he just got very mad."

"What was the next thing that happened?"

"Like I said, he forced himself between my legs."

"His body, his head?"

"His head."

The questioning continued in this vein for some time, with Janice describing her fear and her attempts to leave, much of which she had already told Ben Hall. Further on in the questioning, after she'd said she broke off her relationship with Pierson, she was asked when she'd last heard from him. She said she hadn't heard from him for a while until four days after he was arrested.

"You heard from him in jail?"

"Yes."

"What kind of things would he say to you?"

"He asked if I was going to prosecute. He asked me to lie."

"What did he ask you to lie about?"

"To say that I was lying. He says, 'Janice, please tell them you are lying. I can't go to the electric chair. Please lie.' I said, 'I can't do that.' "

Ferrero and Lehr both questioned her further about the rape experience and what Pierson had said to her after Staci's murder, most of which had already been covered by her with Ben Hall. They wanted to know all she could tell them about any peculiarities of personality and behavior she had seen in Pierson, particularly violent behavior, before they concluded the deposition. She couldn't tell them much more than they already had from her, from the homicide and sexual-battery files, and from depositions previously taken from Angela, Peggy, and Jimmy May, who were going to be deposed again that afternoon.

Peggy May was first. Bruce Lehr questioned her briefly, but since he was interested in the homicide rather than the sexual battery, he got more from her than she had given in her deposition with Ross. She mentioned that Pierson had lived with her and the family on two separate occasions. The first time she'd asked him to leave because "he was mean to the kids. Rough and abusive." She said that once Pierson had gotten mad at her son and tried seriously to choke him. Then he accused her husband of stealing his socks and underwear. But she said she felt sorry for him, he had no place to live, and she let him come back. It was during his second stay with her that he told her he'd raped Janice Langhorn. Nobody asked him, he just came out with it.

Lehr: "How did the conversation come about?"

Peggy: "He said he did a terrible thing, the worst thing that he was most sorry for of anything that he ever did in his life. He was upset because she wouldn't have anything to do with him after he had been questioned by the police about the killing of the little girl."

"Did he ever tell you that he killed a little girl?"

"Only on the phone since he has been in jail, he has sworn that he didn't."

"Was there a time before he went to jail when he told you anything about the murder?"

"Just when I said, 'Exactly what happened?' Because I only had seen sketches of it on the news and I said, 'How was she killed?' and he said, 'She was shot.' This is after he told me the police picked him up to be questioned, and that is why Janice was upset. He had lost his job and everything."

"Are you aware of anybody else that he might have confessed to?"

"He told all of us. There was no secret about Janice."

"How about the little girl?"

"He didn't say he had done anything to the little girl. He said he had been accused of it and that she was shot and that after she was shot, somebody had picked her up in their arms and hugged her like they were sorry for what they had done."

"Did he tell you anything else?"

"That the guy that he had worked with had been acting suspicious, that he had left for a while and just that he didn't have anything to do with it. He said that they gave him a lie-detector test and he passed them all with flying colors."

"Why did John eventually leave your house a second time?"

"I had to tell him to go again. There was just problems with John there. There was always turmoil. I had to ask him to leave. I still felt sorry for John, but I didn't want him around the kids. He was too rough."

Lehr and Ferrero both questioned Jimmy May. He had little to add to what he'd told Ross, except some details about Pierson's violence that interested Ferrero, as Wasko's defense attorney. Jimmy described how he and Pierson had been fooling around one night, wrestling, when for no reason Pierson began shaking, Jimmy said; his face changed, his eyes bugged out and his face got red. Pierson hit him in the head and started choking him until his sister, Angela, came in, grabbed Pierson by the head, and threw him to the floor. Jimmy said he had marks on his neck next day.

Finally, Angela told Lehr that Pierson had admitted to her that he'd raped Janice, and asked, "Do you want me to tell you everything he said?"

Lehr: "Yes."

Angela: "He said that he raped her and it was because she had heard something about his being a suspect in a murder case of a little girl and she would not have anything to do with him and he forced her."

"Did he ever tell you anything about that murder?"

"Yes."

"What did he tell you about that?"

"He didn't say he did it. He said that they were questioning him and that his parents had paid $5,000 for a lawyer and that he had not done it, and then he said—I said, 'Well, what happened?' and he said that somebody had shot her and picked her up and hugged her."

"Did you ever see him get a nosebleed?"

"Yes."

"When?"

"When he gets mad or upset."

"How many times?"

"A lot."

"Would it be a gush of blood or a little blood?"

"It would be a lot. I would make him put his head back."

"Did he make any admissions to you about being in the house of Staci Weinstein?"

"No."

Ferrero took over the questioning:

"He said that whoever shot her had hugged her after the shooting?"

"He said they picked her up and hugged her like they were sorry they did it."

"Do you remember when he told that to you?"

"It was right after he moved in the second time."

"Which was around January?"

"Yes."

"Did he say how he knew the person that killed her hugged her?"

"No."

Angela then told Ferrero that there had been several incidents in which Pierson was very rough with her son, shaking him, slamming him to the floor, throwing him against the wall, things like that. She explained that her son tended to be hyperactive and could get on people's nerves. Pierson couldn't take it and would become violent.

"Other than what Pierson said about the person that did the shooting hugged her, did he say anything else about the killing to you, the murder?"

"He said that somebody had shot her."

"Did you ever see Pierson with a gun?"

"No."

"Did he ever talk about guns?"

"When he was talking about the little girl, he told me that there was a gun that was missing and he thought it belonged to the guy that he was with, because he had a paper bag or something in the car and it was missing after that."

Lehr came back for a few final questions:

"Tell me what he told you about his friend with the gun. Was that friend Eddie Wasko?"

"He didn't say what the name was. He said the guy he was working with that day."

"What did he tell you?"

"He said there was a paper bag in the car and that the guy had disappeared for a couple of hours and that they had thought that John disappeared for a couple of hours and John was gone, the bag was gone when the guy came back, and he thought there was a gun in it."

"He told you that his friend was the one that owned the gun?"

"Yes."

That terminated the deposition session. From Lehr's point of view, it favored Pierson's insistence that Wasko had been the principal perpetrator of the crime, that Wasko owned a gun, that it was Wasko, not he, who had disappeared for a time while at the home of the Morgenthalers'. If Pierson stuck to that story and was believed by a jury, it was a strong factor in mitigating against the death penalty. However, for Ferrero, the depositions exposed Pierson's violent nature and sexual inclinations, indicating that he was not the innocent bystander, the protector of Staci, as he had claimed. Thus in their search for mitigating factors, each attorney had gleaned a little from the depositions.

Chapter 14

During the weeks of September and October, the prosecutors had been busy debating their course of action against Pierson and Wasko. The state's cases were not exactly airtight. What it had, essentially, was a confession from each man blaming the other for the crime. There was no physical evidence at the crime scene incriminating Wasko; nothing had been found even to prove he had been at or inside the Weinstein home.

In Pierson's situation the fact that his blood enzyme profile was "consistent" with that of the blood found on Staci's bed and on her panties was not absolute identification. This was not as strong as a piece of evidence as the DNA genetic fingerprint in use today. The defense could attack the blood evidence by pointing out that the one-in-ten-thousand-enzymes match meant that there could be dozens of men in south Florida alone with the same profile. The saliva samples proved nothing at all. True, Pierson was also in the neighborhood that day, but probability does not ensure a first-degree murder conviction.

Conferences were held at the office of the state attorney with Abe Laeser, just one step below Janet Reno in rank, who had the responsibility to make final decisions on how prosecutions should proceed. As a routine courtesy, he would keep her informed on the progress on complicated cases such as this one. Attending these strategy conferences on a regular basis were the two prosecutors, David Waksman and Jayne

Weintraub, detectives Sessler, Ratcliff, and Hall, and sometimes Marvin Weinstein.

Initially, thought was given to trying the defendants together. There are advantages to this strategy. The state doesn't have to do it twice. The witnesses and the family do not have to go through a trial twice. And since the Dade County Courthouse was among the busiest in the nation, the state doesn't have time to try things twice.

Another significant point is that from expensive, frustrating experience, prosecutors know that when the accused in the same crime are tried separately, a favorite tactic of each defense attorney is to say to the jury, "The other guy did it. Don't worry, I'm sure he'll be convicted next week. Let this guy go." And sometimes two guys walk because each jury agrees yes, the other guy did it.

However, trying them together did not fly. In Wasko's statement, considered "a good statement," by Waksman, he said in effect, "I was there, I beat her, I told John to shoot her." That in and of itself calls for separate trials because when Detective Sessler takes the stand and says, "Wasko said that Pierson shot her," that evidence is hearsay. You can't cross-examine the man who made the statement, Wasko, because he has the right to remain silent.

That decided, they agreed to go for a first-degree murder prosecution on Eddie Wasko. Pierson was a more difficult proposition.

In analyzing the strength of this case Waksman had to weigh the chances of his winning. For one, what Pierson had given them could hardly be called a confession. "He gave us a statement, which considering his limited mental ability, he was very wise in the way that he worded it. For a guy who looked and appeared to be a walking idiot, he covered everything: his blood, his presence, he was afraid, he didn't know, Wasko punched him and so forth."

Examining that statement and whatever little else of useful evidence he had against Pierson, Waksman wondered if he had a case against him at all. If so, for what crime? As Waksman explains, "Few people outside of a courthouse understand that part of a prosecutor's obligation is to be a little judge—in effect a quasi-judicial officer. The judge on the bench has the final ruling, but if the prosecutor thinks something is unfair, then as a result of a U.S. Supreme Court ruling called the Brady Bill he has a number of obligations. If he thinks somebody is lying, he's not allowed to present them. If he finds a witness that would help the defendant, he can't tell the witness to take a trip to Alaska. He must inform the defense attorney that he has found a witness for him. He is not supposed to present a doubtful case for trial and see what happens. For example, if there is enough evidence for an indictment but the prosecutor thinks the jury probably will acquit, his obligation is not to file the case, not to drag the accused through a long, drawn-out fight with the hope that possibly some jury might convict. That is a very difficult decision for any prosecutor to make. But he has to make it based on his experience, his gut feeling—and his honesty.

"There are good prosecutors and there are bad prosecutors, there are *gonifs* and there are prosecutors who'll try to put anybody in jail."

So, what does he have on Pierson? The key word here for Waksman in a felony murder is *participant*. Pierson said he was merely a witness. On the other hand, he is in the house. If burglary is added, if he enters the building with the intent to commit a crime in the building and someone dies—it doesn't matter how—he's responsible for first-degree murder. There's no doubt he's in the building. Did he intend to commit a crime there—the crime being forcible rape or consensual rape with a person under twelve? Pierson said he just intended to watch.

Harkening back to the Brady Bill obligations, does Waksman have a first-degree murder case here?

"Maybe. Will you give me a maybe?" he asks. "A possibly? Some people would say probably."

For the purposes of an indictment the prosecutor has a little leeway. He's not supposed to file an automatic loser, but the grand jury rule is "probably."

Waksman can go with a "probably." He can indict. He thinks Pierson was a participant. Wasko said he did it, he shot her, and for the purposes of a grand jury indictment that statement can be used, but it can't be used in court.

So the next question became: is there enough hard evidence to convince a jury "beyond a reasonable doubt" that Pierson intended to commit a crime in the building?

A consensus developed that a felony murder case against Pierson quite possibly would not be proven to the satisfaction of a jury. They could very well find him not guilty and send him home. That possibility, to all concerned, was too disastrous to contemplate. Second, since against Wasko there was only his confession, perhaps a deal should be cut with Pierson, as a witness, to add his evidence as insurance.

Abe Laeser concurred: "It's hard to quantify all the things that go into a decision of what is the right or appropriate disposition of a case. We knew we had certain problems as to each of the defendants. The quality and volume of evidence was limited, and certainly there were areas where a defense attorney could attack. The second factor that we had clearly put into the analysis was that we really felt there was a substantial difference in criminal responsibility between the two parties.

"By that I mean that as to the homicide itself we felt that Wasko's participation, the physical acts involved, and the actual homicide were his responsibility and that Pierson was a low IQ follower who may have been present but certainly didn't come up with any plans to kill and wasn't an actual participant in the homicide. Given all of that we felt that a substantially more lenient plea would be appropriate in order to secure his testimony.

"It's a bit like a poker hand. If you're sitting with a pair of threes you may be in one position, and if you've got a full house you may be in a different position."

Negotiating a plea bargain for Pierson was a calculated risk, but the consensus was that it needed to be taken. Definitely there was the problem with Wasko's confession.

Laeser adds, "In my own mind the confession was strong enough to go to the jury, but because of the type of case that it was, with at least the contemplation of the death penalty, my realistic evaluation is that juries are hesitant to convict on this evidence and this evidence alone. When they know there is a possibility that they will have to at least consider either first-degree punishment or the death penalty, my personal experience has been that juries look for more evidence. They are almost trained by television and movies to look for something in addition to a confession.

"Because of my feelings about that I was more than willing to approve the negotiations concerning Pierson because it would solidify the prosecution, make a conviction much more likely, and make the possibility of the death penalty more likely."

Marvin didn't like the idea of the plea bargain at all. He wanted the electric chair for Pierson or life imprisonment if he had to compromise. While he had no legal position in the decision, the approval of the victim's family in a murder case plea bargain is considered to be important in presenting it to the judge for approval. It required the utmost exercise of Waksman's rhetorical skills to bring him around to agree. He spent three hours at Marvin's house one night explaining to him why he and everybody else concerned thought the plea bargain was necessary. Exhausted but victorious, Waksman went to the wall phone in the kitchen and called Laeser to tell him Marvin had agreed.

Neither Sessler nor Ratcliff expressed enthusiasm for a plea bargain, either, but they accepted the constraints of the situation. Homicide detectives always do when they are given the state's picture. They really don't have much choice. All the same, they hate plea bargains with a passion. They deplore the revolving door of the justice system and its early release programs. They work ungodly hours, risk their lives, ruin their marriages in the course of tracking down violent and dangerous criminals, only to find the same felons back on the street again in all too brief a time. Too many are the cops killed by a career criminal out on parole or on early release—never mind the civilian casualties. But, as Cold Case Squad veteran Greg Smith commented, "You have to go with what you can get. It's a dirty business."

On the defense side, Bruce Lehr also had to weigh the possibilities. If he thought the state had a weak case, if he was confident he could get a not-guilty verdict, he wouldn't be interested in a deal. He also had a difficult decision to make; what was in the best interests of his client? What were the risks against the gain? Could he say in effect, well, it's a crap shoot. If we win, you go home, if we lose, I go home, and you go to the chair.

He decided that the state's evidence was strong enough to win a first-degree murder verdict and opted for the plea bargain.

On the night of November 3, Waksman, Lehr, and Pierson met in the Dade County Jail and thrashed out an agreement. Pierson would plead guilty to second-degree murder in court the next day. Judge Morphonios would give him the maximum, seventeen years. He would get statutory gain time, which meant that in reality he would serve less than the seventeen years. How much less depended on the vagaries of the state legislature and the rules of the prison system that kept score on gain time, a scheme so arithmetically convoluted that few lawyers and judges even bother to try to calculate the sums in advance of a sentence.

As one important concession by Waksman, he agreed to drop the rape charge. Pierson, for his half of the deal, agreed to testify against Wasko at the trial, which was scheduled for November 14.

At nine o'clock on November 4, John Pierson appeared before Judge Ellen Morphonios at the Metropolitan Justice Building on NW 12th Street in Miami to make his plea and take his punishment. The charges against him on the indictment in addition to murder first-degree were burglary while armed or assaulting someone therein, and attempted sexual battery with a firearm. To that indictment he had pleaded not guilty.

Appearing for the state were David Waksman and Jayne Weintraub. For the defendant, Bruce Lehr. As an observer on behalf of Eddie Wasko, his defense attorney, Brian McDonald. For himself, Marvin Weinstein. "He wants to make a statement when this is all over," Waksman said before the proceedings began.

"I don't blame him," said Morphonios. Then, "Calling John Pierson . . . why are we here?"

Lehr: "Your Honor, at this time the defense would withdraw the previously announced plea of not guilty, and at this time there is a negotiated plea with the state. This is a plea to second-degree murder and the other two counts of the indictment as charged. Under the guidelines that comes to seventeen years of sentence as agreed.

"In addition the state, I believe, will be announcing a nol-pros [will not prosecute] of the sexual battery, also against John Pierson."

Morphonios: "State?"

Waksman: "That is correct, Your Honor. I spoke with the mother of the alleged rape victim in the totally unrelated case. They really have no desire to come to court and be cross-examined on these personal and private matters and said as long as he is going to jail on something else they would like me to drop the charges. So I will.

"We have agreed to reduce Count I to second-degree murder and accept guilty pleas to the reduced count of second-degree murder and guilty pleas to counts II and III. And the defendant is further agreeing to testify if subpoenaed."

Morphonios: "That is important.""

Waksman: "Yes, ma'am."

Morphonios: "He understands that, Bruce?"

Lehr: "Absolutely, Your Honor."

Morphonios: "Swear him."

Pierson was sworn in, then asked by the judge: "Do you understand you are under oath?"

"Yes, ma'am."

Judge Morphonios questioned Pierson on his understanding of what was going to happen; did he agree he was entering a guilty plea of his own free will, because he was guilty and for no other reason, without force or threats from anyone? Did he understand that he was agreeing to testify for the state in the trial of Eddie Wasko? Pierson affirmed that he understood all that.

Morphonios: "You understand, sir, that by pleading guilty you are waiving your right to trial, your privilege against self-incrimination, your right to confront those who have accused you of a crime, and your right to appeal?"

Pierson: "I don't understand."

Morphonios: "Well, read my lips." The judge then repeated those items, one by one, as Pierson replied he understood.

Satisfied that Pierson understood what he was doing, and that he had no complaints about the services of his attorney, Morphonios said she would proceed with sentencing.

Lehr interrupted: "Your Honor, I would ask that any psychiatric evaluations that were done would go up to the prison system. Also that a specific request be honored that at no time Edward Wasko be placed in any facility that John Pierson was in."

Morphonios: "I don't mind making the request. That is up to the corrections authorities otherwise. Mr. Pierson? Are you specifically admitting that on October 14, 1982, that you murdered Staci Weinstein together with another by shooting her with a firearm, either you yourself or together with another contrary to the Florida law?"

Pierson: "I did not shoot her, but I was there."

Morphonios: "All right. Are you specifically admitting that on the fourteenth of October, 1982, that you burglarized together with another the home of Staci Weinstein, either holding a pistol yourself or with someone who was holding a pistol and the intent to commit the offense therein of sexual battery was the reason for the burglary either yourself or with another?"

Pierson: "Yes. Eddie Wasko is the one who went inside with intentions to have sex with the little girl, and he is the one that had the gun. I just started working at Stanley Steemer."

Lehr: "Yes or no?"

Pierson: "I'm sorry. Yes."

Morphonios: "That's all right. And are you also specifically admitting that as to Count III of the indictment that on October 14, 1982, you or together with another did attempt to commit sexual battery upon Staci Weinstein, a person eleven years of age or younger, and committed certain acts in the course of that event, and you yourself or together with another had a pistol?"

Pierson: "He is the one that committed the acts, Your Honor."

Morphonios: "And he is the one that had the pistol?"

Pierson: "Yes, ma'am."

Morphonios: "Does the state wish to make any inquiry?"

Waksman: "Your Honor has asked him several times. I don't know if he has given you the answers that are going to satisfy this plea."

Morphonios: "You ask him. It doesn't matter who asks the questions. Ask him the question."

Lehr: "Your Honor, at this time I have gone over all the evidence in this case, and the state does certainly have the amount of evidence which would be necessary for a reasonable jury to find guilt in all of the above charges, whether it be most probably in a felony murder situation.

"I have explained to Mr. Pierson felony murder, that he does not have to do the act. His being there with any sort of knowledge is sufficient."

Morphonios: "Right, principal in the first degree. You have explained to him the legal theories of principal in the first degree?"

Lehr: "Yes, Your Honor. He is saying yes to each of those. I believe the admission is sufficient for the plea. He does understand."

Morphonios: "Well, I don't mind, David, if you go through it. I don't want there to be any element of doubt."

Waksman: "Are you acknowledging you entered the home that the judge has mentioned with Edward Wasko, and you participated with him when he did some other acts?"

Pierson: "Yes, sir."

"And did you enter that house knowing he was going to do some crimes?"

"He was talking about having sex with that girl."

"You knew that when you entered the house?"

"Yes, but I didn't believe him at first."

"But you knew that when you went into the house?"

"Yes, sir."

"And you are pleading guilty because you are guilty and for no other reason?"

"Yes, sir."

Morphonios: "Anything further prior to the passing of sentence? Anything anyone wishes to say prior to the passing of sentence?"

Waksman: "At this time I will tell Your Honor that I have had lengthy conversations with Mr. Weinstein and with Sergeant Ratcliff, Detective Sessler, Detective Ben Hall. We are all in agreement that this is the best thing for the community in this case. After he pleads and Your Honor passes sentence, Mr. Weinstein would like to make a brief comment."

Morphonios: "Yes, sir. I noticed Mr. Weinstein in the courtroom, and he was affirmatively nodding his head up and down at your statement.

"Okay. Under the sentencing guidelines of the state of Florida as they presently exist, the court has before it category one sentencing guideline sheet which gives him 165 points for the primary offense at conviction, which is murder. Additional offenses at conviction give him an additional 35 points. He has no prior record. He was under no legal restraints and he receives 21 additional points for death or severe injury to the victim, giving him a grand total of 221 points under the sentencing guideline system.

"Under the sentencing guidelines system the court is mandated as to that which it could sentence him to. I can sentence him under the law to no more than 17 years in the State prison, the range being from 12 to 17 years.

"It is the judgment and sentence of this court at this time that the defendant be adjudicated guilty, that he be sentenced to 17 years in the state prison under the sentencing guidelines to be served mandatorily without benefit of parole, but he is to get statutory gain time.

"Print him."

The clerk: "Each count concurrent?"

Morphonios: "Yes, it has to be concurrent under the sentencing guidelines. File the sentencing guidelines sheet, and I think one has to go with the judgment and sentence to the prison system."

Brian McDonald asked Morphonios if they could discuss a trial date for Wasko after Marvin made his statement. She agreed. There was some question of whether the original November 14 date was practicable.

Marvin had to be sworn in before saying his piece. He told Morphonios he was the father of Staci Weinstein and he would like to address the judge at this time. He explained to Morphonios that he had prepared a little speech.

"This is a terrible day in my life," he said. "I wrote this out so I could remember the words a little better, if you don't mind."

Morphonios: "Certainly, sir."

Marvin: "I understand the implications of the guilty plea by the defendant. I have discussed the proceedings with Mr. Waksman and some close family friends. I am in agreement. At least part of this case will come to an end.

"Justice for my little girl will be partially served. By his admission of guilt the defendant is saying two things. One, that he came into my home without my permission, and two, that he either solely murdered my daughter or helped or participated in this brutal act.

"I hope that for every sleepless night that I and my daughter now suffer and for every hurt, mental pain, and anguish that we go through daily that he does the same. He can never live down this terrible thing that has happened no matter how many years pass. I have received and my daughter have both received a life sentence. The seventeen years that this man is getting is nothing compared to what I have."

Morphonios: "Amen!"

Marvin: "I thank you for listening to me, Your Honor."

Everybody, including Marvin, then began to discuss the trial date for Wasko. Marvin said he'd been through a lot of problems on the job because of the time spent in meetings and on other chores related to the case. The week of the fourteenth, just ten days away, was not comfortable for him. The attorneys wanted a postponement as well to give them more time for preparation. Morphonios agreed a postponement would be a good idea. "We don't want to walk into any appellate error by reason of publicity that is bound to come from this." The media people were well represented in the courtroom, and thus there was no doubt in anyone's mind that the day's court proceedings and Marvin's speech would be on the TV news that evening and in the newspapers next day.

"RUG CLEANER GETS 17-YEAR TERM IN SLAYING OF GIRL," the *Miami Herald* would headline its story next day.

Back in the courtroom, a tentative January date was decided upon for Wasko's trial, with a definite date to be announced the following week.

As Marvin left the courtroom, he passed Brian McDonald, who was standing at the rear, near the exit doors. As Marvin came up to him, McDonald said, "They're lying to you, Marvin."

Marvin stopped short. "What do you mean, lying?"

"He'll never do the seventeen years."

"You're crazy. Didn't you hear the judge say seventeen years to be served mandatorily without benefit of parole?"

"I'm telling you, Marvin," McDonald repeated, "he'll never do the seventeen years."

Marvin brushed by him and left the courtroom, shaking his head. Crazy, he said to himself. The man's crazy. Mandatorily without parole, she said. That's what she said.

A time bomb with a long fuse slowly began to tick away. . . .

Chapter 15

The new trial date for Eddie Wasko was set for Monday, January 9. This suited everyone. It gave all the players in the Staci Weinstein case—with the exceptions of Wasko and Pierson—the time to enjoy the coming holidays as they continued preparations for the trial. Marvin even made the point that postponing the trial until after the new year had its merits for the prosecution: "If you try Wasko before Christmas, when people are supposed to forgive and all that stuff, the jury might decide to let the bastard off!"

Holidays or no holidays, the attorneys on both sides worked hard between their festive breaks to prepare for trial. The rehearsing of witnesses about what they will say is legal, proper, and indeed necessary. Detectives are experienced witnesses, know the law, and can handle themselves under cross-examination. Civilians can be confused, made to contradict themselves, and become useless blabberers whether for defense or prosecution. These are the ones who need preparation by the respective attorneys, coached on what they will be asked and how they should answer—truthfully, of course—under direct examination, what they are likely to be confronted with under cross, and how best to cope with that.

McDonald was busy preparing Wasko and taking depositions from Sessler, Hall, and Ratcliff. He needed every bit of detail he could extract from them about the course of their investigations, in particular from

Sessler and Ratcliff about their questioning of Wasko in Ohio, comparing their account with his client's version. That information went into the defensive armament.

He had an important deposition from Janice Langhorn which alleged a vicious rape, indicating Pierson's violent sexual nature. The sex acts Janice said he had performed with her, though consensual for the most part, were consistent with the evidence of a sexual assault on Staci: the saliva traces found on her thighs and around the vaginal area. An important part of McDonald's strategy was convincing the jury that Pierson by his nature was capable of committing those acts, that he alone had done them.

McDonald was convinced that Pierson was a liar. Aware that the plea bargain with Pierson included his giving testimony against Wasko at trial, McDonald wanted to be able to convince a jury that Pierson was, in McDonald's words, "a monumental liar." Therefore whatever he had in the past said even in a sworn statement, or would say on oath on the witness stand, could not be credited.

On the morning of December 9, 1983, McDonald got Pierson out of jail and into the Metro Justice Building in Miami for a deposition he hoped would confirm that, and give weight to his cross-examination of Pierson if and when the prosecution called him.

Jayne Weintraub attended, representing the state. Wasko was there, too, as he was entitled to be, though there had been some question of his presence intimidating Pierson, affecting his statement. In the event, it didn't.

At the outset Weintraub instructed Pierson to tell the truth and answer all McDonald's questions, "unless I make an objection and instruct you not to answer."

McDonald began: "You have been convicted of the murder of Staci Weinstein?"

Pierson: "Yes, sir."

"You did that pursuant to a plea-bargain arrangement?"

"Yes, sir."

"You received seventeen years in the state prison as your sentence?"

"Yes, sir."

"In connection with that plea, did anyone ever describe to you what gain time is?"

"Yes, sir."

"And how that would affect your possible sentence?"

"Yes, sir."

"During the course of your plea colloquy—that's where the judge was asking you questions when you were pleading guilty—about doing this voluntarily, et cetera, you stated several times that you did not kill anybody?"

"Yes, sir."

"Is that your position today?"

"Yes, sir."

"Did you attempt to have sex with anybody on that particular day?"

"No, sir."

"Did you lick any person on the inside of their thighs, around their vagina, or anywhere else on their body?"

"Yes, sir, my ex-fiancée."

"On that particular day when you were licking your fiancée, was that a consensual act between the two of you or not?"

"She—yes, we both agreed to it."

"Were you present when Staci Weinstein was killed?"

"No, sir."

"Were you ever present in Staci Weinstein's bedroom?"

"No, sir."

"Were you ever in Staci Weinstein's house?"

"No, sir."

"Have you ever owned a gun?"

"No, sir."

McDonald reviewed Pierson's schooling and his work record, including how he had got the job with Stanley Steemer. Pierson said his cousin's wife worked there and helped him get the job. From his discovery information, knowing what Pierson had told Detective Ben Hall about the childhood abuse by his mother, McDonald asked:

"During your childhood, would you consider yourself a victim of child abuse?"

"Well, I really don't know what to say because I was young at the time. Maybe and maybe not, I don't really know. Ask my father, he's maybe more aware of that than I am. I mean, I have got hit like any other kid did."

"That's what I was going to try to clear up. You don't recall any particular violent episodes by either of your parents where you were injured seriously?"

"No, not really."

McDonald asked Pierson to review in detail the jobs he and Eddie Wasko had done on the day of the Staci Weinstein murder, specifically to describe the work they had done cleaning the carpets at the Morgenthaler home. Pierson claimed that at one point, while he was inside the house cleaning the carpet in the dining room, Wasko left the house for fifteen or twenty minutes. Said Pierson, "When Eddie came back, he looked very nervous. He was very shaky . . . very sweaty."

McDonald: "Did Eddie have any bloodstains on him when he came back and he was nervous and sweaty?"

"I wasn't looking for no blood."

"Well, if he had any large amount of blood on him, you would have noticed it, right?"

"Well, yeah."

"You didn't notice?"

"I didn't notice. I mean, I wasn't—"

"Did you notice any cuts on Eddie?"

"I—the only thing is, I wasn't paying attention. All I was doing was doing my job."

"I understand that. And I am just asking. Did you notice any cuts?"

"No, I didn't see any on him."

"Did you notice any bruises?"

"No."

"But he did appear nervous and upset and sweaty?"

"Yes."

Pierson said that when the job at the Morgenthaler house was finished and Wasko was working on the truck, he passed around about six Stanley Steemer flyers, as ordered by Wasko. "On the same side," said Pierson. "I never crossed that street."

"And you have never been in the Weinstein residence?"

"No. I have never-never, God's honest truth."

"Except for the time when you left and passed out about half a dozen circulars without crossing the street, you never left the Morgenthaler residence?"

"Not until we finished the whole entire job, no, sir."

"You have never been in the Weinstein residence?"

"I have never, never. I didn't step one foot on the property, never. I admit that I lied."

"John, if you have never been in the Weinstein residence, how were you able to draw up for Hall that map of the residence?"

"Because before we went down, Hall—I had Jeff Weiner—I had hired a private investigator, he showed me where the house was, where Staci Weinstein lived."

"I am not talking about a map of where the house was, I am talking about a map of the house."

"A map of the house?"

"A drawing of what the house looked like."

"I just drew anything, I did not draw exactly what the house—I just drew anything because the thing was, Detective Ben Hall was working at me the wrong way, he was hurting me many times. He was keeping me for hours and stuff like that so what I did was I just drew anything, just to have him leave me alone. I don't even know if that's the house or not."

"Did he scare you?"

"Yes, very much—yes, he did and it was getting worse."

"But you actually struck him on two different occasions?"

Pierson denied that. He insisted that during the questioning Hall had in fact hit him, and hit him again when he was taking the polygraph test at Kent Jurney's office. He claimed Hall refused to let him call his family.

McDonald: "Why did you tell Detective Sessler that you were present when Eddie Wasko committed the murder?"

"The real reason is that after I have been harassed all the time, that another thing, he lied on me."

"He?"

"Eddie Wasko had lied on me, saying that I was the one did this and that and this and that. So what I did, I thought, you know, I said, okay, let me just make up the whole story, which I heard from the news, the paper, radio, and I made up what I heard from, you know, detectives and just like that, what they had told me. And I made up into a big story because I was being followed up all the time, I was—every time I had— when I left a job or something like that, he kept on saying that I am a suspect to a murder.

"I mean, it was looking really bad on me so I just—I started coming to the point of saying, hey, listen, if they don't want to believe me, that's—I gave up on it because I kept on telling the truth. I kept on going down there, everything voluntarily, gave them hair samples, blood samples, saliva, everything they wanted I gave to them, all voluntarily without an attorney because I wanted to prove my innocence."

"But then you pled guilty to it?"

"Yes, I did."

"Why?"

"I just told you. I had—because I was in the position I was scared, I was afraid that I was going to get framed anyway for something I didn't do and if he did do what he did, if he did do it, I don't know, okay? Then he just put me in his shoes or to make it lighter on him and put me inside that category, and if anybody looked at him that same day he probably would have done the same thing to them."

"Did Eddie carry a gun on the truck?"

"I have never seen a gun, but Eddie did mention that he had a gun."

"How did he happen to mention that he had a gun? How did it come up?"

"What I remember is we went to a black neighborhood or something like that and I didn't really like the area too much and he just said something. He said, 'Don't worry, I have a gun,' or something like that. I don't know the exact words he did say—but I do know that he did mention that he had a gun."

"That plea you took, the plea is guilty?"

"Yes, sir."

"That also involved negotiations where they dropped some charges against you, right?"

"Yes, sir."

"Those charges related to—"

"Janice Langhorn."

"Janice Langhorn, and I believe it was charged as an attempted rape, sexual battery?"

"Yes."

"Do you know what sexual battery means?"

"No, I don't."

"Do you know what rape means?"

"Raping, yeah."

"Did you understand that the sexual battery—as the

state wants us to put it—is basically the same thing as rape?"

"I didn't know that, no."

"Did you know that you were charged with rape?"

"That's what I got arrested on."

"Well, that's what I am getting at. I mean, the charge, the way it read for the court papers was sexual battery, but you understood that you were charged with a rape, right?"

"No, I didn't understand that, I didn't think it was rape—sexual assault or something like that."

"Okay. Those charges related to an incident that Ms. Langhorn described as having occurred on the thirtieth of December, 1982. Do you remember the incident?"

"Yes, I do."

"Was that a sexual assault by you on her?"

"In a way yes, and in a way no."

"Could you explain what you mean by that?"

Pierson said he and Janice had driven around to various trailer parks looking for a place they could live when they got married, which they planned to do, he said, and they did a lot of drinking on the way around. Then, because his parents had left town, she asked her parents if she could go with him to his house for a while. "The reason was that she wanted to spend some time with me. I think you might have an idea of what kind of time. But it's not the first time I had sex with Janice. I had sex many times with her."

"So you went over to your place?"

"Went over my place. What I was doing, I was straightening up the house and stuff like that. She was sitting at a table reading a book or watching some TV inside the living room while I was straightening up and I asked her, I said, 'Would you like to, you know, make love?' Something like that. First she said, 'Yes, okay,' and then we went back into my sister's room and from there on, she—she is the one took her clothes off. I did not force her to take her clothes off. She took it off herself and all of a sudden we are in bed together, she started screaming for some reason. I was saying, 'What's wrong? What's wrong?' and I put my hand over her mouth to try to keep her quiet. Now she is trying to say that I tried to suffocate her."

"During that incident, did you lick her all over her body?"

"I had done that before. Also, I had done it in her mother's house, I have also done it in her aunt's house—I mean, her grandmother's house. That was not the first time I had done that."

"Why did she start screaming this time?"

"I have no idea. I honestly don't have any idea."

"Do you have any way of explaining how Janice Langhorn's version of what she describes as sexual assault coincides with what happened to Staci Weinstein before she was killed?"

Jayne Weintraub interrupted with an objection. "Form of the question. Instruct him not to answer."

McDonald explained to Pierson that he could either take Weintraub's advice and not answer, in which case a judge would rule on it, or he could ignore her advice and answer. Pierson appeared to be willing to answer, but couldn't quite understand what McDonald was getting at. The attorney tried rephrasing his question to put it more simply:

"You understand that Janice Langhorn talks about being licked all over her body during this supposed sexual assault, do you understand that?"

"She's done it to me also."

"But it's not so much whether it happened or not, you understand that's part of what she is saying happened?"

"Yeah."

"And you understand that she is saying that you tried to suffocate her?"

"Yes, she says that."

"Now, the evidence the state intends to introduce

shows that Staci Weinstein was licked on parts of her body, not necessarily all over, and the evidence that the state intends to introduce shows that somebody tried to suffocate her. Do you have any way of knowing or have any kind of an explanation why those two incidents should be—"

Weintraub: "Excuse me, which question is it? Does he know or are you going to ask for an explanation?"

McDonald: "First, do you know? Second, do you have an explanation? Do you know why those two things would be identical?"

Pierson: "I have no idea."

McDonald again asked if he had an explanation. Weintraub objected that he'd already answered. McDonald gave up that chase and went on to other areas. He turned to the depositions given by the May family in which they alleged that Pierson had shown streaks of violence, had hit the young lad, Jimmy, and had admitted to all of them that he'd raped Janice Langhorn. Pierson denied their allegations, said it was all horseplay, and had never told them he'd raped the girl, but that she had said that he had done it and he'd denied it.

McDonald went back to the murder: "Do you have any explanation for your blood being on Staci's bed?"

"I don't know why it got there. I mean, I was not there and I will keep on admitting until the day I die that I was not there. So I don't know why my blood got there."

"Did Eddie ever ask you for a blood sample?"

"No."

"Any explanation for how your spit got all over Staci Weinstein's inner thigh and vagina?"

(Pierson shook his head.)

"You have to answer out loud."

"No."

"Did you ever say anything to Angela May, or Peggy May or Jimmy May, about how you were charged, or suspected, I guess would be more appropriate?"

"Yes, I did."

"That you were suspected in the Weinstein homicide?"

"Yes."

"Did you ever say anything to them about that you were suspected of committing a homicide where somebody hugged the person who was killed like they were sorry?"

"Detective Hall told me something about that, and I probably did mention it to them."

"Did you hug Staci Weinstein after you killed her?"

"No, I didn't, no."

"Prior to arriving at the Morgenthaler residence, there was some conversation involving a young girl?"

"What young girl?"

"I don't know. On the way to the Morgenthalers', was there some kind of contact between you and/or Eddie and some young girl?"

"No, sir. No, sir."

"So in your statement of the thirtieth of August, 1983, to Steve Sessler and Sergeant Ratcliff, where you discussed Eddie seeing a girl and talking to her and talking to you about possibly having sex with her and you having sex with her as well and your declining the offer, all that is bullshit?"

"Yes, sir."

"Now, I am kind of looking at your statement on pages nine through seventeen. You are describing driving to a residence, Eddie talking about getting some pussy, teasing you about you not getting any pussy, and the conversation that you had back and forth and then getting to the house, meeting the girl, flirting, some screaming, you rushing in and getting into an altercation with Eddie, and then later hearing two shots. All this is bullshit?"

"Yes, sir."

"Page seventeen where you talk about Eddie having blood on his shirt and pants, showing you a gun, page eighteen, you talk more about the gun, cleaning the clothes—"

"I am not sure if he had changed his shirt or not. He also had like a yellow shirt also. I don't remember exactly if he had that shirt on after we had gone to the other job."

"But on pages seventeen and eighteen where you are talking about him showing the gun, having blood on his clothes—"

"That's all lies, too."

That closed down the deposition. Weintraub had no questions for Pierson. McDonald told Pierson he could have a copy of the deposition transcript sent to the jail if he so wished, so he could read it and refresh his memory of what he had said in it before testifying at Wasko's trial.

If he testified. So much for the state's eyewitness to Wasko's crime. By recanting his entire "confession," the statement that had got him a grand jury indictment for first-degree murder, that had brought him a second-degree murder plea bargain and seventeen years in jail, Pierson virtually guaranteed that the prosecution would not dare put him on the stand. McDonald had perhaps proved his point too soon.

However, Waksman had always had harbored reservations about using Pierson as a witness, unsure of his stability. Now, following this deposition, he was convinced Pierson would be worse than useless. Actually, Pierson had double-crossed him. An integral part of his deal was that he would testify against Wasko, and that was based on his sworn statement implicating Wasko in the sexual assault and murder of Staci.

Waksman had every legal right to void the plea bargain and send Pierson back to square one, and face a trial for first-degree murder. Normally, that would have been his reaction. But the most important thing to him was that if he went to trial with Pierson, the case might not survive appellate review. In fact, he says, "it might not even survive the jury's review. And I was happy to get not sixty days in jail or a year on the farm but a number of years in the state prison. I even used to tell Marvin, where he's going is hell, it's miserable, they get raped, they get knifed. It's a horrible life, and however many years he does it's going to be a miserable existence."

For those reasons Waksman didn't consider hitting Pierson with a perjury charge. It was possible; he had lied on two sworn statements. But Waksman just wanted him out of the way. Today, he says, he ties up a plea bargain that includes testimony with a virtual contract, in writing via a steno-reporter, ensuring that the defendant will repeat substantially, on the witness stand, the sworn statement he has made to the police. If he reneges, the deal is off, and he faces the original charge.

As the new year began, with the trial of Eddie Wasko due to begin in a week's time, Marvin was a bundle of nerves. Never had he considered himself simply a spectator in the campaign to find and punish the perpetrators of the horrendous crime against his daughter. From the moment he had discovered Staci's battered and abused body he had taken upon himself the role of the determined hunter. Get out of my way if you can't help.

Now he was ready to witness the kill. If he couldn't thrust home the sword himself, it would be enough to see the state do it for him.

Chapter 16

The holiday period caused a postponement not only of
Eddie Wasko's trial but other murder trials as well.
Judge Morphonios's calendar was backed up. Now she
had three murder trials scheduled for the same week.
All judges try to clear their overburdened calendars as
expeditiously as possible; of the three murder cases,
only Wasko's contained the possibility of the death
penalty. In the other two the state had waived it.
Morphonios calculated therefore that she could clear
those two within a week, whereas the more complicated Wasko trial probably would drag out over a
longer period. She chose to hear those two cases and
get rid of them, and asked Judge Arthur Snyder if he
would take the Wasko trial. His calendar was lighter
and he agreed.

A quiet, silver-haired veteran of the major-crimes
bench, Snyder was well liked and respected. A no-
nonsense judge, he was eminently qualified to hear this
case.

Prosecution and defense attorneys knew him well,
for they had been in his court before. The first thing he
told McDonald and Waksman was that if they had any
special pre-trial motions to file, he wanted them heard
on the morning of the day the trial opened, not before.

Accordingly, on Monday morning, January 9, 1984,
Eddie Wasko's defense attorneys filed a pre-trial motion "to suppress as evidence at the time of trial . . . all
written and oral statements made by the defendant to

the police or other agents of the state of Florida."
McDonald stated that Wasko was repudiating his confession because it had been coerced from him over the
course of his interrogation in Ohio by detectives
Sessler and Ratcliff and the polygraph examiner,
Randy Walker. Wasko was now claiming that he had
been "brainwashed," mistreated, threatened, and forced
to sign a confession that was dictated to him by the detectives. Therefore, stated the defense motion, the
prosecution should be barred from using that confession as evidence in the trial.

This obstructive tactic to suppress Wasko's confession was potentially a fatal blow to the prosecution's
case. If the judge ruled in favor of the defense, the
prosecution would be left with no case against Wasko.
There was no physical evidence to implicate him, nothing to prove he had ever been in the Weinstein residence. Pierson was now a non-starter as a prosecution
witness. McDonald would tear him to shreds on cross-
examination no matter what he swore to on the stand.

At the same time, the motion to suppress showed a
certain amount of desperation. Should Judge Snyder
deny the motion, and permit the prosecution to introduce the confession as evidence, it would then become
a jury decision either to believe Wasko's claim of coercion or believe the prosecution's version of events.

In effect, upon Judge Snyder's decision arguably
hinged the outcome of the trial.

Before the actual defense and prosecution arguments
could begin, however, Brian McDonald insisted that
Marvin Weinstein be barred from the courtroom during
both the motion proceedings for suppression and the
trial.

"Mr. Weinstein is under defense subpoena and will,
in all probability, be our first witness," said McDonald.
He said he had no objection to Marvin's watching the
trial from the newsroom nearby, since "we're apparently going to be on camera," the attorney said.

Judge Snyder explained to Marvin: "Mr. Weinstein, under the rules of criminal procedure, a witness that is going to testify or there's a possibility that he's going to testify is excluded from the courtroom. Is there anything you'd like to tell me that perhaps puts you outside the normal scope of the criminal rules?"

By now Marvin was well armed to respond: "According to my understanding," he said, "in some of the states they allow the family of the deceased to even sit at the desk of the state attorney. This is something that's being allowed in the state of Georgia, and I had mentioned to the state attorney that rather than file a motion against my Constitutional rights to being kept out, because it is being done in other states, that I hoped that good justice in court would see that as long as there is no emotional outbreak by me, and there will be none, that I do nothing to the jury, that hopefully you will allow me to be here.

"She was my daughter," Marvin said, clearly checking his emotions, "and I feel if anybody has a right to be in this courtroom it's myself, more than anyone in this whole world, and it would be a travesty of justice not to allow me."

Judge Snyder: "I understand that, but so far I haven't heard any good reason other than the fact that perhaps Georgia does it, but every state has its own laws and in Florida we go under the Florida rules of criminal procedure, and frankly, if I were to allow you to stay I would just be allowing an appellate court, if there is a conviction in this case, to set it aside on the grounds that you were present and there's really no reason for that. . . . So I'm afraid I'm going to have to deny your motion."

The judge told Marvin that he would, however, allow him to be in the courtroom after all witnesses had been called, to hear closing arguments and the judge's charge to the jury. And he could sit in the press room and watch the proceedings on the closed-circuit television. This Marvin would do and in fact would video-tape the entire trial. But as for being barred from the courtroom during the trial itself—the state of Florida had not heard the last of Marvin Weinstein on this rule.

For the pre-trial motion to suppress Wasko's confes-sion, David Waksman called as his first witness Phil Ryser, the Ohio attorney for Stanley Steemer Interna-tional. Ryser related his recollection of the events.

Waksman asked him, "Did you direct [Wasko] as an employee that he must speak with these police offi-cers?"

Ryser: "Well, I didn't have to, because he indicated that he was willing to talk, and I never indicated one way or the other whether he had to or not."

Waksman: "Did you, at any time, threaten him with firing or some administrative sanction if he wouldn't cooperate with the law enforcement authorities?"

Ryser: "No, not at all."

The Ohio attorney said he had seen Wasko again that evening. He noticed nothing unusual; Wasko "seemed a little tired, but he had a long day, obviously."

The following morning, Ryser related, after Sessler and Ratcliff had told him they wanted Wasko to take a polygraph test, he told Wasko, "Eddie, all Steems cares about is that you tell the truth and let's get this thing over with."

Waksman: "Did he indicate to you that he didn't want to see these policemen again?"

Ryser: "No."

"Did he indicate to you any improper conduct on their part the evening before?"

"No, not at all."

"Did you have any conversation with him about whether or not he should obtain some legal counsel?"

"Yes, that would have been late Thursday evening."

"Why don't you tell the court about that, please?"

"Well, what happened was, after the polygraph test . . .

I felt at that point as the company attorney and also as an acquaintance and somewhat of a friend of Eddie's, I brought him into my office and sat him down. . . . I advised him at that point in time, I said, 'I don't know what's going on here, but if I were you I would either talk to or hire a lawyer, because I can't represent you. I represent the company.' "

"Did you make any efforts to assist him in getting a lawyer?"

"I offered to refer him to someone in town, and Eddie indicated that he didn't feel it was necessary. He had some friends that were attorneys if he needed them."

Under cross-examination by Peter Ferrero, Ryser said that Sessler and Ratcliff had told him that though Wasko was being cooperative, he was somewhat inconsistent in the stories he had been telling.

Ferrero: "Did they show any concern about any particular area of their questioning, specifically a gun?"

Ryser: "A gun was mentioned, yes, but I can't recall the substance of the conversation."

"Did the detectives tell you that if Eddie was concerned about having a gun, he could get into no trouble for having it? Florida law says it was okay or words to that effect?"

"Yes."

"Did you advise [Eddie] of what the detectives had told you that there wouldn't be trouble? Florida law said it was okay concerning the gun?"

"I advised Eddie that what the detectives had told me was, if he had a gun, there was no problem and that was basically the extent of that."

Ryser reiterated, in response to Ferrero's questioning, that he had told Wasko he should "just tell the truth."

Ferrero: "Did you mention anything to him or did he show any concern about immunity?"

"No."

"Was that term ever brought up?"

"Not by me, no."

"Approximately how long Thursday evening did you talk to him?"

"About forty-five minutes to an hour."

"What were Eddie's main concerns during that discussion with you?"

"He seemed to me like he felt he had told everything he knew and that he was trying to cooperate. That he did have some doubts about what he had said before. As the company counsel in conducting our investigation into the matter, I simply went through the story with him again, and after we went through the facts, it was at that point that I said, 'Eddie, you were questioned last night, you have been polygraphed today. I really feel that you need to consult with an attorney.' "

Ryser was then excused, and Waksman called Randy Walker.

The polygraph examiner testified that before he had begun the interview with Eddie Wasko, he advised him of his Constitutional rights, and gave him a form to read that included his rights. Walker said he spent about a half hour explaining to Wasko about his rights, line by line, as Wasko read the form. He advised Wasko that he did not have to talk to him, and that he was free to get up and leave at any time.

Walker said that Wasko had agreed to waive his rights and participate in the interview and that Wasko told him that he had slept for seven hours and was well rested.

Waksman: "After he agreed to speak to you, did you then speak to him for some time?"

Walker: "At great length."

"Now, at any time during the course of the day did you ever stop to allow him to have certain breaks, either for food or water, going to the bathroom or just to get up and take a little walk?"

"Certainly two things. Not only did I give him the

breaks, but also told him, 'If you need anything while
you're here, rest room, water, whatever, let your needs
be known.' "

"Did you deny him the right to go to the bathroom
or get some water or to get up and take a walk at any
time?"

"Absolutely not."

"What, if anything, did he say when you asked him
if he wanted to continue?"

"At numerous times throughout the course of talking
to him . . . Eddie indicated to me that he liked me and
he liked talking to me. As we talked, he seemed to feel
better about talking with me and talking about it."

Waksman then took Walker step by step through the
entire polygraph examination that had taken place over
the two days of July 7 and 8.

Waksman: "At any time on Thursday did you
threaten Mr. Wasko?"

Walker: "Absolutely not."

"Did you make any promises to induce him to continue talking to you?"

"Absolutely not."

"Did anybody in your presence threaten him or
make any promises?"

"No."

"When did you see him again Friday?"

"The next time I saw him would have been noon on
Friday."

"Was he wearing handcuffs when you saw him Friday at noon?"

"No."

"Was he there voluntarily?"

"Absolutely. If he hadn't been there voluntarily, then
I wouldn't have talked to him."

"How do you know he was there voluntarily?"

"I asked him."

"What, if anything, did he say?"

"He said he wanted, once again, to talk to me."

"Did you have occasion to advise him of any of his rights?"

"Absolutely. Same form as we had gone through the first day."

"Was Mr. Wasko your prisoner at this time?"

"No."

"Was he under arrest at this time?"

"No."

"Why did you advise him of his Miranda rights?"

"Because I wanted to make sure he was there voluntarily, and I wanted to make sure he understood his rights and understood that he didn't have to talk to me."

"Did the topic of the gun ever come up during this Friday afternoon interview?"

"Yes."

Walker explained that at this time Wasko had still been considered only an important witness to the crime, and that there was a possibility Wasko was afraid to admit possession of a .22-caliber gun. "I felt on Friday," Walker said, "that Eddie was afraid that maybe someone had used his gun in the course of a felony and Eddie was responsible for it. So the conversation of the gun was continuous on Thursday and Friday."

"At that time were you familiar with the Florida statute on possession of firearms?"

"I wasn't. It was explained to me."

"Did you ask the Miami detectives what the law was of people having guns in their cars in Florida?"

"Yes, they assured me that a person was able to carry a weapon for self-defense."

"In the vehicle?"

"Yes."

"And did you explain this to Mr. Wasko?"

"No, I let the detectives themselves because I'm not familiar with Florida law. I wanted to make sure everybody understood where everybody was coming from."

"Now, other than the breaks, you were speaking with Mr. Wasko from 12:23 up until 9:00. Why did it take eight or nine hours this Friday?"

"Well, there were so many different versions, and it wasn't so much that the versions changed, it was just that each time we would go through the events of 14 October or the events shortly thereafter, or the events just before the afternoon of 14 October, a new little piece of information would come out."

"From who?"

"From Mr. Wasko. So then we go back over the entire thing again and I point out to him, 'We've got to get all this thing together.' "

Walker went on to testify that when Wasko had opened up to him and confessed late that Friday evening, he then turned the interviewing over to Sessler. "I more or less removed myself from the entire interview," Walker said, "since Detective Sessler knew so much more about the case than I knew." He then reiterated, under questioning by Waksman, that at least in his presence no one had threatened or coerced Wasko at any time or ever denied Wasko's requests for food or breaks. Neither had Wasko ever told him he was tired and wanted to stop talking.

Peter Ferrero then cross-examined for the defense. Since it was the defense contention that Wasko had been variously coerced, "brainwashed," and otherwise forced to sign a confession, Ferrero sharply questioned Walker on his entire polygraph procedure and interview sessions with Wasko. Initially, however, perhaps to reveal by implication that Walker might have certain prejudices, Ferrero brought out via questioning Walker's involvement in the shoot-out that had seriously injured him, and the fact that he approved of the death penalty where legally applicable.

Walker testified under cross-examination that from Thursday morning until Friday evening he had been with Wasko about twenty-one hours.

Ferrero: "Was this the longest polygraph examination you have ever had in your life?"

Walker: "Yes, it was."

Walker said he knew from a conversation he'd had with Kent Jurney that Wasko had passed the polygraph test Jurney had given him in Dade County. Nevertheless, almost immediately Walker noted discrepancies in Wasko's story as it began to unfold. On Thursday afternoon, Walker said, "I told him that I felt he was purposely trying to distort the instrument and that I felt he was not telling me the truth. At that time it was my purpose to try to find out what it was as to why he couldn't tell me the truth."

Ferrero: "So at 3:11 on the seventh of July, the Thursday, is when Eddie is first told that he's a liar, would that be correct?"

Walker: "Oh, no, I wouldn't have used that term. That's your term."

"You said to him that he wasn't telling the truth, is that correct?"

"It would have been more to the effect in this situation: 'There's something bothering you. Something you are holding back. I don't have any idea what it is at this point, but let's try to get this thing straightened out.' "

"Did you tell him that he passed the polygraph test?"

"No."

"Did you tell him that he failed the polygraph test?"

"I told him that I felt he had failed it because of the way he had distorted the polygraph charts."

Walker described, in reply to Ferrero's questions, the many areas in Wasko's story that had changed during the course of the interview. He asked Wasko why there were those discrepancies; for example, about his story about the blood on Pierson's shirt, and then, Walker testified, Wasko would say, "Now I remember," and relate a different version of events.

"Did he say that first day that he had participated in the murder of Staci Weinstein?"

"No, he did not."

"Who concluded the polygraph examination?"

"I did."

"You stated in direct examination that, I believe, that Eddie concluded—Eddie said he wanted to stop."

"No, he did not."

"Was it to be continued the next day?"

"At his request."

"Was it to be continued the next day?"

"Yes, it was."

"Did you want it to continue the next day?"

"I felt as though there was still some information that Eddie needed to share with somebody."

"Did you want it to continue it the next day, yes or no?"

"Yes."

"From the time you were with Ed Wasko at 10:43 to 9:01, did he ever eat solid food?"

"To my knowledge, no. There could have been a time when he was furnished with food by one of the two people and it was not brought to my attention."

"To the best of your knowledge he didn't eat any solid foods?"

"Potato chips."

"And that was it?"

"I offered. He didn't accept."

"He didn't eat anything other than potato chips during this interview or polygraph examination of ten hours. Is that correct?"

"Not to my knowledge."

"Was he tired?"

"He didn't appear. Not at all."

"Did he appear to be in the same condition that you saw him in at 10:48?"

"Yes."

"No change?"

"Not that I could note."

"The man had been in your office for nine and a half hours, not eaten anything but potato chips, told that he had been less than truthful in a polygraph examination, questioned or interviewed or talked to for a period of eight or nine hours, looked exactly the same way that he did when he came in at 10:48. Is that your statement?"

"Yes, it is. That was one of the things that amazed me about Eddie. He never gets tired."

And so the cross-examination by Ferrero continued at length, attempting to paint a picture of a physically and psychologically harassed Eddie Wasko kept under pressure without proper rest or sustenance. Ferrero asked Walker about the time during the second day of questioning when he and Wasko both had broken into tears:

"Approximately what time was that?"

"I can't say for sure. I would say approximately seven to eight on Friday."

"Approximately three hours before he gives his taped statement to Detective Sessler?"

"That would be correct."

"I guess this second day there was a little more than talking in that room, if there's two people crying at about eight at night, would that be right?"

"Well, I wouldn't say that would be correct."

"You have got someone in your office that you have managed to put in tears. You consider that a friendly conversation?"

"I don't."

"You consider psychology being put in that?"

"Counselor, I don't feel that I was the one who put . . . Eddie in tears. I feel it was the events of 14 October that put him in that state."

"Randy, how much psychology did you use on him that second day? Did you try to twist his mind?"

"Twist his mind would be your term. I don't know what you're referring to."

As they neared the end of this extensive cross-examination, Ferrero said to Walker:

"You knew that Ed Wasko had passed the polygraph examination before he came to you, the polygraph examination given to him by Kent Jurney down here, that he was not involved in the shooting of Staci Weinstein?"

"That's correct."

"Yet after a period of some nineteen hours with you, Ed Wasko gave a second version in which he implicated himself. Is that right?"

"Well, there had been a lot of versions in between, but, yes, he did implicate himself."

"Because this was an out-of-town case, this was a Miami case, you were in Ohio ... when you saw Ed Wasko the first day, did you smell something like maybe you could get someone?"

"Absolutely not."

"That second day you were with Ed Wasko, did you feel that you could get him to admit to homicide?"

"Absolutely not."

"Because it was an out-of-town case, did you bend the rules a little bit?"

"That's absurd."

"Did you read the statement that he gave the police?"

"Yes, I did."

"Isn't that equally as absurd?"

"I don't understand the question, Your Honor."

With that, Ferrero concluded his cross-examination of Randy Walker.

Barbara Robinson, the Columbus Police Department stenographer, next testified briefly to the fact that she had transcribed the Wasko tape recording, that Wasko had read it and made several corrections. Judge Snyder then called a brief recess, and the court reconvened at

1:35. Jayne Weintraub took over for the prosecution. She called Steve Sessler.

Responding to the prosecutor's questions, Sessler related his version of the events. He testified that he and Detective Sergeant Ratcliff had gone to Ohio to see Wasko because they believed he was a potential witness against John Pierson, who was the focal point of the homicide investigation at that time. After questioning Wasko on the evening of their arrival in Ohio, said Sessler, Wasko agreed to talk to Randy Walker the next morning and take a polygraph test.

Sessler testified that during the course of Wasko's questioning he had been given several breaks, had been told he was free to stop talking and leave at any time. Sessler said there was a canteen in the police headquarters building, and at one point he had brought hamburgers back for everybody, including Wasko, and cigarettes for him. Sessler further testified that he and Ratcliff had planned to return to Miami on the five o'clock flight on Friday, hopefully with a useful statement from Wasko as a witness to the Staci Weinstein murder.

On that Friday morning, Sessler said, he and Ratcliff checked out of their hotel and picked up Wasko around eleven at the Stanley Steemer building and took him to police headquarters for another session with Randy Walker. At that time, Sessler said, he felt Wasko was still holding back information, and he related the conversation he then had had with Wasko, asking him to tell the truth, and that he, Sessler, understood the reasons why he was holding back: his loyalty to the company and, as John Pierson's supervisor, his responsibility for Pierson's actions.

After Wasko had been with Walker from about noon to three o'clock, they all took a break—that significant break during which Sergeant Jim Ratcliff went into Walker's office, closed the door, and spent a half hour alone with Wasko.

Sessler then went into the office with Ratcliff, heard yet another version of Wasko's story, and promptly cancelled the detectives' five o'clock flight back to Miami, convinced that Wasko would be able to give them a strong statement implicating Pierson in the murder.

The final break came, testified Sessler, about ten that evening.

Weintraub: "At approximately a quarter to ten, did you have a conversation with the defendant about what he had seen or heard on October 14, 1982?"

"Yes, ma'am, I did."

"How long did that conversation last?"

"I would estimate from about a quarter to ten to about ten-twenty or ten-fifteen."

"Up until that conversation, was Eddie Wasko free to leave?"

"Yes, ma'am, he was."

"Up until that time, was Eddie Wasko a suspect?"

"No, ma'am."

"At the end of that conversation at ten-twenty p.m., was Eddie Wasko a suspect?"

"Yes, ma'am."

"Did something new come up in that conversation that you had with the defendant at a quarter to ten to ten-twenty that previously had not come up before?"

"Yes, ma'am."

"What was that?"

"The fact that he assisted by giving the firearm to John Pierson and told John Pierson to shoot the girl and finish her off."

Sessler then concluded his testimony with a description of how he had advised Wasko of his rights, had Wasko sign the rights waiver, and, with Wasko's agreement, tape-recorded his statement, which was then transcribed by Barbara Robinson and read and initialed on every page by Wasko. Sessler said he had explained to Wasko about extradition procedures and arranged to have the group photograph taken, again with Wasko's approval.

With Sessler excused, defense attorney Ferrero reiterated his motion to suppress that stirred a minor defense-prosecution skirmish. Now the defense wanted to suppress Wasko's statement after he had been brought to Miami, during the search for the missing murder weapon.

Judge Snyder said he would allow the amended motion to be entered, but would defer a ruling on it along with his ruling on the principal motion to suppress the confession.

Weintraub then brought Sessler back, asking him to explain in detail both the extradition hearing in Ohio and, back in Miami, his unsuccessful attempt with Wasko in locating the firearm.

Finally, after Sessler was questioned and cross-examined about the perjury warrant issued out of Miami but never served on Wasko, the state rested its case, and Ferrero called Wasko to the stand.

As with Pierson, his story had changed completely.

Chapter 17

Well known for his pride in his appearance, Eddie Wasko took the witness chair smartly dressed in dark blue trousers, light blue jacket and vest, blue shirt and tie. After the usual formalities of swearing-in and background questioning by defense attorney Peter Ferrero, Wasko described his meeting on Thursday morning, July 7, 1983, with detectives Sessler and Ratcliff.

Calm and cool, Wasko stated that during the Thursday morning meeting Sessler had "explained to me different things, mostly pertaining to that in regards to state immunity."

Ferrero: "What did he explain to you regarding that?"

Wasko: "He told me that I was granted state immunity."

Ferrero: "What did you understand that to mean?"

Wasko: "He explained that to me. What he explained was, that state immunity meant that I was free from all involvement in this crime."

Wasko was then taken by Ferrero through his first meeting with Randy Walker. Wasko said Walker had given him a polygraph test, then retested him twice, each time leaving the room for a time and returning for another test.

Ferrero: "What happened after that test the third time?"

Wasko: "... he came back in, and he just kind of

looked at me, and he told me . . . through the charts he was looking at—he did not think I was telling the truth.''

"What was your reaction to that?"

"I was kind of stunned."

"Did his mood change at all at that time?"

"Yes."

"How did his mood change?"

"He started asking me questions about my mental health."

"Did he accuse you of controlling your breath?"

"Oh, yes."

"How long were you with him that time after he confronts you with the fact that you were holding your breath?" (Holding one's breath can distort polygraph results.)

"After that . . . he spent a few hours with me."

"What was he doing during those hours he spent with you alone?"

"Questioning me."

"Was he talking with you?"

"No."

"Or was he questioning you?"

"He was questioning me."

"In what manner was he questioning you?"

"Various ways. Sometimes he could be real soft, you know, like he wanted to be my friend, and cuddle with me, and talk with me, and become really chummy, and then sometimes, you know, he'd just get violent-looking and kind of get real forceful, like he wanted me to say what he wanted to hear, not what I was saying . . ."

"Were you scared?"

"Yes."

"Did you want to leave?"

"Yes."

"Why didn't you?"

"I was compelled to sit down and respect the law."

Later, Wasko said, he had been left alone in the room with Sergeant Ratcliff, who questioned him about his memory of events during the time of the murder.

Ferrero: "Did Detective Ratcliff scare you in any way?"

"Yes."

"How was that?"

"He jumped up—the first time, okay, that he talked to me alone—he got up, and it was like he made—he tensed all up, and his face got real, real red, and like his veins started coming out of his neck, and he kind of like looked at me and he says, 'You're going to tell me the truth.'"

"Did you get scared when he did that?"

"Yes."

"Were you telling the truth?"

"When I was telling everything that—everything that was coming out of my mouth was the truth."

Wasko said that Ratcliff, Sessler, and Walker had kept rotating in and out of the room, questioning him, "always one on one."

Ferrero: "At nine o'clock when you left, what was your mental state?"

"Confused."

"Were you scared?"

"Very."

"Very frightened? Were you frightened of the police?"

"Yes."

"Had you cooperated with them in every way they asked you to?"

"I felt that I cooperated with the police from the very beginning of this whole endeavor."

"Did you think they were cooperating with you?"

"At that moment, no, 'cause everything I said they contradicted."

Wasko then related how he had slept poorly that

night, that he had eaten nothing since noon and was not feeling well the next morning when he was taken by Sessler and Ratcliff down to Randy Walker's office about noon on the next day.

Ferrero: "Did you want to go down?"

"Not by myself."

"Did you want to go with anyone?"

"Yes."

"Who did you want to go with?"

"I had talked to Phil Ryser that morning, and I had talked about the legal representative that he wanted to come down there with me, and he told me himself that he would try to come down. He felt the way I looked, the way I felt, that I should have some legal representation."

"During the course of the questioning on Friday at Columbus Police Station, did you ever bring up the fact that maybe you need an attorney, maybe you should get an attorney?"

"Yes."

"When did that happen?"

"I felt that after the first night, after what the detectives had told me that they felt they couldn't believe anything I was telling them. Well, that they felt I was lying. I felt that I needed some help."

"Did you mention that to the police?"

Wasko said he mentioned it to Sessler and asked to use the telephone to call a lawyer.

"What did he advise you?"

"He told me not to worry. That I didn't need a lawyer."

Judge Snyder interrupted the questioning then to talk to the attorneys for both sides. He told them he wanted to break into the proceedings temporarily to bring the fifty prospective members of the jury panel down, who were waiting upstairs, to talk to them and give them instructions, before sending them home for the night, not to watch television or read the newspapers, because learning about the testimony at the suppression hearing and its result could preclude their serving on the jury.

Ferrero resumed his direct questioning of Wasko:

"What was Randy like on Friday?"

"At the beginning of the day he was talking nicely. We were conversing. Then once we started getting into the interrogation, he got a little bit frustrated, and then he gave me—toward the latter part of it, of our conversation or interrogation, like he had given up on me."

"Did he try to make you feel any certain way in your mind?"

"He made me feel very, very guilty."

"Would it be a fair statement to say that your emotions were going on a roller-coaster ride during this?"

Waksman interrupted: "Objection! Leading."

Judge Snyder: "Sustained."

Ferrero: "How would you characterize your emotions at this period of time?"

"Well, during that whole day, I displayed at least seven or eight different emotions."

"What emotions were you feeling?"

"Confusion, happiness, sadness. I felt bitter. I felt in pain. I felt really confused most of the time, though."

"By the time Detective Sessler came in the office, eventually took that taped statement from you, how would you characterize your mind? How did you feel?"

"To be honest with you, I felt totally brainwashed."

"Were you going to say anything they wanted you to say?"

"Yes."

"Did you feel that if they asked you whether you shot President Reagan, you would say yes to that?"

"Probably."

"When they read you the Miranda rights, were you at eleven-thirty, midnight, that night, understanding them?"

"No."

"The next day during that taped statement, were they your own words coming out of your own mouth as to the true events that occurred that day?"

"No, sir."

"Whose words were they?"

"They were Officer Sessler's written-down statements. I was reading off a piece of paper."

"Why did you make those statements about the murder of Staci Weinstein?"

"Because he told me that if I didn't make a statement, that John Pierson could turn around and testify against me. I could get convicted of first-degree murder."

"Did you believe you were going to be charged with first-degree murder after you gave that taped statement?"

"No, sir."

"What did you think was going to happen?"

"I thought I was going to come down to Miami and testify against John Pierson."

"Did the police lead you to believe that that was the purpose—one of the purposes—in taking the statement?"

"Yes."

"You gave statements to the police on October 28, 1982. Is that correct?"

"Yes."

"You gave a statement to Kent Jurney, polygraph examiner, sometime after that?"

"Yes."'

"Do you recall passing that polygraph examination that Kent Jurney gave you?"

"Yes, sir."

"Did he tell you you passed that lie-detector test regarding Staci Weinstein's homicide?"

"Yes."

"Do you recall telling the police on July 6, July 7,

the entire two days that you were not involved in the killing of Staci Weinstein?"

"Yes."

"When did they let up on you? Was it after the taped statement?"

"No, it was after Sessler read it to me and I read along with him for all the mistakes."

Ferrero had no further questions. Judge Snyder asked Waksman if he wanted to start his cross-examination immediately or wait until the fifty prospective jurors came in for instructions. Waksman, however, said he wanted to make a motion, "that [Ferrero's] outburst about the polygraph should not be made in front of the jury."

Judge Snyder excused Wasko from the witness chair for the moment, reminding him that when he returned, he would be cross-examined, and that he would still be under oath at that point.

Waksman resumed by stating that he'd already instructed Walker that he was a civilian employee for Columbus Police Station. Since polygraph results were inadmissible in court, he wanted the word *polygraph* to be avoided.

Judge Snyder: "Would you like to argue that, Mr. McDonald?"

McDonald: "I'm not quite sure exactly—I'm not supposed to use the word *polygraph* at all? Is that the basic crux of the motion?"

Waksman: "Yes."

McDonald objected, and this was batted back and forth before Judge Snyder said he'd think about it and make up his mind about the use of the word *polygraph* during the voir dire—the jury selection.

The legal term *voir dire* is Old French: "to speak the truth," which is in turn derived from the Latin *verus* (truth) and *dicere* (to say). In law it refers to the preliminary examination by both prosecution and defense attorneys of prospective jurors to determine their competence to serve. In practical terms, attorneys for both sides, who are allowed a certain amount of "challenges," use the voir dire to try to pick the twelve jurors most likely to favor their cause—or, at the minimum, be without prejudice, fair, and open-minded, which in theory of course is what a jury is supposed to be.

The suppression hearing paused then while Judge Snyder had the bailiff, Harry Lambert, bring in and seat the fifty prospective jurors. After explaining to them the trial procedures and reading the indictment of Wasko with all the charges against him, he told them all to return the following morning at eight-thirty for the selection of the final twelve. Finally, he cautioned them that they were not to watch television news that evening or read the newspapers, lest it taint their objectivity about the case. Then he dismissed them.

The suppression hearing then continued with the lengthy cross-examination of Wasko by David Waksman.

Waksman: "Now, you told us that Phil Ryser told you you were granted immunity. Is that correct?"

Wasko: "Yes."

"Did you ever hear of the word immunity before you got involved in these proceedings here?"

"Yes."

"And Mr. Ryser said, 'Granted'? He didn't say they're *giving* you immunity?"

"No, I was given immunity."

"Well, you said before, 'granted.' Had you ever heard of that concept before you got arrested?"

"No, sir."

"Did he tell you to go out and get a lawyer?"

"No."

"Were you sitting here when he testified earlier this morning?"

"Yes."

"He even told you he could refer some names to you. Do you remember that?"

"Yes."

"And you said, 'No, I have an attorney. I have got some friends who are lawyers. I can call somebody if I want.' You said all that, didn't you?"

"No."

"Are you saying Phil Ryser never told you—are you saying that you never told him, 'I've got some friends who are lawyers. I can call somebody if I want'? You're saying that never happened?"

"I told Phil Ryser if I needed a lawyer that I would ask him for one."

"Why didn't you get a lawyer?"

"I was hoping he would come down and represent me."

"Did he tell you, 'There are two detectives here from Miami, if you want to talk to them that's okay, and if you don't want to talk to them, that's also okay'?"

"No."

"He never said that to you?"

"No."

"Why did you talk to the police?"

"Because I had no reason not to talk to them."

"What does immunity mean?"

"I don't know the definition in the dictionary."

"Well, when Phil Ryser said, 'You have been granted immunity,' what does that mean? Somebody is buying you a drink for your birthday? Is immunity a party? Is immunity a sickness? What is it?"

"Immunity to me meant that I would not be arrested for anything."

"That's what Phil Ryser told you?"

"Yes."

"Did he say you wouldn't be arrested?"

"Yes."

"Did you hear him say that here this morning before lunch?"

"No."

"You think he just conveniently forgot about that when he was testifying?"

"I couldn't answer that."

Under continued, rapid-fire questioning by Waksman, Wasko denied that anyone had ever told him he could get up and leave at any time, or that he had ever lied to Randy Walker or the detectives. When Waksman asked him how was it, if he had never lied, that he told different versions of his story to all three men, Wasko replied that he had been fed information about the events surrounding the murder by Walker and the detectives; they had suggested things to him, and then claimed he had volunteered the information.

Waksman: "Who was the one who suggested to you that the girl was wearing pink shorts and a light blue top and no shoes?"

Wasko: "Officer Sessler."

"When did he tell you about the clothing she was wearing?"

"Right before the statement was taken."

"Did you ever tell Randy Walker she was wearing pink shorts and a light blue or sky blue top?"

"No, sir."

"Did you ever tell Detective Sessler it felt good to finally talk about it and get it out?"

"No."

"How many times did Randy Walker get out of that wheelchair and start kicking you?"

"Not once."

"How many times did he stay in the wheelchair and just jab out and hit you?"

"Never once, but may I add something?"

"Please do."

"Frequently he got real close to me and was lifting his foot up toward my face."

"Lifting the foot?"

"Like—can I show him?"

Judge Snyder: "Sure."

Wasko: "He was sitting like this [indicating] and he was lifting his foot up like this [indicating] right at my face."

Waksman: "Is that the foot that doesn't work, because he got shot in the spine?"

"I don't know which foot."

"I would like the record to reflect he lifted his foot two or three times above the ground."

McDonald: "Through the use of his hands."

Waksman: "Are you saying Randy Walker used his hands to lift his foot up?"

Wasko: "Yes."

"And is that how he kicked you?"

"I didn't say he kicked me, sir."

"What was he doing when he was lifting his foot up with his hands?"

"I don't know what he was doing."

"Did that make you afraid?"

"It intimidated me."

Waksman showed Wasko his signed statement and asked him, "Is that your signature on the bottom?"

Wasko: "Yes."

"And on the bottom where your signature is, right above it, does it say, 'I've been treated well since I've been here'?"

"Yes."

"Were you lying when you said, 'No one has coerced me'?"

"Yes."

"Why did you sign it?"

"I signed everything that they put in front of me."

"Remember Randy Walker saying you kept injecting new facts all the time, so he had to keep going over it?"

"Yeah, *he* was injecting facts."

"He was. So he also lied today when he told us about you changing the facts?"

"Yes."

"Phil Ryser lied, and Randy Walker lied, and Detective Sessler lied. . . . Now, on the tape recording you told us everything that you said, you said because Sessler had written it out for you on paper and you read it off the notes?"

"Yes, sir."

"Did he actually write it out for you and say, 'Here is the pad and when I ask you the question, that's the answer'?"

"What had happened, was he and I sat in the room, and we talked. He explained to me what happened and he said he was going to write it down on a piece of paper just so that we wouldn't forget it, and he wrote out sentences, and in between the sentences he told me what to say and I said it."

"Did he write out what answer you were supposed to give?"

"Yes."

"Then when the tape recorder was turned on, did he give you that pad so you see what the script was?"

"No, he held it, and when I couldn't answer something, he would show me and he'd point."

"He would point to the answer?"

"Yes."

"Did he ever afford you the opportunity to give your statement to a court reporter, just like we have in court? To have somebody write it down and just as it was coming out of your mouth?"

"No."

"Randy Walker told us that when you left his office Thursday evening at 9:01 you said, 'I'm sorry I wasted your time. Everything was a lie. I'll straighten it out tomorrow.' "

"No, I don't remember saying that."

"I know you don't remember saying that. Did he lie when he said it here in court?"

"Yes."

"Who was the one who brainwashed you?"

"I'd have to say it was Mr. Walker, and I'd have to say it was Mr. Ratcliff, and I'd have to say it was Mr. Sessler."

"How about Phil Ryser?"

"As far as I listened to him."

"Let me ask you this. After they brought you back to Miami—strike that. They took you to a judge Saturday morning, didn't they? And you told that judge, 'I'll go back to Miami with these policemen'?"

"No, they asked me—the judge asked me if I waived extradition."

"Why didn't you say, 'Judge, they've been threatening me for three days. God bless America, thank God I'm going to be saved now'?"

"Because Officer Sessler told me to waive extradition."

"So that's why you didn't ask the judge to protect you from these threatening policemen?"

"I didn't know I could ask the judge for protection."

Waksman turned back to the statements that Wasko had signed and/or initialed, and about his understanding of his Miranda rights as explained to him by Walker and the detectives. Wasko's response was that he had been "scared" to exercise his rights, that he hadn't really felt he could exercise his rights to leave, to refuse to talk to Walker or the detectives.

Waksman: "Did anybody threaten you with physical harm?"

Wasko: "I don't understand the question."

"Did anybody threaten to punch you?"

"You mean, like say, if you don't answer these questions the way we want you to or else, you know? I mean, leading me to think that something was going to happen to me physically?"

"Did that happen?"

"Yes."

"By who?"

"Officer Ratcliff."

"And what did you think he was going to do to you?"

"I couldn't tell you that."

"Did anybody offer you money to testify? To talk to the police?"

"No."

"So if we can cut all of this down to just one or two words, the only reason you spoke to those people was because you thought Ratcliff was going to beat you up?"

"The only reason I talk to who?"

"Randy Walker, Steve Sessler, Jim Ratcliff. Was it because Ratcliff yelled at you and you thought you were going to get hit?"

"No, that's why the statement changed."

"Oh. That's why you had a different version, because he yelled at you?"

"That's why I had several different versions, according to you."

"Your overall reason for talking to these guys was because you wanted to talk to them? Because you just wanted to talk to them?"

"I wanted to talk to them because they came up to see me and I felt if I didn't talk to them they would arrest me."

"Did they tell you they would arrest you?"

"No."

"Did Phil Ryser threaten to hit you?"

"No."

"And did Barbara Robinson, the stenographer, did she yell at you at any time?"

"No."

Waksman said he had no further questions.

Ferrero said he had no further questions, and that the defense rested on the motion to suppress.

Judge Snyder asked Waksman if he had any rebuttal. And that started another row between Waksman and McDonald. Waksman said he felt forced to bring Ratcliff on in rebuttal either to admit or deny Wasko's allegations, despite the fact he had said previously he would not call Ratcliff as a witness but had requested he be allowed to sit at the prosecutors' table to provide assistance.

McDonald objected strenuously. He said that the prosecution "knew this was coming. Knew that [Ratcliff] was present, that he was there." But, said McDonald, they had said they would not use Ratcliff as a witness under any circumstances and "now they're changing their minds."

Waksman countered: "That shouldn't be a license for them to go in and say for that twenty or thirty minutes they were alone, God knows what happened and that's why the state didn't rebut it with Officer Sessler's testimony. Once a brand-new allegation is made of severe misconduct, we have no choice but to rebut it."

The argument raged back and forth for several minutes until Judge Snyder finally stopped it by granting Waksman permission to call Sergeant Ratcliff to the witness chair in rebuttal of Wasko's allegations of threats, but to testify only about those allegations.

Ratcliff, of course, under Waksman's questioning, denied all the allegations. Ferrero cross-examined.

"Whose idea was it for you to go alone with him, Mr. Wasko, at 3:30 p.m.?"

"I don't believe it was anybody's idea. It might have been Eddie's."

"You didn't threaten him at all. Would that be correct?"

"That's correct."

"Did you call him, quote, 'a bullshitter'?"

"No, I believe that was your terminology."

"Did you call him that?"

"No, sir, you did."

Ferrero's cross-examination continued with his questioning Ratcliff about what actually had occurred when he was alone with Wasko. Ratcliff said Wasko had given him a new version of his story about the events.

Ferrero: "What did he say?"

"He said he wanted to tell me exactly what happened. The truth about the fourteenth of October, 1982."

"Did you have any advance warning that was going to happen?"

"No, I rather expected it to happen."

"Did you expect that because Randy Walker told you that he had his mind twisted?"

"No, I expected him to tell me that he was going to advise me of the truth of that day because he had told me that a number of times. A number of times he had told a number of other people that he was going to quote, unquote, now tell the truth about what had occurred."

"Did he?"

"I did not expect what he told me."

"Did it implicate him in the homicide of Staci Weinstein?"

"No, it didn't."

After a few more questions, Ferrero concluded his cross-examination. Waksman said he had no further questions but said that he'd like to bring Sessler on in rebuttal the following morning, since the judge had already indicated he would not rule on the suppression motion until the next day. Judge Snyder agreed, and court was recessed until 8:30 A.M.

The following morning the first item of business was a discussion before Judge Snyder about the admission in evidence that Kent Jurney and Randy Walker were polygraph examiners. Waksman had wanted the word *polygraph* to be inadmissible. McDonald wanted to mention the fact that they were polygraph examiners, but would not mention the results of the tests. "But I do want to talk about what they do for a living."

Judge Snyder: "The whole issue comes down to you gentlemen can either by an accentuation of your voice or some other means get over to the jury the fact that a polygraph was taken, and perhaps the results were favorable or unfavorable to your client.

"I would suggest to you strongly that you don't do that. I don't think I've ever had any trouble with either one of you—and I don't anticipate that problem. I think we all understand that you can ask them what they do for a living. I don't think it's a matter of dwelling upon it to the point where you can possibly get the inference across to the jury as to the results of the test. I think both of you know how you can keep it within those parameters."

Both attorneys agreed.

They were waiting now for the appearance of Steve Sessler. The detective had been working all night as the leader of a SWAT team that even at that moment was still involved in a serious disturbance in nearby Liberty City. Sessler had just been released from duty and was on his way to the courtroom, so Judge Snyder suggested that in the meantime they begin the voir dire of the jury.

In due course the detective arrived, took the witness chair and, questioned by Waksman, completely denied all of Wasko's allegations. He said Wasko had never asked him for a lawyer, he had not written out answers to questions for Wasko during the tape recording or in any way indicated to Wasko how those questions should be answered. Further, that the judge, Judge Smith, in Ohio, had advised Wasko that he had a choice of returning to Florida voluntarily or fighting extradition.

Attorneys for both sides having rested their cases for and against suppression of Wasko's confession, Judge Snyder immediately stated his decision:

"Based upon the testimony that I heard of all the witnesses that have testified, I rule that the confession or statements given prior to the defendant returning to Dade County, Florida, were freely and voluntarily given and the motion to suppress regarding that testimony is denied."

The judge did add, however, that he was going to suppress "any statement after the defendant was returned to Dade County, Florida," because ". . . the detectives knew that, or should have known that, they should not have talked to him without the consent of an attorney and without a new rights waiver form having been issued at that point."

A major victory for the prosecution.

After a lunch break the jury was selected: nine women and three men who would decide the fate of Eddie Wasko.

Chapter 18

The courtroom—court No. 4 at the Metropolitan Justice Building in Miami—is an imposing wood-paneled room. Two long, rectangular tables for the defense and for the prosecution face the judge and the jury box, which is set to the right of the judge and the witness chair. Behind the attorneys' tables, separated by a low wooden railing, is the gallery for the public. A podium on wheels is placed between the judge's bench and the attorneys' tables from which the questioning by the attorneys and opening and closing statements are made.

With the jury selected and sworn, Judge Snyder proceeded to explain briefly to the jurors about the proceedings to follow, about rules of evidence and what—as judge—his function would be. He mentioned opening statements and the importance of how they should be received by the jurors: "The opening statement," the judge told them, "gives the attorneys a chance to tell you what evidence they believe will be presented during the trial. What the lawyers say is not evidence, and you are not to consider it as such."

The stage was now finally set for the trial to begin.

The case had attracted enough media attraction to fill the gallery with journalists. There were as well some friends and neighbors of the Weinstein family, and the mother and sister of Eddie Wasko. Marvin and Hilari Weinstein, as we know, had been excluded because they were to be called as witnesses. Along with a group of journalists, Marvin was in a nearby press room, where a closed-circuit television had been installed.

Jayne Weintraub went to the podium for the opening statement by the prosecution. An attractive young woman with shoulder-length blond hair and large, round designer glasses, Ms. Weintraub did not look like the experienced assistant state attorney she was.

She began by explaining to the jurors, "The purpose of an opening statement is to give you what we consider, we the lawyers—both lawyers—what we feel the evidence will be in this case. It's an overview. It's sort of like going to read a movie review before you go to a movie."

She then read out in its entirety the grand jury indictment with its three charges against Wasko, and explained in detail, "There are two different ways that the state can prove first-degree murder." One of the ways, she said, was "by premeditation." The other was "felony murder." Premeditation in this case, she said, included the testimony "that the defendant meant to kill the victim, Staci Weinstein.

"There is no specific time that is required to show that premeditated intent or that thought process," she explained. "There is no amount of time that a plan had to be between John Pierson and Edward Wasko for them to think about the killing of Staci Weinstein. Premeditation is as long as it takes to think about committing that crime, whether it's two weeks or five seconds. As long as the thought goes through the defendant's mind—I'm going to kill—that's premeditation.

"The defendant, Edward Wasko, acted with another, John Pierson. The law states that when two people act together while in concert with one another, each is individually guilty of each crime by themselves.

"So, what does that mean with first-degree murder and premeditation? It means that the thought to kill her went through the defendant's mind. In this case you will hear that the defendant handed a gun to John

Pierson and he said, 'Shoot her. Finish her off.' That's premeditation. That's first-degree murder."

Weintraub then discussed felony murder. She explained that felony murder exists "when you have a felony and a death together." She told the jurors that Wasko and Pierson had entered the home of Staci Weinstein unlawfully ("under the pretext of giving her a carpet-cleaning estimate") for an unlawful purpose: "To commit a crime, which was the crime of sexual battery. The defendant went there with John Pierson to have sex with the victim, Staci Weinstein. The unlawful entering of that house, or remaining, staying in that house to have sex with a ten-year-old girl is a felony."

In effect, Weintraub explained, if Wasko was in the house and in any way helped to commit sexual battery on Staci Weinstein, and she was then shot and killed, then it didn't matter who actually pulled the trigger. "Under the law they are both equally guilty. One is responsible and guilty for the other one's acts if and while they are acting together." Therefore, "Edward Wasko is guilty of first-degree murder under the felony-murder theory because of the law that states they were together."

Under Count III of the indictment, Wasko was also charged with attempted sexual battery. Said Weintraub: "You will hear that the defendant entered that house with John Pierson, belonging to Staci Weinstein, a ten-year-old girl, and that Edward Wasko took his fist and he struck Staci Weinstein. Why did he strike her? Because she was resisting, and she was struggling. Why? She was being kissed all over her body. She resisted, and she struggled. So, what did they do?

"Edward Wasko was beating her, but that wasn't good enough. He then had to hand John Pierson the gun and say, 'Finish her off.' And that's just what happened. Staci Weinstein was shot and killed."

Weintraub continued her opening statement by telling the jury how the state would prove the charges: by testimony, by scientific evidence, and by physical evidence. She described how Marvin Weinstein had found the body and the subsequent police investigation. She told how Pierson was connected to the crime, and how the detectives had gone to Ohio to interview Wasko as a possible witness, and that eventually he had confessed to participating in the murder.

She concluded: "You will hear from many witnesses ... all of the evidence, and more. You will hear and you will see for yourselves the evidence against Edward Wasko. And, after you do ... there will be no reasonable doubt that this defendant, Edward Wasko, is guilty of first-degree murder as charged."

Assistant public defender Brian McDonald, stylishly suited and with a dark, trim Vandyke beard, launched an attack on the prosecution's case. He told the jurors first that "you are going to learn that there is physical evidence in this case, physical evidence which points to John Pierson as Staci Weinstein's killer, and which points to John Pierson alone as Staci Weinstein's killer."

He said that when the testimony was put together, the jury would find the Eddie Wasko couldn't have been involved. "This is a case involving emotions," McDonald said. "Marvin Weinstein got home and found his daughter and went nuts." McDonald talked about the detectives assigned to the case and said they, too, had become emotionally involved. "Detective Ben Hall was assigned to handle this investigation ... and Detective Hall got so emotionally involved in this case that he's not with Homicide anymore. It contributed to the breakup of his marriage.... Steve Sessler took over the case from Ben Hall. He fell into it, too. This case has worked itself up to an emotional crescendo that is beyond belief," said McDonald.

He continued to hammer away at the emotional aspects of the prosecution's case. "What's going on here," he said to the jury, "is the state, the police department, everybody has become so emotionally involved in this case that they're getting ready to sentence an innocent man to the electric chair. And they know he's innocent. That's the most bizarre part of it. They know he's innocent.

"They have the evidence. They know what happened in Staci's bedroom. Staci Weinstein was killed by a sex pervert named John Pierson." McDonald then attacked the validity of Wasko's confession. "The state knows that the confession was obtained under rather dubious circumstances," McDonald said, and that he would call Marvin Weinstein to the stand. "I am going to go through the statement with him [referring to Wasko's confession] and show you that out of the twenty-seven pages that he can tell that twenty of them are impossible. The things in that statement could not have happened. . . .

"This is a statement made by a prisoner of war having been subjected to psychological torture, who confessed just like those pilots that were shot down over Vietnam, just like those guys that were—"

Prosecutor Waksman interrupted him: "I'm going to object unless he intends to call these people."

But Judge Snyder overruled him and told McDonald to proceed with his speech to the jury.

"—just like the soldiers that were captured during the Korean War and were held in Communist China for years after it ended, came back after having made statements about the war crimes they committed. That's what this thing is. This is a situation where the state is looking for a conviction. It is looking for an electrocution. It is looking to give some authenticity to this. But in all honesty they know it's not accurate, they know it's not true, and I'm going to prove to you it's not true, that it is a fabrication, that it is an invention. Once the statement [confession] goes out, there is no evidence against Eddie Wasko, none whatsoever.

"If you can find the strength necessary to look at

this case intellectually, with your brains," said McDonald to the jury, "and put the feelings that you're going to have in your hearts aside, and do the duties that you have sworn to God to do, you're going to end up returning a verdict of not guilty.

"You have to put your emotions aside, you have to look at it intellectually because you will be given proof that this statement is garbage. . . . You will be able to throw it in the garbage can and you'll be able to sit back and say what other evidence have they got, and you'll be able to determine that they don't have anything."

McDonald concluded: "There is going to be a lot of stuff coming at you real quick, so take it all in. I need you to do that. I need you to listen to every single piece of evidence and find its place in the overall scheme. I need you to do that so that an innocent man does not die in Florida's electric chair."

Weintraub called as the state's first witness Marvin Weinstein. But before she could begin the questioning, McDonald asked for a discussion with the judge and with David Waksman outside the hearing of the jury. He objected to the fact that the prosecution intended to introduce as evidence poster-size photos of the crime scene, including that of the body of Staci. McDonald claimed they were legally prejudicial because they would tend to be sensationally graphic, and the prosecution should be limited to eight-by-ten photos. Waksman argued that the reason for the blowups was so that the twelve-person jury could all see the photos at once instead of his passing around smaller photos. "It's done routinely," Waksman said. Judge Snyder said he didn't see anything wrong with the blowups, and overruled McDonald's objection.

This interruption by the defense was to be the first of many. It was intent on breaking the prosecution's rhythm with continuous demands for a mistrial, a delay, conferences—whatever tactic possible to confuse the jury.

It is a well-known ploy to defense attorneys: they cannot allow a smooth, unbroken rhythm of prosecution witnesses to take the stand and, one after the other, recite a litany of evidence against the accused. If that sequence is allowed by the defense to be presented without interruption even before cross-examination, it presents a picture difficult to erase. Thus whenever possible, on the slightest pretext, a defense attorney will ask for a mistrial or go sidebar—a conference at the judge's bench out of the jury's hearing. This gets the jurors thinking, breaking their concentration on the evidence being brought out by the prosecution.

Once McDonald's objection to the photos was overruled, Marvin then testified about what had happened on October 14, 1982: what he saw when he came home and entered Staci's bedroom. He identified a poster-size photo of Staci's body. Again McDonald objected to the size of the photo. "I don't see any reason to turn this into a circus," he said. The judge overruled him again. Marvin continued to describe how he had run to the home of his neighbor, Stanley Saul, and how they dialed 911 and the police arrived. For the record, Weintraub asked him:

"Did you ever give Eddie Wasko or John Pierson permission to enter your home on October 14, 1982?"

Marvin: "No way."

"Did you ever give anybody permission to enter your home on October 14, 1982?"

"Absolutely not."

"Mr. Weinstein, did your children have authority or permission to hire workmen to come into the house?"

"That's ridiculous."

McDonald's cross-examination was brief. He discussed Ruth Ann's illness with Marvin and the troubles he'd had over the past two years. Then, referring to

Staci's murder, he asked, "You want to see the people responsible for killing Staci punished?"

Marvin: "Wouldn't you if it was your child?"

"Yes. I'm not saying there is anything wrong with that. You do want to see that happen?"

"That's obvious."

"And you went to the extent of talking to psychics during the course of this investigation to try to get some leads, right?"

"That's correct."

"And a characterization of what you found on October 14, 1982, is that your whole world went up in smoke?"

"It did. She was my baby. What would you expect?"

McDonald had no further questions.

Weintraub called Stanley Saul, who described his recollection of events on the evening of Staci's murder.

Weintraub: "Did you go into the bedroom of Staci Weinstein?"

"Yes."

"What did you see?"

"We saw a little baby all brutally beaten and bloody. I wish the Wasko family saw it."

McDonald bounded to his feet and asked the judge for an attorneys' conference at the bench, outside the hearing of the jury. "I'm moving for a mistrial due to that comment," said McDonald angrily.

Judge Snyder: "On what grounds?"

"On the grounds that it is totally out of place. It's designed solely to poison the minds of the jury, and it's a deliberate attempt to circumvent the justice issues that are going on here today. He's appealing to these people's emotions, and the state is not keeping him under control."

Judge Snyder: "Unless you can show me some connection between what the state is showing, I'm not going to grant a mistrial."

McDonald: "I'm going to ask you to excuse the jury

and instruct this guy to keep his mouth shut and answer the questions properly."

Waksman: "Let's get to the photographs and the legal ID. I can assure this court I did not expect to hear this answer."

McDonald: "There is no way we can be sure he won't do it again."

Judge Snyder: "I'll handle it, okay? That's what I'm here for. I denied your motion for a mistrial." The judge instructed the jury to go to the jury room, and he then cautioned Stanley Saul about making comments. "I can understand your being emotional about this case, but this is an American courtroom," Snyder said to him. "In this courtroom everybody is innocent until proven guilty, okay? You are not on this jury, you are not one of the twelve people that will help us decide whether Mr. Wasko is guilty or not guilty.

"By making gratuitous statements like you just did . . . is almost, but not quite, reason for a mistrial. We would have to start all over again. Two days right down the drain. I must caution you to just answer the questions. You're only a witness. You're here to give the facts."

Saul: "I thought I was answering the question."

Judge Snyder: "You're making comments. We will determine, or these twelve people will determine Mr. Wasko's guilt. Do you understand?"

Saul: "A little."

Judge Snyder: "Well, I've got to make sure you understand me because I can't let you continue testifying."

Saul: "I understand what you're saying. I should only answer what [Jayne Weintraub] says."

When the jury returned, the judge told them that he had warned Saul about making comments and that they should disregard what he'd said. However, the man was obviously still emotionally affected, particularly when asked to identify the photo of Staci's body. Mc-

Donald therefore kept his cross-examination to a minimum, eliciting from Saul the fact that except for what he'd seen in Staci's bedroom, he knew nothing about the case except what he'd read in the newspaper about it.

"So, you don't know whether Eddie Wasko did it or not from your own personal observations?"

"No."

"So there was no basis for your outburst, was there, sir?"

"I think there was a serious mistake. I read that he confessed and that's a pretty basic—"

"But that's what you *read*," McDonald interrupted.

As its final witness of the long day, the state called Officer Earl Higginbotham, who related his part in the events of October 14, 1982. McDonald, still trying to impress upon the jury the emotional aspects of the case as he had outlined in his opening statement, asked Higginbotham: "Did walking in on this scene cause you to have any thoughts about your police career?"

"Yes, sir, it did."

"What thoughts were those?"

"Seeing a ten-year-old child in this position is the closest I've ever come to leaving police work."

"It was an emotional situation?"

"The scene itself was an emotional situation, yes."

The following morning David Waksman took over for the prosecution and called Detective John King. Waksman took King through the crime scene and had him explain the meaning and cause of blood spatter, showing him a number of different photographs.

McDonald challenged the testimony on blood splatter. In part this was more obfuscation on the part of the defense trying to interrupt the flow of evidence. At the same time, McDonald was making a legitimate point. Not all the blood was spatter. Nobody had known that until Theresa Washam at serology cleverly spotted that: a drop of blood as though from a bloody nose, whose enzyme profile proved consistent not with Eddie Wasko but with John Pierson. This supported the defense contention that John Pierson had done it all by himself. It gave the jurors something to contemplate.

Waksman continued with King, asking him about the area canvass.

"In the course of this area canvass were many people interviewed?"

King: "Yes, there were quite a number of people interviewed."

"Was anybody found who had received any Stanley Steemer handouts?"

"Not by myself, no."

"Okay. Did you find any Stanley Steemer door hanger-type handouts in the neighborhood?"

"No, I didn't."

Waksman began to question King about some results from the autopsy, using photos and sparking off a round of sarcastic interplay between Waksman and the defense lawyers about the size of the photos, to which the defense was continuing its objection. Following one exchange of remarks, McDonald said, "We're turning this into a sideshow." Moments later, after showing King for identification a large photo of one of Staci's head wounds, with the head shaven to show the wound, Waksman left it up as an exhibit. McDonald, obviously annoyed, said, "Just leave it up there for everybody to look at for a couple of hours." And Ferrero added from his seat at the defense table, "Could I see the trial and have that removed from in front?"

Judge Snyder stepped in: "Will you check with Mr. McDonald? I don't know whether you want it up or down."

McDonald said dryly: "We'll leave it up. State wants to make it a sideshow. I'm more than willing to accommodate them."

Snyder had heard enough of this. "I wonder if I

could have the jury step back in the jury room, please."
When they'd retired, he said, "Can I see the attorneys
sidebar? And the court reporter." The attorneys and the
court reporter approached the bench. Judge Snyder
looked down on them, his expression bleak, cold.

"Can you all hear me? I want this to stop now, okay?
The next lawyer that makes anything other than a legal
objection or any other remark other than is necessary
to make the objection—all these side innuendoes are
going to stop now.

"The first time it's going to be a large-figure fine.
The second time you're going to go to jail, okay? Do
you all understand that? Let's go."

When McDonald followed Waksman with his cross-
examination of Detective King, he continued to peck
away at what he had termed the tactics of the prosecution to play on the jury's emotions, at the moment via
the enlarged photos of Staci's wounds. So he said to
King, pointing at the large photo on display:

"Does that picture accurately depict in any way,
shape, or form the way you found the body when you
went to the Weinstein residence on October fourteenth?"

King: "No, sir."

"The picture is staged, is it not?"

"No. It was shaved for the purpose of photographing
the trauma and its relationship to the trauma on the
arm, the gunshot trauma to the head, and the blunt
trauma to the head directly above the gunshot trauma."

"And that photograph was staged for the purpose of
taking that photograph?"

"I wouldn't use the word staged, sir."

"Posed?"

"Graphically illustrates the trauma to the victim's
head. The trauma would not be visible with the hair."

"My question really relates to the relationship of this
mark on the arm and the bullet hole in the head. That

has no relationship whatsoever to what you found at the crime scene, does it?"

"Only its consistency to the location. And when we lifted the arm up, it kind of matched up to that particular projectile."

"But you had to lift up the arm to see it?"

"Yes, sir."

"So, it is staged for the purpose of showing this?"

"Yes. It's an illustration of that particular trauma."

McDonald had no further questions.

Tedious as some of this testimony, with much more to come, might have seemed to some members of the jury, and indeed some visitors in the gallery, it was necessary for the prosecution to lay the foundation of their case before proceeding with witnesses who might have a more direct bearing on the crime and the alleged guilt of the defendant. In legal terms, the state first has to prove that a homicide was committed, and, certainly in this case, that it was a uniquely brutal killing, so that should the jury find the defendant guilty, the state could ask for the maximum penalty—the electric chair—on the grounds that it was a particularly heinous crime with the victim a ten-year-old girl. Squeezing every drop of horror out of available evidence was hardly an invention of this particular set of prosecutors.

In the press room, viewing all this on the closed-circuit television system, Marvin Weinstein found these graphic pictures of his daughter's wounds agonizing. But he refused to turn away. It was as though that consuming hate he bore for his daughter's killers and the nagging guilt he could not expiate (should I have stayed at home with her?) needed to feed off those photos, to burn those graphics indelibly into some part of his fevered brain like stigmata.

Mea culpa.

Chapter 19

The next morning Waksman called Medical Examiner Charles Wetli. After stating his credentials—B.S. from Notre Dame, St. Louis University School of Medicine, University of Miami, six years with the Dade County Medical Examiner's office—he was questioned in detail on the results of his autopsy.

In the dispassionate manner of medical examiners specializing in criminal pathology, Dr. Wetli described the various trauma to Staci's body.

What killed Staci Weinstein?

"She died of gunshot wounds of head and chest and abdomen."

The medical examiner was shown a large color photograph.

"This photograph depicts a contact-type gunshot wound to the right side of the chest. The wound is right here [pointing], what we call the mid-axillary line, straight down from the apex of the armpit, and it's got an abraded margin, which you can see a portion of it here and another here, and the blackening inside are characteristic of a contact gunshot, meaning the muzzle of the gun is placed directly against the surface of the skin and then the trigger is pulled."

Dr. Wetli was shown another large color photograph.

"This photograph actually depicts three separate wounds. First, again, is a contact type of gunshot wound to the right temple area. It's characterized by darkening in the center of it without any distinct abra-

sion around it in this particular case. The other wound
is a laceration of the scalp, approximately two and a
half inches long, and just below and almost behind that
is another triangular-shaped laceration. These particular wounds have got very irregular margins, characteristic of blunt-force trauma."

The lacerations were consistent of strikes by a gun
butt, which would have caused blood spatter on the
headboard of Staci's bed, testified the doctor.

What caused the bruise on Staci's right cheekbone?
Consistent with a closed fist, said the doctor.

The lacerations on the skull, what did the autopsy
find?

"Once I reflected the scalp, it disclosed the presence
of a large skull fracture. Consistent with blows from a
gun butt. Considering all the lacerations to the head
and their pattern and that the gun was a small .22,"
said the doctor, "it would probably take three blows
from a .22 revolver to create that pattern."

Based on the doctor's experience, asked Waksman,
in what order did he conclude the injuries were suffered?

"In my opinion, one or more blows to the scalp occurred first. The second was the gunshot wound to the
chest and the abdomen region. The third is the gunshot
wound to the right temple. The reasons for this, the
laceration is very large. We have this one, the large one
here [pointing at the photo] and then the two on the
other side of the head. We also have blood spatter on
the headboard and adjacent wall, and there is also a
large amount of blood on the pillow here. The scalp
lacerations are the only wounds that are going to have
any degree of external bleeding.

"The gunshot wound to the chest and abdomen went
through the liver, the stomach, and the spleen. The
liver and the spleen bleed very profusely once they're
injured. She had 750 cc's, almost a quarter of blood, in
her abdominal cavity. She also had another half a pint,

if you will, in the chest cavity, about 300. This means the heart had to be beating for a period of time for that to occur."

Waksman: "If you're going to be shot in the chest and you die instantaneously, will you expect to find a large amount of blood inside the body?"

"If you die instantaneously, no."

"Why?"

"Because the heart is no longer beating, you're going to get a small amount of staining of the blood. The heart has to keep functioning as a pump for a period of time."

"What does that assist us in determining as to when this occurred in relationship to the chest wound?"

"It tells me her heart was beating for at least a couple of minutes before the heart actually stopped pumping blood. In other words, if she was, for example, shot in the head first, and then shot in the chest, it would be extremely unlikely that you would have any accumulation of blood in the chest and abdomen. She'd be dead."

"Did you see anything in your autopsy that would cause Staci Weinstein to gasp or sigh sometime before death?"

"Well, gasping and sighing is generally part and parcel of death which is not instantaneous, such as loss of blood with or without the lungs filling with fluid, and so forth."

"So, you would expect that there might be some gasping before death in this particular case?"

"Yes, from air hunger, anyway."

The doctor said he had found no signs of forced sexual activity, no signs of sexual intercourse. Staci died a virgin.

This dissertation by Dr. Wetli had even hardened crime reporters in the press room shaking their heads. "Bastards," someone said. Marvin sat silent, tight-lipped.

Judge Snyder's timing, it must be said, was awful. When Dr. Wetli concluded his testimony, the judge announced, "We're going to break for lunch now, folks."

Following the lunch break Waksman called serologist Theresa Washam. She said she had been certified as an expert in serology in the courts of the state of Florida, and McDonald did not challenge her.

Waksman knew the limitations he could expect from her testimony, and rather than fall into a trap and allow McDonald to expose them on cross-examination, he did it himself, thus blunting the defense attorney's attack. He discussed first with Theresa the blood traces she examined, and which she found by enzyme analysis to be Staci's blood.

Waksman: "Blood is not like a fingerprint, is it?"

"No, it's not."

"So, all you can tell us is the blood you found on the pillow was the same type that had the same enzymes as Staci Weinstein's?"

"That's correct."

"You cannot tell us definitely it was hers, can you?"

"No, I can't."

"But you can exclude that blood as Pierson or Wasko, can you?"

"Yes."

"Is that about the most your science can tell us?"

"At this point, yes." Then Theresa explained that she had found blood at the bottom of the bed that was of a different type. "The enzymes that were found were consistent with the blood of John Pierson."

"Were they inconsistent with the blood of Staci Weinstein?"

"Yes, they were."

"And was the blood and enzymes inconsistent with Edward Wasko's?"

"Yes."

"So, in addition to Staci Weinstein's blood on one of

the sheets, you also found blood and enzymes which
were consistent with John Pierson?"

"Yes."

"Can you tell us what percentage of the people in
the community have certain blood types?"

"Yes."

"And can you also tell us what percentages of the
people in the community have the certain enzymes and
proteins as well?"

"Yes."

"Now, when you multiply all of these numbers out,
are you able to tell us what percentage of the people in
the community would have that particular blood-
enzyme-protein combination that you found on the
sheet?"

"Yes, I can."

"Were you able to come up with a percentage of the
people who had that blood which you testify is consistent to Pierson's?"

"Yes."

"What would that be?"

"That would come out to be .1 percent, or approximately one out of every thousand people."

"Dealing with a community of approximately a million
and a half in Dade County, how many people would have
that combination of blood type and various enzymes and
proteins?"

"Would be approximately fifteen hundred, something like that."

"So, some of the blood on the sheet was consistent
with Pierson and fifteen hundred other people, at least,
in Dade County?"

"That's correct."

"But inconsistent with Staci Weinstein and inconsistent with Eddie Wasko?"

"Yes."

Waksman went on to the clothes Staci had been wearing, and the blood Theresa had found on them and analyzed.

Theresa: "On the orange or yellow set of underwear I found two different enzyme types that were consistent with two of the enzymes of John Pierson." On the pink shorts, she said, "there were also some enzymes present that were consistent with that of John Pierson."

Waksman reviewed the swabbings taken from Staci's body. Theresa said she'd determined that no seminal fluid was present, but swabs from the inner thighs of Staci indicated saliva. She explained that because of the small amounts of the saliva that could be collected, it was difficult to make definitive conclusions.

Waksman: "So the bottom line on the saliva—it's human saliva, but you can't tell us who put it there?"

"That's correct."

The cross-examination by McDonald dealt largely with the mathematics used by Theresa in figuring the percentage possibility of the foreign blood found being Pierson's. That was fine with the defense attorney. Waksman had in effect by preempting an attack also had done his work for him.

McDonald: "You found nothing consistent with Ed Wasko's blood being in the house?"

"No."

After a succesion of minor witnesses, Waksman called Randy Walker on the fourth day. McDonald had no argument with the fact that Staci had been murdered, or that Wasko and Pierson had been cleaning carpets in the neighborhood that day. He would have been well pleased with the testimony of Theresa Washam; he could safely bet the jury would conclude it was Pierson's blood found at the scene, that none of the blood was consistent with Wasko's type. The saliva found on Staci's inner thighs was unidentifiable, but that sex act was one the jury probably would also attribute to Pierson.

McDonald's attention was focused on the testimony

of Walker, Sessler, and Ratcliff—Walker in particular, since he had spent those many hours over three days talking to Wasko. The jurors, it will be recalled, had not yet been selected at the time of the suppression hearing on the first morning of the trial, so all that direct testimony and cross-examination would be repeated—but in much greater detail.

As per the agreement between prosecution and defense, Walker was allowed to say he was a civilian polygraph examiner with the Columbus Police Department. He described how he was called in to interview Wasko and give him a polygraph test as a witness in a homicide investigation in Florida. Specifically, the detectives wanted him to ask Wasko to tell the truth about his possibly seeing blood on Pierson's shirt. Walker said that because he had been interviewing Wasko solely as a witness, not a suspect, he hadn't been given very much information about the case.

Repeating what he'd testified to at the suppression hearing, Walker said that it was important he satisfy himself that no one had forced Wasko to talk to him.

"Once the two of us were alone," Walker testified, "the first thing I wanted to cover was the idea: have you been forced by these two detectives . . . to come in here and talk to me? Also, have you been forced by your employer or someone totally unbeknown to come in here?

"If an individual comes to me and he says he has been forced in any way, then I am not going to talk to him or continue the conversation. He indicated he was here voluntarily and wanted to do anything he could to assist."

Walker said he had given Wasko a copy of the standard rights-waiver form and advised him of his Constitutional rights, reviewing each form with him line by line, affirming that he understood all of it clearly and had no questions.

Waksman: "Why did you advise him of his rights if

he was not under arrest or a suspect in this investigation?"

"It's very important that he understands he doesn't even have to talk to me, didn't have to stay there, he was under no obligation whatsoever."

Walker didn't get much further into his testimony before McDonald objected:

"Your Honor, we've argued a motion to suppress. This is the witness that took the statement, and we're getting into a series of statements that culminated in the actual statement that the state intends to bring before the court. I'm going to object to him testifying as to anything Eddie Wasko said as not freely and voluntarily given.

"We don't have the rights form in evidence, we don't have any evidence whatsoever that he understood what was on that form. We don't have any evidence as to what else is on that form or what else Ed Wasko was told before he signed it."

Judge Snyder: "Mr. Waksman, are you going to introduce the rights form into evidence?"

Waksman: "Yes."

Judge Snyder: "Well, based upon the state going to introduce it, I'll let them continue."

Waksman: "I'll move it in right now."

Walker read out to the jury what the form said, and what he had read out loud to Wasko to make sure he understood all of it. "I can't be sure whether I read the bottom portion of this form or not. That I don't recall," he said. "Sometimes I'll simply say, 'Read over the bottom portion of this form. If you agree with it, sign it.' "

McDonald pounced on that and asked the judge for the right to question Walker, but for clarification, not as an objection—not yet.

"You said that you're not sure whether you read that to Eddie Wasko?"

"That's correct."

"Did Eddie Wasko read that?"

"Yes, sir, he would have read it before I would have allowed him to sign it."

"How do you know he read it?"

"I know for a fact that he did."

"How do you know that?"

"Well, I would have given it to him, and he would have instructed me—"

"You know that he read that because it was sitting on the table for a period of time in front of him?"

"I would have stated to him, 'Did you stay of your own free will?' and he would have signed the form."

"There is a lot of writing on that particular piece of paper which has not been read into the record, isn't there, sir?"

"That's correct."

Then McDonald objected "to this document coming into evidence at this time."

Judge Snyder: "On what basis?"

McDonald asked for one of his many sidebars. "We still don't know that he was advised what's in the rest of that writing, what he was giving up, what he wasn't giving up, what he was told he could do."

Judge Snyder: "You have a right to do that on cross-examination. Has nothing to do with the admissibility into evidence."

McDonald: "It sure does. You're taking this to understand that Eddie knew what he was doing."

Judge Snyder: "Okay, you'll bring that out, I'm sure. Denied."

Waksman's continuing questioning of Randy Walker detailed for the benefit of the jury the hourly events, with Walker reiterating his testimony of the suppression hearing. Intermittently McDonald objected to something Waksman was asking, or Walker was preparing to answer. When Walker responded to a Waksman question about what he had been trying to find out from Wasko, and Walker replied, "I asked him to speculate what he thought had happened 14 October '82 and he stated to me—" McDonald objected and asked again for a sidebar.

McDonald: "We're getting pretty far afield here, starting to have this gentleman testify as to him asking Eddie to speculate about what could have happened."

Waksman: "It's what the defendant said."

Judge Snyder: "Whatever the defendant said is admissible. He either was advised of his rights or he wasn't. He knows that anything he says can be used against him in subsequent hearings, and he's now testifying as to what he said. Denied."

A few questions later, Waksman was discussing Wasko's original interview in Miami. He asked Walker: "Did he tell you if he prepared himself in any way for that interview?"

"Yes, sir, he did. I don't know whether it was on the seventh of July or the eighth of July, but at one point—"

"Are these the two dates that you spoke to him?"

"Yes, sir."

McDonald broke in with yet another request for a sidebar. His objection was that while Walker had said he'd given Wasko a rights form on the seventh, now he was getting into what was said and done on the eighth without testifying that he'd given Wasko another rights form, that Wasko was still talking to him voluntarily.

Waksman complained: "I have an objection that he's trying to suppress this crucial witness and coming up with what I consider very frivolous objections so the jury doesn't get the gist of this man's testimony."

This argument bounced back and forth, with Waksman trying finally to word the questions differently about the dates to satisfy McDonald's objections. It didn't work. They couldn't agree.

McDonald asked for another sidebar. Waksman objected to McDonald's continuing request for them.

McDonald's objection was that "we're dealing with

the overall issue of voluntariness. . . . If this gentleman cannot limit himself to a specific period of time, then he should not be allowed to testify."

Judge Snyder was beginning to lose his patience. "We have several things, Mr. McDonald. Number one, I've already ruled that this confession was freely and voluntarily made. That's number one.

"Number two, it is impossible when there is more than one interview to have everybody testify prior to the admission of some document, and we all know that sometimes it takes later testimony to bring it out.

"Now, you have a right to comment on all this, and I'm sure you will, in closing argument. You have a jury instruction that tells you exactly what it is on statements that are prepared, and we can talk about voluntariness at that point. And you're going to tell the jury whether it has come in freely and voluntarily. I have ruled on this thing, and we're going to allow these statements to come in.

"If you wish your continuing objection to be noted on anything, fine. But let's not have any further objections on the voluntariness until after the state has concluded their case. If you wish to renew your motion to strike the entire thing as not being freely and voluntarily made, I will listen."

McDonald: "Basically, you're telling me to sit down and be quiet while these statements come in with the understanding that you have entered a continuing objection on my behalf and you don't want me coming to sidebar conferences anymore."

Judge Snyder: "I'm not restricting you from making an objection on any new point. But as far as the freeness and voluntariness of this statement and the fact that I've already ruled on that, yes."

McDonald: "And, in terms of the time restraints and all of those other problems that this gentleman is coming up with—"

Judge Snyder: "You'll have an opportunity to do that on cross-examination."

McDonald: "Well, I believe it's objectionable."

Judge Snyder: "The objection is standing."

Waksman proceeded smoothly for a time, until Walker testified about what had happened when he terminated the interview with Wasko at nine that evening.

Waksman: "Now, what happened at nine o'clock when you terminated the interview?"

Walker: "Shortly before nine o'clock Mr. Wasko said to me, 'Okay. I saw her that day. I talked to her.' And I said, 'Okay. Let's talk a little more about that.' And he said, 'I made that up. I made the whole thing up. Everything I told you today is just a big lie.' And I said, 'Eddie, we've gone in circles the whole day. We have gotten nowhere. I suggest we stop the interview right here. There is no need to continue.' "

"What if anything did Mr. Wasko respond?"

"He responded to me that he was very sorry for 'wasting my time.' "

"Did you believe you were ever going to see him again?"

"I honestly didn't believe that night I was going to see him next day."

"So, what did you do?"

"Asked him if he would mind if I took a Polaroid picture of him for the case file."

"Did he agree?"

"Yes, he agreed."

Waksman introduced the photograph as state's evidence.

McDonald said he had no objection to the photograph.

Waksman: "What happened after that?"

"Mr. Wasko agreed to come back the next day."

"For what reason?"

"In his words, 'to get everything straightened out.' I honestly, at that point, didn't think he'd be back."

"Is that why you took the photograph?"

At this point McDonald was on his feet: "Move for a mistrial, ask for a sidebar."

At the bench, McDonald said to the judge: "This witness is totally out of control. He is doing everything he can to prejudice the jury against my client. I recognize that every piece of evidence the state intends to introduce against a particular defendant is prejudicial, but the Rules of Evidence govern how far they can go. He was asked his opinion. I thought it was improper, but I didn't object to it. But he's out of control. He's going crazy with this thing. He's volunteering information. He's trying to weight this jury improperly and I want a mistrial."

Judge Snyder: "It's denied. I don't think he is, but I'll caution the witness to restrict his answers solely to the questions asked." Snyder told the jury to take a few minutes' break, during which he admonished Walker to restrict his answers to questions asked and not to add anything.

Not without several further interruptions and requests by McDonald for sidebars with the judge, Waksman continued to question Walker in detail about his interviews with Wasko.

Throughout all of this Eddie Wasko sat placidly, without expression, never showing the hint of an emotion, either looking straight ahead or at times turning his head slightly to look at Walker.

In the press room, Marvin was seething. On the television screen he could see clearly, sitting in the gallery behind Wasko, near enough to reach out and pat his shoulder—which from time to time she did—Wasko's mother, and seated with her Wasko's brother and sister. It's all right for them, thought Marvin angrily. They can sit in the courtroom. It's okay for that murderer's mother to sit there and influence the jury. Can anybody tell me Wasko's mother sitting there, shedding tears, wiping her eyes, has no influence on the jury? But me,

I can't. God forbid the jury should look at me and feel sorry for me. No, for me they can't feel sorry . . . for Staci they can't feel sorry! But for Wasko they can feel sorry. It's not fair. It's just not fair.

By the time Waksman completed his questioning of Walker it was almost lunchtime. The judge reckoned, correctly, that McDonald intended a very long cross-examination, so he called a lunch break. After lunch, McDonald got to work on Walker.

He took Walker step by step, virtually minute by minute, through the interviews with Wasko. Here was the heart of the matter: McDonald's purpose was to bring to the attention of the jury the defense allegation that Wasko had been "brainwashed" by the technique of an incessant interrogation over two days that deprived him of rest and food. He calculated, and Walker confirmed, that from the first time Walker had seen Wasko until the tape recorder with his confession was turned off was a total of thirty-nine hours and thirty-three minutes.

The questioning was tedious. McDonald told Walker it would be, but that it was important and please to bear with him. For example:

McDonald: "July seventh he arrives at 10:45. At 10:46 you have a urine sample taken?"

"Correct."

"And at 10:48 you sit down for the polygraph examination?"

"Exactly."

"And that's when you begin the whole process of rights all the way through?"

"Right."

"And you break for the first time at 1:17 p.m.?"

"That's correct."

"I have calculated that to be two hours and twenty-nine minutes. You want to trust me on that?"

"I'll trust your figures."

McDonald mentions a ten-minute break for Wasko,

then: "You picked up again at 1:27? And go straight through to 3:34?"

"Correct."

"For a total of two hours and seven minutes. Took a rest room break and resumed at 3:38?"

"Yes."

"Let me clear something up. After 3:11 p.m. you never ran another chart on Eddie Wasko?"

"I did not."

"You resumed at 3:38 and continued till 6:20 p.m. at which time Eddie was offered some potato chips?"

"No. At that time I was asking specifically if he was hungry because the snack bar in the basement closes, and at that time he told me he wasn't hungry and instead used the rest room and drank water."

"The next break is at 7:19 p.m. and Eddie is offered some potato chips and Pepsi and he accepts?"

"Correct."

"And using the conservative figure of 6:30 so we have a starting point, that's 49 minutes, right?"

Walker nodded in the affirmative.

"Eddie took some time to sit back, sip on the Coke, eat some potato chips, and you started back in and broke at 9:01 p.m.?"

"That's correct."

McDonald continued in this vein, calculating the times spent in interviews and the breaks Wasko had had from the time he arrived the next day at noon until Walker left the interview room at 3:20 and Sergeant Ratcliff took over. Ratcliff went in and talked to Wasko for about a half hour, at which time Walker returned to the interview room.

McDonald: "At 4:59 you picked back up, you're alone with Eddie and the next break is at 10:23, when Eddie drinks some water and there is a break, right?"

"That's correct."

"That's five hours and twenty-four minutes straight?"

"That's correct."

Walker said that Wasko had again had Pepsi and chips at 10:42, when Sessler went into the interview room to talk to him. The next break was at 11:46 p.m. McDonald kept going right through to the tape recording of Wasko's confession statement, at 2:30 a.m., the transcription and on into the early morning hours when the photo was taken, about eight, of Wasko with Walker, Sessler, and Ratcliff and the pizza.

McDonald: "I come up with a figure of 21 hours and 43 minutes of interview time between 10:45 a.m. on July seventh and 2:24 a.m. on July ninth. So, out of 39 hours and 33 minutes, 21 hours and 43 minutes are spent in that interrogation room with you, Ratcliff, or Sessler?"

"Yes."

"Seventeen hours and 56 minutes are left over, and 15 of those hours are the night breaks between July seventh and July eighth?"

Walker nodded in the affirmative.

"Eddie Wasko had two hours and 56 minutes worth of breaks during two days of questioning?"

"If that's what it comes out to, that's what it would be."

"Your notes reflect him eating potato chips during that entire time period?"

"Yes."

"Drinking Pepsi?"

"Yes."

"Smoking like a chimney during that entire period?"

"Whatever he wanted."

"And he was just beginning to show fatigue after 21 hours and 43 minutes of virtually straight questioning?"

"Fatigue or relief."

"Well, which was it?"

"I'd say it's both."

"And Eddie got a piece of pizza at 3:08 in the morning?"

"The entire pizza box was set beside him. He could have had as much as he wanted. I don't know how much he ate."

"When was it you broke down and started crying? What time?"

"I don't have the exact time. It was sometime in the evening of Friday night."

"Why were you crying?"

"I had spent a lot of time with Mr. Wasko, and after sitting and talking to him for that length of time you begin to get a feel for this person. And I knew that there was a fear there, and as we began to talk and we kept talking, and he couldn't tell me the truth, at one point in time I began to cry myself and said, 'Eddie, please just tell me the truth.' "

"You got real bummed out because you were feeling sorry for Eddie's pain in not being able to resolve these issues and that made you start crying?"

"He told me he wanted to get it straightened out."

"Didn't have anything to do with any kind of psychological tricks, psychological coercion?"

"No."

"Just empathizing with Eddie's pain, right?"

"Exactly."

"So in your mind at that time Eddie was in a state of emotional distress?"

"I'm not a psychiatrist."

"You capitalized on Eddie's mental stress to crack him?"

"That's your term, Counselor."

"After that happened you got the statement you wanted, wasn't it?"

"The statement I wanted—the only thing I was after was the truth."

"Is the statement you heard on the tape recording the truth?"

"Yes."

"How do you know?"

"I don't."

"And you cannot state that it's the truth?"

"No, I can't."

There was more cross-examination along these lines until McDonald said no more questions. Judge Snyder called for a brief recess.

Assistant State Attorney Jayne Weintraub took over the direct examination for the prosecution and called Steve Sessler to the stand. A sergeant now and no longer in Homicide, Sessler testified that when he had taken over as lead detective in the murder investigation, John Pierson was the focal point but not a subject to be arrested. He was the focal point, said Sessler, "because John Pierson's blood was found on the bed next to the body of the victim."

Eddie Wasko at that time, said Sessler, was Pierson's coworker but not considered a suspect. Following weeks of investigation, however, he became "potentially a very valuable witness."

Weintraub: "Why?"

"Because I had knowledge he and John Pierson worked together, and I felt that with Pierson being the focal and them being partners, arriving together, that Wasko should have and probably did see something unusual about John Pierson on the fourteenth due to the scene itself with all the blood and trauma."

"Did you also have an occasion to review the statement that Edward Wasko gave to Detective Huetter?"

"Yes, I did need that."

In the course of the investigation he had interviewed a number of people at Stanley Steemer, said Sessler, coworkers and executives of the company, and subsequently decided he needed to go to Ohio with his supervisor, Sergeant Jim Ratcliff, to talk to Wasko.

"Why?" asked Weintraub.

Sessler explained that after talking to those people at the company, "I found out information that Eddie had

related to them about what he saw that was different
about John Pierson on October fourteenth, and coupled
with the statement that Eddie Wasko gave, I knew
there were discrepancies."

"When you went to Ohio to discuss the discrepancies with Eddie Wasko, was he considered a suspect at
that time?"

"No, ma'am, he wasn't."

Sessler then recounted his story of what transpired in
Ohio in more or less the same terms he'd used in telling the story at the suppression hearing. Weintraub
then informed the jurors that she was going to play in
open court the tape recording of Wasko's confession.
Each juror would get a transcript in order to follow the
tape line by line and verify that tape and transcript
were precisely the same.

There followed an eerie silence in the courtroom as
the voice of Eddie Wasko was heard telling of the
events of October 14, 1982, and his part in that sexual
assault and murder. There was this disembodied voice
telling its chilling tale, while the man himself sat between his defense attorneys; not a flicker of emotion
passed over Wasko's stony face, though behind him,
stifling her sobs, was his mother, Mary. And in the media room, Marvin stared transfixed at the TV screen,
with the cameras focusing on Wasko. Marvin had read
the transcript, but to hear the voice, to put a face to
that voice, was almost more than he could bear. He felt
his heart pounding, and he had to press his hand to his
chest to stifle the pain.

McDonald cross-examined and to some extent took
Sessler along the same course as he'd taken Randy
Walker with regard to all the time Wasko had spent in
interrogation with very little break time or food. The
defense attorney was in a difficult position; that tape
recording was a hard act to follow. He tried pressing
Sessler:

"What was the purpose in taking that tape?"

"To have a tape and bring it back down to Miami."

"What was the purpose in having it typed up?"

"So that it could be read by myself in front of Eddie and signed on each page with him indicating that each page was correct, and stands corrected, and then finally signing the back page—hey, this is what I said and this is what I'm saying happened."

"So it could be used in court as evidence?"

"Yes."

"So that the jurors could read it and see that it was freely and voluntarily made?"

"Yes."

"The purpose of taking that tape recording and typing up the transcript of that tape recording is so that they can be used in a court of law?"

"Somewhat, yes."

"So that you can testify and produce hard evidence of what that statement was?"

"What do you mean by hard evidence?"

"Something tangible that you can look at and say: 'This is it.' "

"Well, that's an addition. I consider what I'm saying as being tangible, too, even during the verbal interview. The tape is just an addition. It's something physical, yes. It's more than just what I'm verbally relating. It's something that actually has his voice on it."

"And it's there so that it can be produced for the jury, so that I can't say you're making it all up?"

"Well, you can say what you want to say, in all respect, Mr. McDonald."

"I understand that."

"It's up to the jury to determine whether they believe this tape was done uncoerced and freely and voluntarily. It's not up to me or you, sir."

Referring to the time available on the tape, McDonald pointed out that availability had been thirty minutes on each side. He asked Sessler, "Do you know how many minutes of conversation are on that tape?"

"Somewhere in the high thirties, thirty-eight, thirty-nine minutes."

"Thirty minutes on one side and then some on the other?"

"That's correct."

"How much time is missing?"

"Oh, I'd say, I don't know, anywhere from ten to fourteen minutes is missing."

"We would only have your word as to what happened during the ten to fourteen minutes?"

"My word is on the tape because the tape stopped and we didn't know the tape stopped. We continued on the last coherent question."

"And the reason you make a tape and type a transcript of the tape is so that we don't just have your word when you come into court about the conversation?"

"Partially. It's just another piece of evidence."

"Piece of evidence to let us know what you have told us is true?"

"You know, again we're playing. We seem like we're playing a game, Counsel, with this tape.

"The Metro-Dade Police Department has trained me not only to interview, not only to investigate, but also certain procedures, and part of the procedures is after having interviews with a suspect or a witness, it's our procedure to try to get either, one, a taped interview, two, a stenographically recorded statement, or three, some type of written statement from this person.

"There was no stenographer available to me, and the tape-recording machine was available to me, and your client was very available to me, too."

The state's final witness was Robert Hart, a firearms expert with the Metro-Dade Police Department. Having established Hart's credentials, Waksman had the gun expert identify the pieces of white plastic gun grip found on Staci's bed as pieces from a Rosco RG-10 revolver, .22-caliber.

With that, Waksman formally announced that the prosecution rested its case against Edward Wasko.

Because of what he knew was to follow immediately after the state rested its case, Judge Snyder asked the jury to step back into the jury room.

Assistant Public Defender Peter Ferrero stood up.

"Respectfully, at this time, the defendant would move for a judgment of acquittal.

"We would state to the court that independent of the statement by Edward Wasko, which has been previously litigated, we state that the statement is inherently unreliable. There is no other evidence of guilt against Mr. Wasko other than the statement made after twenty-two hours of interrogation, which the court has previously heard. We believe it to have been a coerced, inherently unreliable, and untrue statement by Mr. Wasko to the police.

"Looking at that evidence in the best light for the state, we still maintain that the evidence is inherently unreliable, should be rejected by the court, and the court should grant a motion for judgment of acquittal as to all counts. On that argument we rest."

Judge Snyder: "Denied."

And so the court battle resumed.

Chapter 20

When the state rested its case on Friday afternoon, attorneys for both sides discussed with Judge Snyder what he had in mind for the rest of the day: perhaps a few opening defense witnesses with brief testimony and then an adjournment until Saturday, or even Monday, at which time the two principal witnesses would be called—John Pierson and Eddie Wasko. McDonald and Ferrero had decided that since the prosecution wasn't going to call Pierson, giving them the opportunity to cross-examine, the defense would call him. McDonald planned to question Pierson about his plea bargain and about the rape charge against him, hoping to prove to the jury that Pierson and Pierson alone was guilty of the charges against Wasko.

Judge Snyder, however, wanted to get on with the trial. He wanted to wind it up on Saturday with nothing else but final arguments and his charge to the jury. He did not want to face either Pierson or Wasko on Saturday morning.

The defense attorneys had problems with that; they complained that they were having trouble rounding up some of their minor witnesses—minor but important nevertheless.

Ferrero in fact told the judge: "Eight o'clock last night we called up one of our witnesses. First words out of his mouth: 'I think Ed Wasko should be castrated in public, and I'm not going to do anything you say.' That's what we start out with."

Judge Snyder shook his head. "We'll just go as far as we can now."

McDonald's first important witness was Marvin himself. Immediately Judge Snyder sent the jury out of the courtroom and asked, "What's the nature of your questioning of Mr. Weinstein going to be?"

McDonald: "I'm going to ask Mr. Weinstein a series of questions about the veracity of facts alleged in Mr. Wasko's statement to the police in Ohio."

Judge Snyder: "Is it going to be done in a cool, calculated manner without any attempt to rile him to a point where—"

McDonald: "Mr. Weinstein and I have reached an accord where he understands that I'm doing my job."

Judge Snyder: "I'm going to tell Mr. Weinstein myself right now that this is going to be no attempt to rile him, and I just want him to answer the questions as they're asked without any side remarks to inflame the situation."

What McDonald did was take Marvin through Wasko's confession and ask him, almost line by line, whether or not the actions and quotations attributed to Staci in that confession were consistent with her normal behavior. McDonald got right down to the details of the sexual assault, Staci's alleged laughter at the size of Pierson's penis, and her vulgarity.

McDonald gave Marvin the line from Wasko's statement: "She said, 'Asshole, if you're going to fuck me, take your pants off.'"

The attorney asked Marvin: "Is that consistent with your daughter?"

It took all of Marvin's promised restraint to check the retort that was on his lips. Taking a deep breath, he said, "I would think during a rape situation like this, she'd be terrified."

McDonald: "Which means essentially that this is inconsistent with your daughter, she would not be laughing and making those types of comments at a time like this?"

"No, she would not. She would be terrified."

What precisely was behind McDonald's questioning of Marvin in this fashion was anybody's guess at that moment. It obviously was an ordeal for Marvin, and his control probably earned him some sympathy from the jury—not good for the defense. Actually, however, what McDonald was attempting to show was that since the Staci references were palpably preposterous coming from a ten-year-old who looked eight and still played with stuffed toys and Barbie dolls, then, as Ferrero had pointed out in his request for a dismissal, the statement that Sessler and that the state claimed was made by Wasko was untrue, unreliable, and coerced. And the jury would see that.

It was a good point and well played. There was a fault in it, however—if the jurors recognized it. If, as McDonald was implying, as Wasko had alleged in the suppression hearing, that he was reading from cue cards held up by Sessler, then that doesn't ring true, either. An experienced homicide detective, which Sessler was, would have written a much more believable scenario for Wasko to read than one in which Staci comes on as a seductive little tease who uses the coarsest of bedroom language. Staci was shy and unsophisticated, and far too young to have said such things.

McDonald called Ben Hall, and got from him the fact useful to the defense that once the blood report had come in from Theresa Washam naming Pierson, the entire focal point of the homicide investigation, to the point of Hall's transfer, was John Pierson and only John Pierson; other trivial leads had been checked out and discarded.

The defense next prepared to call Janice Langhorn. The prosecution objected (with the jury out of the room) that what she had to say about the rape was irrelevant to this case and she should not be permitted to testify.

Not so, said Ferrero. "Ms. Langhorn will testify that John Pierson attempted to have sex with her against her will, that she is under the age of eighteen during the course of that rape and having sex with her against her will. He licked her all over the body, consistent with what happened to Staci Weinstein. She will also testify that he, as she attempted to call out, choked her and tried to suffocate her, consistent with the injuries in Staci Weinstein's case."

Waksman said that was not relevant evidence. "There is nothing that Ms. Langhorn has to say that will prove or disprove a material fact as to what happened in this case."

Judge Snyder agreed, stating that "the testimony of this particular witness shall not be allowed."

McDonald asked him at least to read Janice Langhorn's deposition and see what it was she would testify to. Perhaps it would change his mind. Snyder read it. He didn't change his mind. He would not allow her to testify.

In that case, said Ferrero, "we move for a mistrial on the grounds that the defendant has a Sixth Amendment right, compulsory right of process and the defendant's Constitutional right to have witnesses testify on his own behalf to relevant—we have proferred as relevant and material evidence has been denied by this court, excluding this witness from testifying in this case. So, move for a mistrial on those grounds."

Judge Snyder: "I already ruled that the testimony she would give is not relevant, and therefore your motion for a mistrial is denied."

John Pierson was next, clad in a black open-necked polo shirt. In the chill of the air-conditioned courtroom he appeared to be uncomfortable—some of the jurors were wearing sweaters—so Judge Snyder asked the bailiff to get a jacket or a sweater for him. A red cardigan was produced that appeared to be about two sizes too big for him, but Pierson donned it with thanks to the bailiff and sat down in the witness chair.

Before McDonald could get started, another debate ensued. Waksman said that because he was not calling Pierson as a witness, he could not be allowed to talk about the disposition of his plea bargain. "I've made a decision not to call him. Therefore what I offered him if he testified as a state's witness becomes immaterial."

Ferrero argued the point but lost again. The judge ruled that since the state wasn't calling Pierson as a witness, then what they might have offered him if he was called "is not relevant and therefore inadmissible and shall be limited by the defense attorney."

Now this ruling had to be explained to Pierson, which was not an easy task. Judge Snyder tried and asked Pierson if he understood. Pierson said, "Plea that I got—I can't change it in any way."

Judge Snyder: "No, no, that's not that you can't change it. You can't testify about it, that it was how many years you received or what kind of arrangements were made when you got that sentence, okay?"

Waksman pitched in and helped. "The judge is saying that the jury is not supposed to know that you pled guilty or how much time you were sentenced to. They're not supposed to know what crimes you pled guilty to, either. The attorney won't ask you that. But you're not to let it slip out somehow. You answer all the questions truthfully. You understand?"

Pierson said that he did.

McDonald: "Can we ask if he agreed to testify for the state without any qualifications about how that came about?"

Waksman: "That's the same thing. They want to know was he offered something to do it. He might have gotten something in return."

Judge Snyder: "I agree. It's all part of the same relevancy. That also shall not be asked."

Ferrero again asked for a mistrial, "on the basis of the court's ruling on this particular evidentiary matter."

Judge Snyder again denied it.

McDonald said to the judge that he'd like Pierson to be declared an adverse [hostile] witness or a court witness since, frankly, considering the various statements Pierson had been making, he really had no idea what he might say on the witness stand now.

The reason for that request is that a trial attorney can't impeach his own witness—discredit him. However, if he can have the judge declare that witness to be an adverse witness, then he is free to impeach him. McDonald thought that depending on how Pierson would testify—whether he would give the story in his confession statement about what had happened or stick to his deposition statement saying he knows nothing and never even crossed the street—it might be useful to impeach him.

Judge Snyder said he'd reserve his ruling until he saw the course of the testimony.

McDonald wasted little time on the preliminaries. He asked Pierson: "In October of 1982, did there come a time when you met somebody named Staci Weinstein?"

"I didn't know her name. If that's the girl we're talking about, yes, sir."

"Did you participate in her murder?"

"Yes, I was there."

"How did you happen to meet her?"

Pierson related that after they'd completed a job, Wasko drove to a nearby house where they were supposed to do a job estimate. Wasko told him to wait in the truck while he went inside.

"About five minutes later he opened the door, and he had a towel in his hand. He called me in. Five minutes later I heard a scream, a young girl screamed. There was no one else inside the house. I ran upstairs and I saw Eddie on top of that little girl. He had a pillow over her face."

"Doing what with it?"

Pierson's voice cracked. He began to sob quietly. "Trying to suffocate her. At the time that I went inside the room, he had his pants part down."

"What happened when you saw him suffocate her with the pillow?"

Still sobbing, speaking hesitantly, as he continued to do through the greater part of the rest of his testimony, Pierson said: "He was on top of the girl."

"Where were you?"

"I just got into the bedroom."

"Were they on the bed?"

"She was struggling to get away from him."

"But were they on the bed or on the floor?"

"They were on the bed at the time."

"She was struggling to get away from him?"

"Yes."

"Was she successful?"

"No, she wasn't."

"So what happened next?"

"I came after Eddie."

"What do you mean, you came after him?"

"I came after him, tried to do my best in my power to get him off the girl."

"Tried to save her life?"

"Exactly."

This was too much for Marvin. He leaped from his chair and shouted at the screen, pointing at it, pointing at Pierson. "That lying fuck!" he shouted. "He tried to help Staci? He beat her up! He tried to stick it in her! He ate her pussy! He—"

A couple of reporters came to him and gently sat him back in his chair, calmed him down. "Hey, Marv," one of them said, "if you did that in the courtroom the judge would have to declare a mistrial."

"Yeah, right," Marvin said. "But if I'd been in the

courtroom I'd have jumped the rail and gone after him, the lying bastard." Marvin shook his head in disgust.

The questioning had been going on: McDonald asked Pierson: "What actually happened between the two of you?"

"We were both fighting. I told Staci Weinstein to 'Get the hell out of there.' My exact words."

Pierson described his continuing struggles with Wasko until "Eddie gave me a couple of good blows in the face and I ran out. I ran downstairs. I ran out of the house. Two minutes later I heard two shots."

"What did you do after hearing those two shots?"

"I got back into the van. Eddie came running out. I asked him—I said, 'Did you shoot her?' but he didn't answer me. I asked again. He told me if I said anything to anybody, he said he'd take my life the same way he did hers."

A few moments later, McDonald asked Pierson why, when Detective Ben Hall had interviewed him, he didn't tell him what happened.

"Eddie knew where my mom and my family lived. He threatened me. He like threatened my family. If he couldn't get to me, maybe he would get my little brother or my retarded sister. I was completely petrified. I wanted to go to the cops so bad. It's just I didn't know what to do."

McDonald at that point said to Judge Snyder, "Judge ... I move that the Court declare this gentleman an adverse witness."

Jayne Weintraub said to the judge, "They're going to impeach him with the deposition. At that time I'm not going to have a problem with it, I think."

Remarked Judge Snyder: "Let me say that in all my years as a judge, in all my years as a lawyer, I have never seen a witness that is more adverse to your interests. Therefore, I shall declare him an adverse witness."

And, after running Pierson around the ring for several minutes with questions coming from various directions, McDonald went in for the impeachment blow. He reviewed with Pierson the statement he'd given Sessler and Ratcliff on August 30. Specifically, he zeroed in on the fight with Wasko, and the part where Pierson said he'd been near the bedroom door when he got hit and his nose began to bleed.

McDonald: "Do you know that some of your blood was found in Staci Weinstein's bedroom?"

"I heard of it, yes."

"Were you ever told where in the bedroom it was found?"

"I heard it was on her sheets and on her panties."

"How close did you ever get to Staci Weinstein during all of this tumble mess that you were involved in?"

"I don't know . . . man, you guys are asking—"

"You jump on top of Eddie. Would that be accurate?"

"Yeah. See, but this thing is I don't know how my blood got there after he hit me again, he kept on coming after me. So, maybe some of my blood came off on her, or something. I don't know how it got there."

"On Friday, December 9, 1983, do you recall meeting Jayne Weintraub and I on the ninth floor of this building?"

"Yes, I did."

"Who else was present?"

"Stenographer."

"And?"

"Eddie Wasko."

"Were you under oath?"

"Yes."

"What version of events of October 14, 1982, did you tell us on December 9, 1983 starting at ten-thirty in the morning?"

"I had nothing involved in it—I didn't know anything about it."

"You'd never been across the street?"

"Exactly."

"Say anything about fliers during that statement?"

"I reckon so, I think."

"Do you recall what it was you said?"

"I said—well, if you did ask me a question, I would have said that I did pass out fliers, about three on each side of the house that we were working on."

"Was that statement the truth?"

"No, it wasn't."

"On Friday, December 9, 1983, why did you tell me you didn't have anything to do with it, that you weren't even across the street?"

"At that point Eddie Wasko was in the room with me, and I just didn't want to say that when he was around me, 'cause I am scared of him."

"Still?"

"Yes, he is frightening."

"On the fourth of November, 1983, at nine o'clock in the morning before the Honorable Ellen Morphonios, circuit court judge, you were sworn and admitted your involvement in the case and pled guilty, did you not?"

"I did."

"One month and five days before telling me you had nothing to do with it. You entered your plea of guilty on the fourth of November, 1983. You gave your statement to me that you hadn't been across the street on December ninth of 1983. Correct?"

"Yes."

"Your first three interviews with Detective Hall were to the effect of you had nothing to do with this entire situation?"

"Yes."

"In any of the versions that you've given, have you ever stated that you went into this young girl's bedroom and tried to take her clothes off and tried to rape her and tried to kill her?"

"No."

"Your testimony today is you did not do that?"

"That's right. I did not do that."

McDonald held up two poster-sized color photos of Staci's bloodied back. "That picture on the right—you see the orange undershorts?"

"Yes."

"Tell me, under any of your versions of the facts how your blood would appear when you rolled that waistband down and looked inside those undershorts?"

"I have no idea."

"Neither do I. On October 14, 1982, you killed Staci Weinstein, isn't that correct?"

"It's incorrect."

"You tried to rape her, you licked her all over her body, you tried to smother her with a pillow."

"You're lying."

"She resisted you, you hit her, and you killed her, isn't that what happened?"

"No, it's not what happened."

"And none of the versions of the facts that you have described in this courtroom or at any other time under oath are true, are they?"

"They're true."

"All of them?"

"Right now in here?"

"Yes."

"Yes."

McDonald asked for a sidebar conference and asked Judge Snyder for permission to get into the rape, to show the similarities between the two crimes and that Pierson, who had just denied doing it to Staci Weinstein, had done it to someone else.

The judge denied it. "That is an entirely different situation. It's so far afield it isn't even close."

Denied his request, McDonald said he had no further questions of Pierson.

The state had no questions to ask him.

The time was nine forty-five. Judge Snyder called it a night. He adjourned the court until nine the next day.

The following morning, before the jury was seated and the first witness called, there was a conference before the judge. Jayne Weintraub said that McDonald was planning to call all the witnesses from the rape case: Angela, Peggy, and Jimmy May, and Gary King. And she wanted to make sure that based on the judge's earlier ruling that these people would not be allowed to talk about the rape or the murder.

Judge Snyder affirmed that, leaving McDonald with little testimony from them but that Pierson had told him he was being investigated for a murder and that he told them that whoever committed the murder had picked up the girl after she was dead and hugged her because they were sorry.

The judge allowed that much, and the prosecution did not contest it.

That brought Eddie Wasko to the stand to speak for himself.

McDonald questioned Wasko in detail on his educational background, all the jobs he'd ever had, how he'd come to work for Stanley Steemer and eventually wound up in Miami with the company. It was a decently impressive school and work record, and Wasko explained that during his time with Stanley Steemer he'd gotten to know quite well a number of the company's executives. Interestingly enough, Wasko testified that when he had arrived in Miami in July of 1982 he was called "Electric Eddie."

McDonald questioned him on his functions as crew chief of the two-man truck and the routine used on the jobs they did. Wasko replied clearly and confidently.

Eventually McDonald got around to the murder.

"On October 14, 1982, did you personally have any connection with an incident that led to anyone being injured?"

"No, I did not."

"You have seen all the pictures that have been introduced into evidence. Did you have anything to do with this, Eddie?"

"No, I did not."

"From your personal observations on October 14, 1982, from what you were able to hear and see that day, do you know how this happened?"

"I have my suspicions."

"But you didn't know?"

"But I didn't know."

"Let me ask you this. When you stopped at the convenience store, whatever it was, did you know that there was a dead ten-year-old girl near your last job?"

"No, I did not."

Wasko said he had his suspicions raised about Pierson at a later date when he learned about the murder and was questioned, because Pierson had been acting weird. Anyway, he said, he never liked Pierson, he thought he was a bad worker, and he suggested to his boss that Pierson be taken off his truck; shortly afterward Pierson was fired.

Now McDonald entered into the heart of the matter: what had transpired when Sessler and Ratcliff came up to Ohio and the long series of interviews began.

The question-answer period was virtually a replay of the suppression hearing, but there was a greater need in court to expand on the details. There was a jury to convince, not a judge: a jury can be swayed, can be convinced, or confused, by a torrent of testimony. It has been said by attorneys skilled in criminal trial defense: "If your client is innocent, get him before a judge; if he's guilty, get him before a jury."

It would be the jury's turn to hear for the first time Wasko's contention that he had been "brainwashed," that Sessler had written out on a pad the answers to the questions he was going to ask for the taped statement. Wasko spoke of lack of rest, little food, pressure, harassment, repeated refusal by the detectives to accept his story. He claimed that he tried to be constant in his version of events, was telling the truth, but it was the detectives who continually changed his version of the story and prompted him to go along with them, putting suggestions into his mind as part of their "brainwashing" technique.

One important addition to his testimony concerned the time he had spent alone with Sergeant Ratcliff.

McDonald asked him to tell of his conversation with Ratcliff when the two were alone in the interview room.

Wasko: "What he did was he turned his chair around. It was like one of those chairs you can turn around and you can sit with your arms up."

McDonald (indicating): "Like this?"

"Yes. And he was maybe a foot away from me, and he started talking with me. He started off his conversation like—well, the way he did start off his conversation, to the best of my memory, was that he says I'm a bullshitter, and he says, 'I'm good at what I do,' and he says, 'We've done our homework on you. We know you're a bullshitter. So, why don't you quit bullshitting and start telling the truth about this?' And then he got up, lifted the chair up, and banged it down."

"Like that?" (indicating)

"Something to that effect."

Wasko said he told Ratcliff that he had been telling the truth the whole time, and went over his story with Ratcliff about the events of October 14, insisting to the detective that he'd had nothing to do with it.

At the end of the questioning, McDonald asked him, "Has everything you testified here today been the truth, Eddie?"

"Yes, it was."

After a lunch break Waksman took over for the cross-examination.

The prosecutor went immediately on the offensive, offered a quick "Good afternoon, Mr. Wasko," then:

"Why did you bash her head in?"

Wasko: "Excuse me?"

"Why did you bash her head in?"

"Whose head?"

"How much food did you have Wednesday evening after you spoke to the police?"

"Nothing."

"Was that your choice or someone else's choice?"

"Someone else's choice."

"Whose choice?"

"The detectives."

Waksman had a reputation as an expert at cross-examination, with a cozy manner when he thought it prudent, and a thrusting attack when he thought he needed it. The sword was out of its sheath with Wasko, as he unleashed his questions quickly and concisely. However, Wasko turned out to be an effective swordsman himself. He was totally self-contained, cool and calm, never hesitating, responding politely with his answers. Nothing Waksman could say ruffled him in the slightest. Occasionally swiveling in the witness chair to look at the jury as he spoke, Wasko met every question with a ready answer as though the entire scene had been rehearsed. To some extent it had been because of the suppression hearing, but in any case, well prepared for the cross by his defense attorneys, Wasko knew what would be coming from Waksman and was able to parry the greater part of the prosecutor's thrusts.

It was a virtuoso performance.

Waksman needed to press him about the tape recording, since the entire case actually rested on the authenticity of it. He asked Wasko, "Do you remember the tape recording?"

"Yes, I do, Mr. Waksman."

"Sessler told you exactly what to say on that cassette, didn't he?"

"Not just him—there were two other detectives involved that help create this tape."

"Okay. But when the tape recording was on itself, who was in the room with you?"

"Detective Sessler."

"And he had written down all of the answers, correct?"

"Yes."

"And if you couldn't remember the correct answer he would hold up the pad so you could see it?"

"Yes, he would."

"And that's how you knew what to say?"

"Yes."

"Because you were never in Staci Weinstein's house?"

"No, I wasn't, Mr. Waksman."

"You never bashed her head in?"

"No, I didn't."

"You don't know when you walk into the living room the hallway is to the left and you have to take three steps up to get into that hallway?"

"I didn't know that till Detective Sessler told me that."

"Who told you that Staci was shot in the upper chest area?"

"Detective Sessler did."

"And who told you that the girl was shot twice?"

"I couldn't answer that one."

"What were you told about her being shot?"

"They told me that the girl that's in question, okay, at the murder was killed."

"They didn't tell you how many times she was shot?"

"They didn't tell me how many times she was shot at first."

"They told you what kind of gun you shot her with?"

"Yes, they did."

"Did Sessler hold up a pad and say she was shot in the right side of the head?"

"I don't remember exactly what he said or what was said."

"Well, you never heard yourself on the tape recorder say: 'I shot her in the head,' did you?"

"I don't remember exactly what all is on the tape. I'd have to listen to it again."

"Have you heard the tape recording played in this courtroom?"

"Yes, I have."

"Whose voice do you hear on it?"

"My voice."

"Who else's voice?"

"Detective Sessler."

"You have the transcript in front of you. . . . Toward the middle of page twenty: 'Q. How many times did you observe John Pierson shoot the girl?' What was your purported answer on the tape?"

"I said, 'Once.' "

"But she was shot twice?"

"I didn't know that."

"Well, didn't Sessler tell you that?"

"Like I said, Mr. Waksman, I don't remember everything that happened that day."

"Didn't he hold up two fingers?"

"I don't remember that."

"Didn't he point to the chest and the head?"

"I don't remember that, either, Mr. Waxman."

"Is there an answer you gave without looking at Detective Sessler's pad?"

"I believe the first couple of questions regarding my name and my age."

"How many pages do we have on the transcript?"

"Last page is page twenty-seven."

"And other than your name and your date of birth and your address and your phone number, he wrote everything else out for you?"

"Yes, he did."

"Couldn't you remember a thing he was telling you?"

"No, I couldn't."

Waksman had to attack Wasko's credibility, pit it against the credibility of the state's witnesses. He proceeded to the time following the taped confession, when Wasko claimed he had dozed off while Barbara Robinson typed up the transcript. Waksman reminded him that he had initialed every page of that transcript.

Waksman: "Were you falling asleep while you were initialing those pages?"

"Yes, I was."

"Would Sessler have to shake you up and wake you up every third or fourth page?"

"Couple of times he had to."

"Was Barbara Robinson in that room the whole time?"

"Yes, she was."

"Did you hear her testify you were alert while you and she were in that room together?"

"Yes, I did."

"Were you alert or were you falling asleep while that statement was being read to you?"

"I was awake."

"You were awake when Sessler had to shake you to wake you up; were you asleep, were you awake?"

"I was asleep."

"If you were asleep, you were not alert, were you?"

"I don't believe so, Mr. Waksman."

"So when Barbara Robinson says you were alert, she is mistaken, right?"

"I wasn't alert."

"She said you were alert. She's a liar? Say it. You can say it."

"Well, she's not telling the truth."

Waksman took him back to that first night of the interviews in Ohio, when Sessler and Ratcliff had been driving him back to the Stanley Steemer office. Waxman reminded him: "Did you to say to Sessler back in the car, 'Was she shot with a .22'?"

"No, I did not."

"Did you hear him say that in this courtroom?"

"I heard him say a lot of things. Whether or not he's telling the truth, okay, that's up to the jury, I guess, to decide."

"You know he's lying, don't you?"

"Yes, I do."

"You can say that."

"Okay. Mr. Sessler—Detective Sessler has been lying."

"How about Mr. Ratcliff? Has he lied?"

"I don't believe he's been called to the stand."

"You heard him testify before?"

"Oh, yes. Detective Ratcliff lied."

"He lied, didn't he?"

McDonald interrupted. "I'm going to ask for a mistrial. Ask to come sidebar."

Waksman: "I think you can rule from the bench on this. You heard my question."

Judge Snyder: "Denied."

Waksman: "So, Ratcliff lied, didn't he?"

"Yes, he did."

"And Sessler lied?"

"Yes, he did."

"Barbara Robinson lied."

"Yes, she did."

"And Randy Walker lied?"

"Yes, he did."

"How about Dr. Wetli? Did he lie?"

"No, no. I don't know."

Waksman talked about pressure, the pressure Wasko claimed had been exerted on him to confess.

"Tell us what Sessler did to you that made you confess, [then with sarcasm] the former schoolteacher."

"He told me everything that had happened, okay,

how he thought it had happened step by step, and he told me just to repeat everything and we're going to put it down on paper."

"Why did you repeat everything? These folks want to hear, why did you repeat everything?"

"At that point I felt that I had to repeat everything that they said."

"That's my original question. What did Sessler do to you that made you feel you had to repeat everything?"

"They were pressuring me constantly."

"Please tell us what did they did to pressure you."

"They kept telling me I was a murderer. They kept telling me they knew I was involved in this because of all of the bullshit. They kept saying I was a bullshitter, and I kept telling them over and over again that I was not involved in this. And I clearly told them the same story that I had told them over and over again from the very beginning."

Wasko then said that Randy Walker had pressured him, too, told him he was a liar, and Walker became so frustrated, Wasko said, that he began crying and asking him why he had got himself involved, why he had done it.

Wasko: "And I kept telling him that I wasn't involved. So I guess you'd call that making someone, convincing someone to believe in something almost— what would you call it—brainwashing?"

"Is that what they did to you?"

"I believe so."

"You were brainwashed, right?"

"Yes, I was."

"When did you get over this brainwashing? When did you return to normalcy?"

"I couldn't answer you that, Mr. Waksman, because I'm still not feeling well."

"Well, you didn't confess to any other crimes today . . . the last time you confessed to a crime was July 9, right, 1983, that you didn't commit?"

"As far as the taped confession, yes."

Waksman: "When the pressure started getting too heavy, when you couldn't take any more and you started saying things, the only thing you could do is confess to first-degree murder. Why didn't you get up and walk out?"

"Detective Sessler sat me down, and when he had talked I explained to him that I would like to talk to a lawyer, and he told me it was rather late and that I wouldn't be able to get in touch with a lawyer, why not just make the statement and after I made the statement, okay, I could do whatever I wanted to."

"Detective Sessler advised you of your rights again July ninth about 12:15 a.m. Do you recognize this form?"

"Yes."

" 'Are you willing to answer questions without the presence of an attorney at this time?' And where it says yes, you put your initials. Why didn't you put your initials where it says no?"

"He told me to put it where it says yes."

"Oh, you were afraid of him?"

"Yes."

"When you were on the tape recording, why didn't you just blurt something into the tape—'Help me, they're lying. They're pressuring me. They're threatening me. It's not true.' And then that's what the jury would have heard. Why didn't you do that?"

"I was told to read off the paper and to answer everything that was on that paper."

"Were you afraid of Barbara Robinson, too, the stenographer?"

"No, I wasn't afraid of her."

"Why didn't you say something to her that this is not true and correct and this was not freely made?"

"I was just told to sign the paper."

Waksman switched to the extradition hearing, and asked Wasko why he had agreed to waive extradition. Why hadn't he said, "Judge, get me away from these guys, they're killing me?"

Wasko said he had been told to waive extradition by Sessler and he did it.

Waksman: "Why didn't you tell the judge: 'I don't want to see these guys anymore,' or were you still brainwashed?"

"Let's put it this way. I was still listening to everything I was told to say and do by Detective Sessler."

Waksman returned to the testimony of Randy Walker: "Do you remember about 7:19, 7:20, when you took a break Friday evening and he said to you, 'Do you want to leave?' and you said, 'No. I knew this night was going to come'?"

"I never said that."

"Is that another one of his lies?"

"That's another one of his lies."

"How come everybody is lying against Eddie Wasko?"

"I didn't say everyone is lying."

"Phil Ryser lied?"

"Yes."

"Barbara Robinson lied?"

"Yes."

"Randy Walker lied?"

"Yes."

"Steve Sessler lied?"

"Yes."

"Jim Ratcliff lied?"

"Yes."

"How come these five people all decided to lie on Eddie Wasko?"

"I couldn't answer that, Mr. Waksman."

"John Pierson probably lied when he testified last night?"

"Oh, he lied a lot."

"Everybody is lying on Eddie Wasko, right?"

"Yes."

"Why?"

"I don't know, Mr. Waksman."

Waksman had no further questions.

Chapter 21

McDonald could not allow his client to leave the stand with that final sequence of questions and answers ringing in the ears of the jury. He kept him there for a redirect examination, asking him several questions related to the extradition hearing, indicating, as Wasko had said to Waksman, that he had been more or less hustled in and out of the courtroom that morning and signed whatever he was told to sign.

McDonald then brought out the transcript of the tape recording, saying to Wasko: "A suggestion has been made that in this document you just lay off everything you did on John Pierson, right? That's what David Waksman suggested?"

Wasko: "That's what Mr. Waksman suggested."

McDonald: "If that's true and this document and the tape recording that it's taken from are just you telling Detective Sessler what John Pierson did, then this is an accurate one hundred percent description of the event that happened at Staci Weinstein's house that night except the people are changed around, if that's what this is. Like Mr. Waksman would want the jury to believe? That's what this is?"

"That's what he wants them to believe."

A few more questions and Wasko was excused, completing his testimony.

Waksman wanted time for a brief rebuttal. He called Sergeant Ratcliff, who denied categorically Wasko's allegations about bullying and chair banging.

McDonald cross-examined and asked Ratcliff if he had yelled and done some of the things Wasko had alleged. Ratcliff told him he had not. He considered himself a good police officer, and that would be improper procedure.

McDonald: "A bad police officer would not be averse to taking the stand and lying about an incident like that, would he?"

Ratcliff: "I have no idea."

Waksman in rebuttal called Phil Ryser, who denied Wasko's claim, made both in the suppression hearing and in the trial itself, that he had told Wasko that the governor of Florida, Bob Graham, had granted him immunity from prosecution.

McDonald looked for an angle in cross-examination. He asked Ryser: "Is your company facing the very distinct possibility of being sued for the acts of one of its employees in murdering Staci Weinstein?"

Ryser: "It's conceivable."

"Do you anticipate that that is a good possibility?"

"More likely than not."

"And disassociating the company from the act would go far toward defending such a lawsuit, isn't that correct?"

"I doubt whether it would or not, seriously."

The state rested again. The defense had already rested its case.

There was a sigh of relief among many in the courtroom. This had been a difficult, sometimes agonizing week of trial to sit through, especially having to witness the poster-sized, detailed, close-up color pictures of ten-year-old Staci Weinstein.

Judge Snyder called the room to order and announced to the jury that the case was over "as far as both sides putting on testimony." He explained to them that now they would hear the final arguments of the attorneys, then his own charge to them on the law, after which they would be sent out to deliberate on their decision.

Judge Snyder admitted he was tired; it had been a long, tedious day for everyone, and he said he imagined the jurors were tired, too. Final arguments and his charge would take about three hours. It was important that they listened closely to what the attorneys said, and even more important that they listen closely to what he said to them about the law. Therefore, so that everyone could get a fresh start, he was going to recess the trial until nine o'clock Monday morning.

Since earlier in the trial he had sequestered the jury due to the enormous amount of press and TV coverage the trial was getting, the judge warned the jurors that at their hotel it was important that they did not discuss the case with one another. "Until you hear the final arguments and you hear what the law is," he advised them, "you're just not in a position to discuss this case. Sometime Monday afternoon, that's when I expect you to sit down with each other and really discuss this case, but not before."

When the jury exited the courtroom, followed by most of the visitors in the gallery, Judge Snyder asked if the defense had any motions to make—as he knew it would, and what it would be.

In a standard move, Ferrero asked for a judgment of acquittal. The grounds essentially were as they had been in his earlier motion: that the confession was unreliable, and now, that the evidence was "legally insufficient even to go to the jury."

The judge denied the defense motion for an acquittal.

As Marvin left the court building that Saturday afternoon, he knew he was going to have a terrible time getting through the weekend. How could he possibly sleep, he wondered, or eat, or think, or work, when he had to wait until Monday to get into the courtroom, as he would be permitted to do, to listen to final arguments, to hear the judge charge the jury and to be, physically, that close to Wasko, the murderer of his little girl? Oh, there was no doubt in his mind about that, and he told it to one and all in the media room, though he was careful to avoid doing anything that would give the defense an excuse to bar him for the remainder of the trial.

And yet, confident as he was of a guilty verdict, there remained in the back of his mind a nagging, gnawing fear that for some unfathomable reason the jury would let Wasko walk out of the courtroom a free man. If, God forbid, such a thing should happen, he said to himself, he worried that he might do something desperate.

Monday morning. An air of expectancy in the court-room. The gallery was packed with spectators, this time including Marvin and some of his friends and supporters from Parents of Murdered Children. Just a few rows in front of Marvin and to his right were Wasko's mother and sister. Wasko himself now wore a dark blue suit and a white, open-necked shirt. No tie. This might have been a security measure, since each time during the course of the trial, when he had been escorted by two guards to the men's room, the guards had removed his tie and belt. A rule forestalling any possibility of a hanging suicide attempt in the men's room.

Judge Snyder began these climactic proceedings with a few words to the jury about final arguments: he reminded them that, as with opening statements, what the lawyers said was not evidence, it was their inter-pretation of the evidence. The way the system worked, the prosecution would speak first, then the defense, then a rebuttal by the prosecution. However, to be fair, though the prosecution had two chances to speak, total speech time—as in presidential TV debates— would be equal.

Following the final arguments, Snyder told the jury, "I will try to cram a three-year law school course into your heads in about an hour. It's not difficult. Please don't think that trying to figure out what the law is, is difficult."

Waksman then rose to his feet and began to speak. He explained first about the principles of partnership in a crime; it didn't matter who did what. "It doesn't matter who holds the gun and who takes the money. It doesn't matter who tries to rape a little girl and bashes her head in. It doesn't matter. Sometimes it's impossible to determine." It was so in this case, he said. There was Pierson's statement and there was Wasko's statement. "It doesn't matter who did it all," said Waksman. "They're partners in crime and they're responsible . . . each one is responsible for the acts of the other." He continued with an explanation of the various degrees of murder, and pointed out in somber detail the evidence of the sexual assault, and the law on sexual battery.

"Normal sexual battery is when you force somebody," he said. "However, the law gives a little greater protection to little girls. When a little girl hasn't reached her twelfth birthday yet, the law says we don't care what she wants, we don't care that she went out into the street and solicited you, Eddie Wasko. We don't care that she said, 'Asshole, if you want to fuck me, take your pants off.' The law says we don't care what kind of person that little girl is—if you have sexual relations with her, whether she wants it or not, it's sexual battery 'cause little girls are not supposed to do that with big boys, you see.

"So, the fact is she's under twelve, and her father told you she was ten, and the next door neighbor said she looked like she was eight. But Eddie said she was seventeen. So if you find after hearing all the evidence she was seventeen, you have to find him not guilty of attempted capital sexual battery because she's over twelve. That's a decision you have to make."

Waksman proceeded to the gist of the trial: who

should the jury believe, Eddie Wasko or the prosecution witnesses?

"If you don't believe Randy Walker," said Waxman, "we just roll him back to Ohio. If you don't believe Steve Sessler, he's just a sergeant on patrol now, no better, no worse. If you don't believe Phil Ryser, he's still a corporate attorney in Ohio. If you don't believe Eddie Wasko, that man is in a lot of trouble. He knows it and you know it."

Waksman reviewed all the evidence then, how the detectives had gone about accumulating it, the testimony of the prosecution witnesses, and the principle of reasonable doubt.

"If you have reasonable doubt as to whether Detective Sessler is telling you the truth, if you have reasonable doubt as to whether or not Randy Walker, the guy in the wheelchair who kicked up at Eddie's face—if you have reasonable doubt as to whether he's telling you the truth, as to whether the stenographer, Barbara Robinson, is telling you the truth, if you have a reasonable doubt as to whether Phil Ryser is telling the truth . . . whether Sergeant Ratcliff is telling the truth, you got to find Eddie not guilty.

"Just say, Eddie, I believe you. I think these guys lied. I think they threatened you. I think they staged this interview. I think it's all a put-on and somebody bashed her head in, Eddie, and somebody shot her in the head, Eddie, and somebody shot her in the chest and somebody did all of these terrible things to her, Eddie, but it wasn't you so we're going to find you not guilty."

"On the other hand," said Waksman, "if the evidence convinces you beyond every reasonable doubt of the guilt of the defendant, you should find him guilty even though you may believe one or more persons are also guilty.

"What was my first question to Eddie Wasko? First

question: 'Why did you bash her head in?' What did he say? 'Who?'

"Who? He doesn't know who we're talking about, sitting here all week. He doesn't know who we're talking about. The judge will tell you that is something you can consider, whether he's honest and straightforward. If Randy Walker and Steve Sessler are lying to you, walk him out of here, send him home.

"I'll hold the door open. We'll all watch him walk out the door. We'll understand."

McDonald also reviewed the evidence and the testimony. His theory about what happened hadn't changed, either. He talked about Wasko's statement that he'd sent Pierson around to pass out flyers while he repaired the truck and Pierson disappeared for a time.

"The police didn't find any flyers 'cause John Pierson didn't pass any flyers out. John Pierson went wandering around the neighborhood looking for open doors, John Pierson went wandering around the neighborhood looking for something to steal and John Pierson . . . saw Staci Weinstein and John Pierson went into that house, John Pierson tried to rape and kill Staci Weinstein, and John Pierson did that while Eddie Wasko was in the back of a Stanley Steemer truck, upside down with his head inside a float tank.

"That's what happened that day."

McDonald ridiculed Waksman's contention that Wasko owned a gun. "The state's big piece of evidence that he owned a gun, the earth-shattering fact that lets you know that Eddie Wasko owned a gun and that he was lying . . . he carried a gym bag in his truck. Geez, I might as well throw my hands up and go home. You guys have to vote guilty on that."

Pierson had done it all was still the attorney's theme. He went into great detail about how Pierson had sexually assaulted her. He had called Pierson a sexual per-

vert in his opening statement; now he went back to that
with his own version of the sexual assault on Staci:

"Attempted sexual battery: blood inside panties. The
way that blood got there—John Pierson got on top of
Staci Weinstein. She wouldn't cooperate. He beat her
over the head with his gun. Every mark on her is a result of him hitting her that way, taking the gun and
striking it down on her head, making the damage to the
right side of her head.

"And he continued to beat her, and her head moved
. . . and one missed and he hit her on the cheek, a
glancing blow. He just pounded her into submission.
And after pounding her into submission he took her
pants off. By this time he was wild-eyed, his eyes were
bugged out and his nose was bleeding. He was crazy.
His eyes were weird, his nose would bleed when he
got excited.

"And John Pierson grabbed her pants and pulled
them down, and he put his mouth on her vagina. He
started licking her on her vagina and on her inner
thighs, and a little bit of blood from his nose got on
her panties, a little bit of blood from his nose got
on her sheet, and she started to scream."

He killed her, said McDonald. He realized she was
going to identify him. He shot her in the side and he
shot her in the head.

"And then he was sorry, that sick, disgusting human
being that took the stand a couple of days ago that
killed this girl, and he decided he was sorry and he
pulled her pants back up and hugged her to show how
sorry he was. Those facts weren't in Eddie's statement.
Ed never told you about Staci Weinstein being hugged
'cause Eddie Wasko didn't know about it because
Eddie Wasko wasn't there.

"The only person who would have given you information about the smears was John Pierson. Nobody
else knew how it got there."

So it was John Pierson, all John Pierson, and only

John Pierson, said McDonald before he returned to his claim that Wasko had been lied to and been brainwashed. He said that Sessler and Ratcliff had arrived in Ohio with a preconceived idea: that it was Wasko's gun and Pierson used it. McDonald implied that the polygraph examination had been nothing but a subterfuge. "He was not there for a polygraph examination. Randy Walker was there to crack him, was there to get the story Sessler wanted, and he started in on him."

McDonald played part of the taped statement for the jury and asked them to listen to Wasko's voice, said how different it was from the voice they'd heard from him on the witness stand. "It is not a normal, conversational voice," said McDonald. "It is a flat, mechanical type of voice, somebody who is simply following instructions.

"That statement that's been introduced into evidence is garbage," McDonald said as he concluded. "It is a product of brainwashing and just as much the truth as every statement made by every American pilot who confessed to committing war crimes of the most outrageous nature against the people of North Vietnam."

Waksman said in his brief rebuttal:

"Mr. McDonald is entitled to his theory of the case. I didn't object. I don't mind. He can say anything about it he wants. However, when His Honor instructs you how to look for a reasonable doubt, he will tell you not to speculate, not to look for imaginary or speculative doubts—look for real doubts. So, his theory is based upon his speculation, his theory is fantasies of how this crime happened. It's not supported by anything anywhere along the line.

"His manager told you, and I think even he said, his nickname was Electric Eddie. I asked him: 'How many hours did you used to work?' Sixteen hours, fourteen hours, brought in a thousand dollars a day—a lot of money. He volunteered for night jobs after working all day long. Fellow has a lot of endurance and stamina.

"But these detectives wore him out. I couldn't wear him out. I spoke to him about two hours. They wore him out.

"He never told the judge in Ohio, 'Thank God I'm in a courtroom.' This is an American judge. There is an American flag here. He never told the public defender in Ohio: These guys have been working me over for three days. I don't want to go to Miami with these guys. They didn't feed me for three days. Never said anything about it. Denied he had a lawyer in Ohio until we showed him a transcript of the extradition hearing. He was brainwashed.

"How many times did Mr. McDonald say to Sergeant Sessler, well, we got to take your word for that. That's your opinion. That's what you say. If they come in here and say this is what the defendant told us, this is what he looked like, the public defender says, 'That's what you say.'

"There was no video camera in Staci Weinstein's bedroom. But if there was, you'd probably be told, that guy just looks like Eddie Wasko.

"But that's his job—to defend Eddie Wasko.

"You heard what Sessler said. You don't got to take my word for nothing. The jury will play the tape recorder. They'll do what they want."

Waksman's contention was that if Sessler had been going to dictate a statement for Wasko, why would he make it so outlandish, so illogical; why would he tell Wasko to say this was a sexually aggressive girl, sexually mature? "He knew what he was dealing with. She has the dolls. Marvin says she plays with Smurfs. Her father said the biggest thing in her life was to play with the Smurfs. Yet Sessler tells Eddie: tell me she was aggressive. Tell me she said, 'Asshole, take your pants off.' Remember that? This is what Sessler is telling Eddie Wasko to say because he's an experienced homicide detective and he's going to make an airtight case with no holes in it. Doesn't make sense.

"Sessler knew how many times she was shot. He may not have known who killed her, but he knew she was shot twice. If you can figure out a reason for him to tell Eddie Wasko: tell us she was shot once—if you can figure out a good reason, walk him out the door. Twelve Americans sitting on a jury presided over by a judge don't make mistakes. And if you can figure out why Sessler told Eddie Wasko she was shot once, he's not guilty."

Waksman halted for a fraction of a second—a dramatic, theatrical pause as he looked at the jurors, lifted his right arm, and pointed at the ceiling—pointed a finger heavenward:

"Staci will understand," he said slowly, softly. "She'll understand. We'll all understand 'cause Sessler's a liar.

"Staci is watching this trial. She'll understand."

McDonald was furious at these theatrics. "I'm going to object and move for a mistrial at this time."

Judge Snyder denied it and instructed Waksman to continue. To the surprise of many in the courtroom, Waksman did continue; that dramatic finger pointing to Heaven and the remark about Staci watching seemed like such a perfect exit line. However, Waksman had a few more minutes to talk about the evidence and the tape and the question of why so many people were lying while only Eddie Wasko was telling the truth. What would be the purpose of detectives in framing him for the crime, knowing that by doing so they would be allowing the real killer to walk freely on the streets to commit another child murder?

"You folks know what the last word or two is," he concluded. "Don't be ashamed of what you do. He's earned it. He's had a trial. He's had a fair and impartial jury. Tell him whether he's a liar or eight witnesses that I called are liars."

* * *

Now it was Judge Snyder's turn: his charge to the jury. It was long, as the judge had warned them it would be. He explained to them patiently the various conceptions of the several types of unlawful killing, ranging in seriousness from first-degree murder to manslaughter. Included in that lecture were the criteria needed for legal verdicts by a jury, and how they applied to the killing of Staci Weinstein.

Jayne Weintraub, in her opening statement, had covered some of this, notably the legal definition of a felony murder. Waksman had also talked about conspiracy and dual responsibility. Staci Weinstein was dead, killed. No matter who had done ~~what to her~~, if both had been there in that house when the deed was done, if both had entered aware that there was an intent to have sex with the girl and she died during their illegal presence in that house, then both were equally guilty.

The judge explained reasonable doubt: the state had to have proved Wasko guilty "beyond a reasonable doubt." The defendant pleaded not guilty, which meant that the jury must presume he is innocent through each stage of the trial "until it has been overcome by the evidence to the exclusion of and beyond a reasonable doubt.

"The defendant is not required to prove anything. Your verdict finding the defendant either guilty or not guilty must be unanimous."

At 1:20 P.M. the jury retired to the small, windowless jury room near the judge's chambers to consider their verdict. Lunch was sent in as the courtroom emptied of visitors, but few left the building to lunch at the nearby restaurants and snack bars. People milled about in the corridors and on the courthouse steps, gathering in small clusters, in hushed tones debating the case, pros and cons, betting and guessing about the outcome. Some predicted a quick decision, others that the jury might take days to decide. Marvin, centered among news media and his POMC supporters, dared not predict. Just pray.

At three-thirty the jury sent in three questions, ending in the request: "Please turn on the fans."

The jurors wanted the note pack and notes of Randy Walker, the results of his polygraph tests, and all pre-trial interview testimony.

None of the documents requested had been presented as evidence during the trial, and therefore Judge Snyder sent a note back saying those items were "not available."

A half hour later, they requested the testimony of four prosecution witnesses. The judge called them in and told them that the object of questions was "not to rehear the trial." They should depend on their collective recollections, unless there was perhaps one specific item they wanted clarified; then he might be willing to do that.

At ten, the jury sent the judge a note saying it was unable to come to a verdict. The jurors said they would need several more hours and requested an adjournment to the next day.

Judge Snyder agreed; actually, he and the attorneys appeared surprised that after nine hours of deliberation in this case the jury needed another day. Certainly, however, one more day should be enough for them. "I want you to check out of the hotel early tomorrow morning," he said to the jurors. "Be back here by eight-thirty in the morning and bring all of your stuff over here because you'll be here all day."

He told them to come not to the courtroom but straight to the jury room and get to work, because he wouldn't be seeing them. He was starting another first-degree murder trial in that same courtroom in the morning; however, should they have any questions he would be available.

On Tuesday, January 17, Marvin sat in the press room at the courthouse surrounded by cables and television equipment, waiting, as were all the media people, for something to happen. He was weary. They all were weary. "The jury has been out so long," Marvin said to *Miami Herald* columnist Charles Whited. "I wonder what's in their minds."

As the morning dragged on into lunchtime and on into the afternoon with no decision, Judge Snyder contemplated dismissing the jury at six o'clock and sending them home instead of back to their hotel. He didn't see much sense at this point in keeping them sequestered at great expense to the state. The defense attorneys argued with him about that, about the jurors watching television at home, talking to friends and relatives while they were still considering the verdict. McDonald wasn't even sure it was legal for the judge to cancel his sequester decision. Waksman said, "Judge, we may never reach that point. If we get a verdict soon and if there is a conviction, we'll go right into the second part."

The legal debate remained academic when at six o'clock the jury sent in a note that it had reached a verdict. By then, fortunately, the judge's murder-case trial had been adjourned for the day and the court was clear. The bailiff notified all interested parties that the jury was coming in. There was a scramble for seats; in the press room: full alert, all eyes on the TV screen. Marvin clenched his fists tightly, hardly daring to breathe.

The jurors filed in and took their seats. The courtroom quieted.

Judge Snyder: "Madam clerk, will you read the verdict?"

The clerk: "The state of Florida versus Edward Robert Wasko, verdict: We, the jury, find the defendant Edward Robert Wasko, as to Count I of the indictment, first-degree murder upon one Staci Weinstein, guilty as charged. So say we all.

"As to Count II of the indictment, burglary with an assault, guilty as charged. So say we all.

"As to Count III of the indictment, attempted capital

sexual battery upon one Staci Weinstein, guilty. So say
we all. Marjorie Foster, foreman."

The clerk then polled the jury, calling each by name,
and each answered yes to the verdicts.

Wasko sat unmoved and unflinching in his chair between his glum attorneys. Behind him, his mother pat-
ted him on the shoulder and wept silently. In the press
room reporters called in their story. Marvin breathed a
loud sigh of relief. "Thank God," he said. He put his
head in his hands and began sobbing.

Though it was now past six, the judge and the attorneys agreed to go straight on to the sentencing phase
of the trial. During this phase the defense and the prosecution present evidence and arguments regarding factors in aggravation and mitigation relative to the
sentence that the jury would recommend. Judge Snyder
decreed a dinner break, with court reconvening at
seven-thirty. Wasko was then brought forward to be
fingerprinted. In the interval, Ferrero said that as witnesses he would be calling Wasko's mother, Mary, and
John Pierson. Waksman said he wouldn't be calling
any witnesses.

Marvin approached Waksman during the dinner hour
and said he wanted to testify, since Mary Wasko was being called by the defense. Waksman said he couldn't do
that.

"What?" cried Marvin. "I'm not getting a chance to
talk to the jury? He's not a defendant anymore. He's a
murderer! A convicted murderer! The jury's made its
decision. I can't influence their decision. His mother's
had her chance all through the trial to sit there and let
the jury see her cry for him while I was barred. I had
to sit in the press room. Now she's getting another
chance? Now she's going to sit there in that witness
chair and cry for her son, that murderer, that murderer
who killed my little girl!

"Who will cry for Staci? Tell me that, who will cry for Staci?"

By law, however, the prosecution could not call the victim's family to support aggravating circumstances in quest of a death sentence from the jury. The defense, on the other hand, was allowed to call witnesses in support of mitigating circumstances and a sentence of life imprisonment.

Waksman stated that the only additional evidence he would be offering was the verdict form convicting Wasko of attempted sexual battery.

Judge Snyder advised the jury, before testimony, that "under Florida law, your verdict is advisory; however, you are instructed that the law requires the court give your verdict great weight and serious consideration in determining the sentence to be imposed, and I guarantee you that this court will do so."

Ferrero called Wasko's mother to the stand. She testified about his childhood, relating that he had been a Cub Scout, had been on safety patrol at school, never had been in trouble as a schoolboy or afterward. She was allowed to introduce a photo of Wasko in which he was being baptized a Roman Catholic. He had been a religious child, she said, and often had gone to church with her.

"Eddie was a good kid," she said. "He would do anything, anything you tell him. He never was in trouble."

Marvin was incensed at all this. What did it matter if he was a Cub Scout and a good kid? Eddie Wasko, twelve years old, was not on trial here! Eddie Wasko the grown-up man was on trial. What does it matter what she's saying? He was beside himself with outrage that he had to sit there and listen to this woman crying softly as she told the jury what a good boy her son was. Yeah, give the kid a chance ... just like he gave Staci a chance.

Ferrero asked Mary Wasko: "Mrs. Wasko, do you feel that your son should be electrocuted?"

"No."

"Tell the jury why not."

"Because Eddie wouldn't hurt a little girl."

"How old are you, Mrs. Wasko?"

"Forty-nine."

"If Eddie is released from prison, if he is released from prison in the year 2009, will his home still be waiting for him."

"If I'm still alive."

Marvin shook his head in disgust. If she's still alive. Is Staci still alive? Will Staci ever be forty-nine years old? She never even made it to eleven.

Ferrero called Pierson as his second and final witness in mitigation. The tactic here was to bring to the attention of the jury the fact that this man, who had confessed to complicity in the murder, had gotten away with a plea-bargain maximum sentence of seventeen years.

Ferrero questioned him on all of that.

"Was Mr. Waksman in court when you entered that plea of guilty to second-degree murder?"

"Yes."

"Was that plea—was that seventeen-year sentence a mandatory minimum number of seventeen years?"

"No."

"Did you have a discussion with your lawyer concerning this case?"

"Yes."

"About how many years did your lawyer tell you you would actually have to serve before you are released into Dade County, Florida, John?"

"Not really certain."

"Did he give you a ballpark—?"

"He told me something—maybe about—maybe eight to ten."

"So you're—hopefully you can become a productive member of society in eight to ten years, right?"

"Yes."

"Did they drop another rape case against you for a rape of a seventeen-year-old?"

"My ex-fiancée, yes."

"That ain't bad, huh?"

"Lucky."

Following the rest of testimony, Waksman and Ferrero each had his chance to speak to the jury: Waksman on why the jury should recommend the death penalty for Wasko, Ferrero on why the jury should recommend a life sentence, which would carry a minimum mandatory of twenty-five years. Both attorneys were passionate and eloquent. Waxman harped on the particular viciousness of the crime and Staci's age; Ferrero concluded his speech with a mental picture of Pierson laughing outside the gates of his prison after serving his short sentence; it would be grossly unfair, Ferrero said, for his client to be sentenced to death for the same crime; a life sentence would be punishment enough.

It was three minutes before eleven when the jurors were sent out to decide. Forty-two minutes later, they filed back into the courtroom.

Again the clerk of the court made the announcement:

"We the jury advise and recommend to the court that it imposes a sentence of life imprisonment upon Edward Robert Wasko without possibility of parole for twenty-five years."

In the press room Marvin broke into tears. "I guess you could call them tears of joy," he said to the *Miami Herald*. "This man murdered my daughter, and it's been a long haul to get him into court."

The recommendation of the jury was just that: a recommendation. Florida was one of just four states that allowed a judge to make the final determination of the sentence in a capital crime. Alabama, Delaware and Indiana were the others.

What followed was a period of pre-sentencing investigation, including psychological and medical reports, confidential background checks on Wasko's childhood seeking any evidence of child abuse, and a thorough reexamination by Judge Snyder of all the homicide records, medical examiner's reports, and evidence introduced by both the state and by the defense.

The final stage before the judge decided Wasko's fate was a hearing scheduled to take place on February 16. At this hearing he would hear from a number of people who wished to testify either for the death penalty to be imposed and from those who were against the death penalty. In this instance both Marvin and Hilari would be allowed to testify.

During the four-week interim between the jury verdict and this hearing, Judge Snyder was deluged with letters, for the most part from former classmates, friends, coworkers and girlfriends of Wasko, pleading for the judge's mercy, relating their memories of Wasko as a good fellow who never did anybody any harm. Many letters, too, came from Staci's classmates and former teachers, from some POMC members, and some of Marvin's neighbors, asking the judge for the death penalty, telling of Staci's sweetness and innocence and expressing their horror at the bestiality of the crime.

In the courtroom on the hearing day, Judge Snyder asked those who wished to testify to raise their hands: first for the state, then for the defense. The show of hands was about equal, so the judge said he would call them alternately, after which he would hear final legal arguments from the attorneys.

Alan Sacharoff testified first for the state, then Wasko's sister, followed by the principal of Staci's school, a man from the American Friends Service Community opposed to the death penalty, Nelan Sweet of POMC, and so forth. Hilari and Marvin were the last two to speak.

Hilari asked for the death penalty for her sister's killer. "I miss my sister very, very much," she said, "and nothing or nobody will ever replace her. The last few years of my life have been miserable for me. First my mother died and it was only four months later when these two animals, Edward Wasko and John Pierson, came into my house and brutally murdered my little sister."

Hilari mentioned that since Staci's death her school grades had gone down considerably. She said that giving Wasko the electric chair "is letting him off too easy. To have to worry about Edward Wasko ever being on the street again, may it be twenty-five years or fifty years, I will always be afraid. With the electric chair I know he'll be somewhere where he'll never be able to hurt or kill again."

Marvin's speech was much longer. He had it all prepared and written down.

"Now that Edward Wasko has been found guilty of Staci's murder," said Marvin, "I would like to say that he had an exceptionally fair trial with ample opportunity to prove his innocence, and that is a hell of a lot more than he gave Staci.

"She didn't have two public defenders to argue on her behalf; nor did she have a judge and jury to decide her fate. Instead she had Edward Wasko brutally beat her and shoot her to death in her own bed, in the security of her own home. . . . My life and that of my daughter, Hilari, will never be the same as long as we live.

"Wasko took one life and ruined two others, our penalty as victims of this crime. His own life should be no less. Edward Wasko took it upon himself to be Staci's arresting officer, judge, jury, and executioner."

Marvin talked of the possibility that if given a life sentence with a twenty-five-year mandatory, he might be released in seventeen years with gain time. "The electric chair allows Wasko to have the same gain time he gave my baby. Staci didn't have two attorneys to argue her innocence, and whatever crime Wasko executed her for, neither was I or my daughter or any of her friends able to testify in open court on her behalf.

"Ed Wasko did everything he could to avoid being caught. His purpose for being in court today is to try to convince you that his life still has some value and that maybe someday he should be set free and allowed into society.

"Well, Staci can't be here now to ask for the same. She won't get any time off from the grave for good behavior, and she can't appeal for a new trial.

"I have here, Your Honor, a picture of Staci's classmates during her last year at school, and I would like to show you this, if I may.

"The only thing is, Your Honor, Staci is not in it. She was murdered before the picture was taken. This will show you the peer group or age group my daughter was in."

In closing, Marvin said, "If there ever was a crime that justifies the maximum penalty that the court can impose, it's the brutal death of a little defenseless girl. I urge you to impose the death penalty on this cold-blooded, heartless murderer."

Two weeks later, on March 1, after due deliberation, Judge Snyder overruled the jury and sentenced Wasko to death in the electric chair.

He called the murder of Staci "a hideously evil, shocking, and violent crime. This homicide was extremely heinous, atrocious, and cruel. If there ever was any case wherein the death penalty is called for, it is this case," the judge said in his written opinion.

Judge Snyder also sentenced Wasko to life in prison for armed burglary and suspended a sentence for attempted sexual battery.

"Justice has been served," said Marvin. "I'm satisfied Judge Snyder did the right thing."

End of story? Not quite.

Chapter 22

Marvin should have been elated, but he wasn't. He was depressed. He didn't know why, but somehow something was missing. He wasn't feeling the pleasure he had expected to feel about Wasko being sent to death row at Florida State Prison. Not that he had any misgivings about that—no, none of that, no moral backlash about taking Wasko's life. He'd pull the switch himself if they'd let him. It was, rather, sitting there in his home in the evenings, with Hilari at the dining room table or in her room doing her homework, he felt an emptiness, a weariness. All the energy seemed to have drained out of him in a rush, and he was overcome with a lassitude he could not fathom. He had no energy. He did not want to go to work. He didn't want to do anything, really, but sit around the house and . . . and not even think. He was not at peace with himself, and it disturbed him terribly. At times, inexplicably and suddenly, he would burst into tears.

At such times he would wander into Staci's room and sit on her bed. Then, at least, he knew why he was crying. He missed her so.

It didn't help that he was about to lose his job. All the Grand Union stores in Florida were closing down. He didn't know what he would do then, but he would do something to keep the house. He would find a job as a baker. Or maybe sales. He had experience. Or maybe in some kind of job where he could help people in distress, people like himself who had suffered tragedy and who needed help.

After all the many months of being fueled by his anger and his pain, the comedown was like falling off the edge of a cliff. There was nobody to fight anymore, no need to charge angrily downtown to argue with Matthews, or Morrison, or Hall, or Waksman—or anybody.

What kind of future lay in store for him and Hilari? Could they ever live a normal life? Could they ever get over the pain-racked, lingering death of Ruth Ann, of the terrible murder of Staci?

That was the hardest part. Thinking about Staci, how she died, how they killed her. The details so clinically, so dispassionately, unveiled during the trial were too terrible to think about, but there was no way he could chase them from his mind, not now—not ever. That they had killed her was awful enough, but to know that she had been so afraid, that she had suffered so, was devastating. He remembered how shy she had been, how she hadn't liked to be touched. She was just starting to develop and go through physical changes. And what those beasts did to her! The anguish she must have felt! The shame! The disgust!

And maybe worst of all was that as they beat her about the head with that gun butt and she lay there bleeding and semiconscious, she must have known that they were going to kill her, must have known that she was going to die. Ten years old. What could have gone through the terrorized mind of a ten-year-old girl who knew that she was about to be killed?

When he thought about that, rage built up in him again. He didn't cry then. He hit something. A wall, the dining room table, the refrigerator—each object the face of John Pierson, the face of Edward Wasko. And they—those despicable human beings—they would be alive and breathing, eating three meals a day, watching television in prison, talking to other people—existing. His little girl no longer existed.

And I was not there to protect her.
He knew no peace.

One evening in March at a meeting of Parents of Murdered Children, Marvin heard speeches by Florida state
representatives Dexter Lehtinen and Ileana Ros, who
were trying to push through the legislature a victims-
rights bill they were sponsoring. During the course of
his talk, Dexter Lehtinen mentioned as a case in point
Marvin Weinstein, who had been kept out of the courtroom during the trial of his daughter's murderer and
had fought against it. Lehtinen said this common-law
court rule was grossly unfair and he wanted to change
it. He was there that night to win support from the
members of POMC.

When the meeting was over, Marvin introduced himself to the two legislators. They chatted for a time
about his case and other cases, and Marvin wished
them well in getting their bill passed. Several weeks
later, Marvin was on the phone with Lisa Hardemann,
then president of the local POMC group and one of its
founders, when Lisa told him she was going up to Tallahassee, the state capital, to represent POMC at hearings then talking place before the Criminal Code
Subcommittee of the state legislature on the Lehtinen-
Ros Victims Rights Bill. Marvin said he'd like to join
her. She thought it was a great idea, and in her station
wagon she and Marvin and two other members of
POMC drove to Tallahassee to attend the hearings.

In the committee room the next day Marvin sat there
listening to speeches by representatives of various
victims-rights groups, and he thought: nobody is getting up there and talking with any real emotion. It all
seemed rather matter-of-fact and even boring. He
looked around the room and saw that conversations
were taking place among people in the room even
while someone was at the podium speaking.

"Wait a minute, nothing's happening here," he said

to Lisa. "Look, last night I wrote out some things that I would say if I had a chance to speak. Here, read what I wrote. Somebody's got to tell these people what's really going on out there! What do you think?"

There was just one opening remaining for a speaker—a two-minute slot that Lisa was supposed to fill. She and Dexter Lehtinen held a brief conference, and they gave Martin the slot. Two minutes.

Well, it takes Marvin Weinstein two minutes just to hitch up his trousers and say "Good afternoon, ladies and gentlemen." And when he gets going on a speech, when the adrenaline flows and his emotions take over, it's a juggernaut at full speed. Two minutes? Forget the stopwatch.

Marvin got up there and gave the committee members both barrels from his heart. He gave them case histories. He said the public, the people out there, people like him, ordinary people, whether members of Parents of Murdered Children or not, were sick and tired of all the protection violent criminals seemed to be getting. "They get do-gooders, social workers, psychologists, all worried about murderers' Constitutional rights. How about our rights? All these people are out there asking for a break for these rapists and these killers. How about a break for the victims and their families?

"It's not just me standing here I'm talking about. It's not even the people out there I'm talking about. It's you . . . you . . . and you!" he shouted, pointing his finger at the committee members. "While we are sitting here, right now, it could be your child who's being murdered! How do you know? There has got to be changes made in the law, changes to care about what happens to the victims and their families, and if Dexter Lehtinen here is trying to make changes for victims, he's trying to make it for everybody—and that includes all of you."

He told of his own case. "I and my daughter Hilari

were barred from the courtroom during the trial of
Eddie Wasko, the murderer of my ten-year-old daughter Staci. We were made to feel like we didn't matter.
Why? Because a couple of sharp public defenders
listed us as potential witnesses. They were afraid my
presence would affect the jury. So they list me as a potential witness. What could I testify to except that I
found my daughter's body? Hilari they never even
called. Meantime the mother of that killer, Eddie
Wasko, she was allowed to sit behind him all through
the trial and cry for him.

"Who was allowed to cry for Staci?"

Marvin brought the house down. When he finished,
he got a standing ovation.

The Criminal Code Subcommittee sent the bill on to
the full Judiciary Committee by a 7–0 vote. The Victims Rights Bill was passed by the legislature and
eventually became the Victims of Crime Amendment
to the Florida Constitution. Marvin was deluged with
letters of thanks and praise from families of victims
and from attorneys and legislators.

Spurred on by Dexter Lehtinen, "Who will cry for
Staci?" became the rallying cry for victims-rights
groups as they pushed the Victims Rights Bill higher
up the ladder until it became part of the state Constitution.

It reads: "Victims of crime or their lawful representatives, including the next of kin of homicide victims,
are entitled to the right to be informed, to be present,
and to be heard when relevant, at all crucial stages of
criminal proceedings, to the extent that these rights do
not interfere with the Constitutional rights of the accused."

In practice, judges sitting a homicide case would not
allow defense attorneys to bar next of kin from the
courtroom by listing them as witnesses unless they
could prove that the testimony would be important
enough to have an impact on a jury's verdict.

Talk shows love people like Marvin Weinstein: articulate and angry. So he appeared on several of them in the ensuing weeks, and spoke before a number of victims-rights groups. However, none of these were paid performances, and Marvin was hurting financially. The baker's job was gone. Using his van, he worked for a time as a courier, delivering packages. Then Audrey Sweet of POMC introduced him to a man who was in the business of laying carpets and was looking for a partner. He would teach Marvin the business. Marvin thought it strange to be a carpet layer, considering that Wasko and Pierson had been carpet cleaners. However, this sounded as though it could be a good trade to learn, and since this prospective partner already had accounts with stores, he would begin earning money immediately. So, Marvin became a carpet layer. And, though he could scarcely afford it, he went into therapy, visiting a psychologist once a week who he hoped would settle him down and help him normalize his life. He tried to get Hilari to go too, but she refused. She said she didn't need it and didn't want it. In many ways Hilari was stronger than her father, mentally tougher.

A lawyer friend who did not handle that kind of case suggested to Marvin that he might have a suit against Stanley Steemer, because a company of that kind would undoubtedly carry insurance. Marvin found a lawyer who specialized in negligence cases, sued the company, and agreed to a generous out-of-court settlement.

Now Marvin found himself in an attractive financial position; the question was, what should he do with the money? At the top of the list, he put aside enough money to pay for Hilari's college education. She was not enthusiastic about going to college—she thought she'd rather go to work fresh from high school—but Marvin sat her down and talked to her about it.

"I want you to have that education. I never even fin-

ished high school and I regret it. You'll have plenty of
time in your life to work. It doesn't even matter if you
never use your degree to get a job. What's important is
that you stay in school and get the education. You'll
never regret it."

Marvin is a bulldog of a persuader, as many a homicide detective can confirm. Hilari agreed to buckle
down, improve her grades, and go to college.

He quit the carpet-laying business. He paid off his
mortgage, fixed up the house, which had fallen into
disrepair since Ruth Ann died, and decided that since
he had a fair amount of money behind him now, he
would devote all his time to Parents of Murdered Children. He wanted to help people. He had the experience,
he had the contacts.

Marvin became a veritable whirlwind from one end
of Florida to the other. If he saw a story in the paper
about a young child murdered, he was at the parents'
door, offering to help. He telephoned, he rang door-
bells, he read every newspaper, watched every television program about crime. He got Marcía involved
when he came across a case in which detectives were
stymied, recommending to the victim's parents that
they bring her in on the case. According to Marvin, she
helped solve several cases.

Knowing the legal and investigative system as he
did, Marvin would go to court with families, sit with
them, comfort them, advise them of their rights, help
them fight the system if he thought it necessary. As he
had done in his own case, he would badger detectives
for information on behalf of bereaved families.

All was well until 1987. Hilari was a fine young
woman of seventeen ready for Broward Community
College. Marvin had money invested and was living
off the interest. He was doing what he wanted to do—
help victims of crime. For a time he even thought of
going back to school to get a law degree, or at least to

qualify as a paralegal. It was a notion that was lost in the swirl of his frenetic activity.

In February Marvin discovered that the Florida Supreme Court was preparing to rule on Wasko's appeal for a reversal of his sentence.

He got in touch with Julie Thornton of the Attorney General's Office, who was the attorney of record for the state, which of course was resisting the appeal. He asked permission to accompany her to the Supreme Court hearing and make a speech before the court. He couldn't do that. It wasn't done. The Supreme Court looked at the law, looked at precedents, looked at the trial record, the basis of Wasko's appeal, and the state's rebuttal—and would decide.

On March 5, the Supreme Court announced that it had upheld Wasko's conviction for first-degree murder, but overturned the death penalty. By a 5–1 vote the court ruled that Judge Snyder "improperly overrode the jury's recommendation."

The basis of the court's decision was that "the jury and trial court relied on the same facts in this case. The killing of a child is especially despicable. On the other hand, Wasko had no significant prior history of criminal activity and presented testimony of his good character, good employment record, and a good family background. Moreover, the jury may have questioned the respective roles of Wasko and Pierson in this homicide. These factors gave the jury a reasonable basis for recommending life imprisonment.

"The trial court is directed to resentence him to life imprisonment with no possibility of parole for twenty-five years. Because we have determined that Wasko should not be sentenced to death, the trial court may wish to revisit the sentences for the other convictions."

Justice Ehrlich agreed with the decision, but added a separate opinion of exceptional strength:

"Death-penalty cases are never easy and nice. This one is particularly gut-wrenching to me.

"The defendant's depravity as shown by his confessions is complete. He is a Jekyll and Hyde and should never be permitted to return to an open society. The evidence established that he was a totally upright, hardworking conscientious young man who had never before run afoul of the law. The jury found that he had committed a heinous, repulsive, senseless crime, totally out of character. He became a monster whose bestiality is utterly revolting. Although the jury recommended that the defendant should not receive the death penalty, and I agree for the reasons articulated in the court's opinion, he should never again be given the opportunity to revert to his dark side.

"The imposition of a sentence which makes him eligible for parole in twenty-five years is inadequate. If his sentence for burglary and attempted capital sexual battery were made consecutive to his mandated life sentence, defendant may never be able to walk the streets again and the interests of society will have been served without the taking of his life by electrocution. Anything less will, in my opinion, be utterly inadequate."

Predictably, understandably, Marvin was bitter at the court's decision. As soon as he found out he rushed to Hilari's school to tell her before she found out from somebody else. She broke down in tears when he gave her the news. "It's not right," she cried. "It's not fair. How could he murder her and they let him off?"

It was a good question, and duly challenged.

Marvin, together with Julie Thornton, presented written arguments to the court on the basis of the fact that since in principal the court ruled solely on the letter of the law, it erred by speculating on what the jury had in mind regarding Wasko's background and the relative culpability of Wasko and Pierson in recommending the life sentence.

The court did not agree.

Eventually, the matter of a judge's right to overrule

the jury went all the way to the United States Supreme Court. As mentioned earlier, only four states allowed the judge to do that. The Supreme Court ruled in effect that this was a state's rights issue. It would not interfere with the right of a state to have such a rule. If a state wished it to be that the trial judge has the final word in sentencing, so be it, and it did not deprive a defendant of any of his Constitutional rights.

David Waksman's comment on the Florida court's decision was: "The good news is that the conviction is affirmed. The bad news is, what do you have to do to get the death penalty?" Brian McDonald, naturally, was relieved that Wasko was escaping the electric chair. He was as convinced as ever that John Pierson had attacked Staci and killed her while Wasko was working on the truck.

The other good news was that Judge Snyder now had the option of resentencing Wasko. That, however, required yet another hearing, with prosecution and defense attorneys giving arguments before the judge. And even Marvin would be allowed to speak his piece.

The hearing was set for September 17, and in July State Attorney Janet Reno submitted a memorandum of law, in which she quoted the Florida Supreme Court and Judge Ehrlich, and a number of precedent cases, concluding:

"The state of Florida, based on the aforesaid authorities, respectfully recommends to this honorable court that the defendant's previously imposed sentences for burglary while armed and attempted capital sexual battery be changed to two consecutive life terms each consecutive to each other and consecutive to his life sentence in Count I and each bearing a three-year mandatory minimum, concurrent to each other yet consecutive to the twenty-five years mandatory minimum sentence imposed on Count I."

That would not satisfy Marvin. He wanted the chair, and he wanted to know how the Florida Supreme Court

could overrule the judge—and at the hearing before
Judge Snyder he quoted the U.S. Supreme Court decision mentioned above.

Judge Snyder told him, "Mr. Weinstein, the Supreme
Court of Florida is my boss." That was the fact of the
matter; Marvin had misinterpreted the U.S. Supreme
Court ruling. As it was explained to him: the court said
it was fine if Florida wants the circuit court judge to
override a jury's recommendation. But then the Florida
Supreme Court has the right to override the judge.

Following the September hearing, Judge Snyder
changed Wasko's sentence to a life sentence on Count
I with a minimum sentence of twenty-five years plus
three for the gun before eligibility for parole, followed
by a consecutive life sentence on Count Two, and on
Count III guilty with a suspended sentence. It was unlikely that Wasko would ever be set free.

Marvin was not completely satisfied. He always
found it difficult to understand why judges and courts
constantly disagreed with him, difficult at times to the
point where he felt the entire system was a conspiracy
by judges, courts, and lawyers to deprive him and every other honest citizen of justice.

Disappointed at Wasko's rescue from death row,
Marvin worried about John Pierson, and when a friend
asked him shortly after the Wasko resentencing, "Have
you ever checked into what Pierson's status is?"
Marvin replied that as far as he was concerned, Pierson
was doing his seventeen years. "It was a mandatory
sentence, but I'll try to find out."

Marvin called around to various officials in the Corrections Department and found out that Pierson was in
the Dade Correctional Facility in Florida City. To his
horror, he discovered that Pierson was stacking up an
enormous amount of gain time. "Wait a minute, wait a
minute!" he said in a conversation with a lady at the
Department of Corrections. "What do you mean, gain

time? Judge Morphonios gave him a mandatory sentence of seventeen years with no parole!"

That sentence, he was told, was incorrect. Impossible. For a conviction of second-degree murder there was no such thing as a mandatory sentence; neither was there a consideration of parole. There was only gain time. Statutory gain time plus a possibility of earned gain time.

Marvin could not believe his ears. He could not believe the follow-up letter he got detailing the gain time Pierson was getting. It added up to the fact that Pierson was due to be released in March 1993—not in the year 2000. And if he earned incentive gain time he could earn an additional twenty days a month off his sentence. And he would be released in Dade County, less than an hour's drive from Marvin's home.

Once again, after an interval in his life of relative quiet, Marvin descended into chaos. He went to see Judge Morphonios, who told him that after sixty days from sentencing she had nothing to do with prison time. He went to see Janet Reno, who said there was nothing she could do. He went to David Waksman, who said they were constantly changing sentencing guidelines and gain time because the prisons were overcrowded. Pierson must be getting gain time under new rules that had come into practice since he was jailed.

Marvin wrote to state senators, he wrote to U.S. senators and congressmen. He wrote to the Florida Department of Corrections. A veritable blizzard of paper descended over Florida as all these people wrote to him, to Janet Reno, to Ellen Morphonios, to each other. The end result of all this paper was nil. Everybody expressed concern. Nobody could do anything about it.

Not good enough for Marvin. He pulled the colloquy record of the case. There it was, he had to admit, along with "mandatorily" and no parole, were the words "statutory gain time." He didn't remember hearing that. He thought about it, trying to recall what the judge had said. He did remember now that Brian McDonald had told him, "He'll never do the seventeen years." He had thought McDonald crazy. Well, he wasn't so crazy after all. Morphonios had said "mandatorily." That's what Marvin had concentrated on, that and no parole. Gain time? He'd never heard it. The words had passed right over his head.

At the Florida Department of Corrections in Tallahassee there was a Victims Coordinator. Marvin made up a flyer, a grotesquely explicit flyer picturing Staci's bloody body and head with a large bold headline: THIS GIRL COULD HAVE BEEN YOUR OWN DAUGHTER.

He drove up to Tallahassee and distributed scores of these flyers to legislators as they entered the Senate building, then went to see Mark Lazarus, the Victims Coordinator. Lazarus showed him the file on Pierson. Marvin mentioned the sentence handed down from Judge Morphonios. Lazarus said it couldn't be, that was not a legal sentence.

"Well, who's giving him the gain time?" Marvin asked him. Lazarus explained that they were required to give gain time by law.

Lazarus kept looking in the file and found the original written sentence. It did not read the same as the judge's colloquy, her oral sentencing. The difference was profound. The sentence read, following the stipulation that Pierson should not be placed in the same facility as Wasko, "Court further orders that the defendant having elected to be sentenced pursuant to RCrP 3.701 Sentencing Guidelines shall not be eligible for parole or gain time."

"There it is!" exclaimed Marvin. "It says no gain time."

That was confusing. Judge Morphonios's colloquy had specified "statutory gain time." The written sentencing form, dated the same day, said, "Not eligible for gain time." Legally, it is what the judge says in open court that takes precedence over what might be stated on the written sentencing sheet. Lazarus was amazed. It shouldn't be. Judges have nothing to do with gain time. He looked further into the file and found another sentencing form, dated the same day, November 4, 1983, titled Corrected Sentence. On this form the phrasing regarding parole and gain time had been deleted. However, this Corrected Sentence form, though dated the same day as the first, for some reason was not put in the file until some five months later.

To Marvin this smacked of judicial error. And perhaps reversible. Maybe he could stop Pierson from getting all this gain time and early release. Whatever, to Marvin this was a scandal of monumental proportions. Judge Morphonios says in open court seventeen years mandatory, no parole. Then she signs a form that says he gets no gain time. Then she signs a corrected form that deletes the references to parole and gain time. Never, never, Marvin said to Lazarus, would he have agreed to a plea-bargain deal for Pierson had he known of gain time of such proportions. Pierson to be released in March 1993? Maybe even earlier with incentive gain time? Never!

Marvin used this new information on the conflicting sentences to continue his agitation for some sort of redress. He wrote to the attorney general. He appeared on television talk shows. He cornered David Waksman and Bruce Lehr, brandishing the two different sentences and a copy of the Morphonios colloquy.

Marvin was in his element. Don Quixote, the Man of La Mancha, was small-time. Marvin Weinstein, the Man of North Miami Beach, was taking on the Florida legal system again.

He didn't care what anybody said to him about what Morphonios said, about what he should have heard, what the law was on gain time. He didn't care that Waksman and others told him that at the time of Pierson's plea bargain new guidelines had just come in and yes, the judge had made a mistake. No question about that. Her colloquy, her sentence handed down in open court, was wrong: there was no such thing as a mandatory sentence with no parole for second-degree murder. There used to be such a sentence but no more. She should have just given him the seventeen years. In fact, there was no good reason for her to mention gain time at all. That falls entirely within the province of the Department of Corrections. Like the Lord, they giveth, and they taketh away.

Marvin didn't want to know.

In April 1990, as he continued to battle in the press and on television and with letters flying all over the state to keep Pierson in jail for the full seventeen years, he received further bad news. A recent Florida Supreme Court ruling—the Waldrup decision— suddenly gave Pierson another 597 days of gain time. That meant he was eligible for release from the Martin County Correctional Institution—where he had been sent from Florida City—in December.

Marvin didn't know what to do next. This was just too much. Getting out in December 1990! Having done only seven years? Merry Christmas, John Pierson! What was the prison system coming to?

He fired up his publicity campaign.

"They're going to free the slimeball who killed my little girl!" ran a four-line headline in the *Weekly World News.* "Those idiots in the court system made this gain time thing to stop prison overcrowding," Marvin said in the newspaper article. "I'll tell you what will stop prison overcrowding—crank up that electric chair. That'll thin them out real quick. Hey, Staci's grave is overcrowded right now. She's not too comfortable down there."

The *Miami Herald* headlined its story: "FATHER'S OBSESSION IS TO KEEP DAUGHTER'S KILLER IN PRISON." It quoted Marvin: "We've created a situation where we mollycoddle these people. Where's the break for Staci?"

However, above and beyond all the headlines he was creating, Marvin thought seriously that he had found a flaw in the Waldrup decision that gave Pierson those extra 597 days. He believed it was possible that the Waldrup decision did not apply in Pierson's case.

He sued the state of Florida and the Department of Corrections. A friend of his recommended an attorney named Kelley Finn. An experienced criminal defense attorney, she examined all the documents Marvin had collected, looked up the law, reviewed the Waldrup decision, and took up Marvin's case. With time running out now, with Pierson due to be released on November 26, Finn worked through the night and drew up papers for an injunction to keep Pierson in prison pending a full hearing.

Early the next morning, November 21, Marvin drove north to Stuart, which had jurisdiction over the Martin County jail in Indiantown. Finn would meet him up there later that morning. The basic plea of the injunction was that the next of kin of the victim had not been "adequately informed of crucial stages of criminal proceedings, to be present and to be heard all in violation of petitioner's rights under the Florida Constitution." The injunction went on to challenge the gain time awarded Pierson and claimed that "Weinstein was not advised of gain time when explained the sentencing guidelines by the assistant state attorney."

At the courthouse Marvin handed the legal papers, some two hundred pages of legal papers, to the clerk of the court, and asked for an appointment with the judge. The clerk disappeared into the judge's chambers. She returned some ten minutes later and said to Marvin that the judge had denied the injunction.

"What do you mean, denied it?" he said. "He read all those papers in ten minutes? Anyway, who asked him for a decision? All I did was ask for an appointment for when my attorney arrives a bit later." He

argued in vain; not only did he fail to get an appointment, he couldn't get his papers back.

Finn arrived then, and a battle royal went on with
Marvin shouting at the top of his lungs that he wanted
those papers back. Coincidentally, a TV crew was
nearby on another matter. Marvin wasted no time telling them what was going on, and he got a TV interview on the spot. He also got his papers back. Finn
meantime was on the phone calling around to see if
there was another court that would listen to them. She
found a court in Palm Beach County, the 4th District
Court of Appeals, that would hear them and let them
file the injunction if they got there before the five
o'clock deadline.

Off they raced to Palm Beach County, the TV crew
trailing behind them. They reached the courthouse and
asked for an emergency hearing on the injunction.
What they didn't know was that elsewhere in the building were three judges waiting for them to give them a
full hearing. It was just after four o'clock. Just as they
were ready to go into the courtroom, on the injunction
hearing, Finn got a beep on her beeper. She called her
office and was told that the Attorney General's Office
and the Department of Corrections had agreed to post-
pone Pierson's release until December 22.

Marvin breathed a sigh of relief. "That will give us
time for a hearing," he said. "That's all I ask. The victim deserves his day in court too."

Finn then filed papers for a full hearing before Judge
Morphonios which would review Marvin's allegations
about her sentencing errors and their impact on the
Pierson situation. And perhaps she would give them a
further injunction pending a full hearing before the
Florida Supreme Court. When they stood in front of
Morphonios with these allegations, she was so angry
she disqualified herself and asked Judge Snyder to take
over. Snyder didn't know what was going on, why he
had been called in. "Where's the defendant?" he asked.

"There is no defendant," said Marvin. "There's a murderer."

As Marvin began talking Judge Snyder stopped him. "Wait a minute, Mr. Weinstein. We are not a kangaroo court. Never have been. Pierson has to be brought into court." Snyder told them to go to Judge Ralph Person, who would schedule a hearing, but Pierson would have to be present.

They went to Judge Person. He looked over the papers, the Morphonios sentencing papers of Pierson, and scheduled a hearing for them the next day before Judge Rothenberg for a further injunction and Marvin's entire case for negating Pierson's additional gain time under Waldrup. Marvin went home filled with hope. Maybe, maybe finally we'll get a proper hearing. All I want is a hearing. I'm entitled to a hearing. Why, he wondered, why are all these people fighting me over this? All I want to do is keep a murderer in jail.

It was three in the afternoon when Marvin returned home. He started to make a cup of coffee for himself when the telephone rang. It was Kelley Finn informing him that her office had just received a fax from Tallahassee saying that the Florida Supreme Court, in a 5–2 decision, had denied them a hearing.

Marvin couldn't believe it. "Denied us a hearing? Not even a hearing?"

"Sorry, Marvin," she said. "That's the end of it."

"No hearing before Rothenberg tomorrow?"

"No, this cancels it out. No hearing. It ends the fight, Marvin."

This was difficult for Marvin to accept. He really could not understand the concept of a justice system that would deny him even a hearing, when he believed he had a legitimate basis for a complaint. And if the result was 5–2, then two judges agreed with him. "Well," he said in despair to Kelley Finn, "let's at least give Pierson a hard time when he walks out of prison. Let's get a group up there and spit on him when he walks out."

Two days later, early on the morning of December 22, Marvin, Kelley Finn, and a group of about twenty members of POMC drove up to the Martin County jail to picket outside the gates as Pierson was released. Several TV camera crews were there for the spectacle, ready to film it for the early evening news. And what a scene they were able to capture: the group holding hands and singing "Amazing Grace" as Marvin, who had begun taking lessons, accompanied them on the violin.

Unfortunately, the subject of their demonstration was not there to witness it. The warden, concerned about the possibility of an ugly scene, had shipped Pierson out the night before to a jail in Daytona Beach, from which he had been released earlier that morning.

The warden was sympathetic, however. He invited Marvin and Kelley in for a cup of coffee and even gave them a little guided tour of the jail. He said he was familiar with the case, and deeply regretted releasing Pierson, but . . .

Marvin nodded and muttered his thanks. As he left with Kelley he said to her, "But . . . but . . . all I get is buts from everybody. They'd like to do something, but . . . I've had more butts than a billy goat."

He was totally depressed by the time he reached home. Wasko had escaped the electric chair. Pierson was out on the street after serving just seven years. Seven years for murdering Staci and doing only God knows what to her first. What a mess our legal system is in, he thought bitterly.

Hilari wasn't home yet from school. He wandered around the house, into Staci's room. Sat on her bed. He smiled up at all her stuffed toys set on the shelf, exactly where she had always kept them. How she had loved them all! After a time he left the bedroom and went into the living room. On the wall, opposite the couch, was a picture of Staci, smiling. Smiling at him. He began to cry.

Hilari walked in the front door. "What's the matter? Did you see Pierson? Did you spit on him for me?"

He looked up at her, his eyes red-rimmed behind his glasses. "They wouldn't even let me have that final satisfaction. To see his murdering face. For him to see my face and see the disgust, the loathing in my eyes. They sneaked him out in the middle of the night, like the thief he is. That's what he is, Hilari. Him and that other murdering bastard, Eddie Wasko. They stole Staci from us, Hilari. They took her away from us ... took her away ..." and he began to cry again.

She came to him then, Hilari did, she came to him and sat down beside him on the couch, and she put her arms around him and she laid her head on his shoulder, and they sat there like that, father and daughter, and together they cried for Staci.

Epilogue

Marvin Weinstein's prominence as a champion of the victims of violent crimes and their families, his head-lined, well-covered battle against the state of Florida in the John Pierson debacle, gave him celebrity status. He was overwhelmed with speaking engagements, press interviews, radio talk shows, and television appearances on such popular programs as *Inside Edition, Jane Whitney and Bertice Berry*. His mailbox overflowed with letters from the victims of family tragedies. His telephone rang constantly with requests, with pleas for help and guidance.

Not all the phone calls, however, were from victims.

John Pierson called. From prison. Before his release, when he knew he was getting out early because of all the gain time.

Marvin wasn't home. Hilari took the call. She could not believe the chutzpah of this man—this man who murdered her sister—not only to call but to call collect. Curious, Hilari accepted the charges, but not before she grabbed pen and paper to make notes of what he would say, in case he threatened her and Marvin.

Pierson said that before he came out of prison he wanted to clear his name. He wished that her sister was alive today, he said to Hilari, because she was the only one who could say that he had never been in their house, that he had never seen her. He told her that he had given his blood and his saliva voluntarily, the hair off his arms and his head, and if he had been guilty he would have not have done that voluntarily.

Hilari was completely calm throughout this conversation, speaking to the killer of her sister as though they were two acquaintances talking about something that had happened to somebody else. She wanted to know how he was able to describe her house if he had never been there. Pierson said he had been describing the house he had worked on earlier that day. She asked him why he had confessed. He said he was nineteen, and he was scared, that Detective Ben Hall had pushed him around and frightened him, and said he was the one that did it, and then later he was told that if he didn't confess and plead guilty, he would go on trial and he might get the electric chair.

Pearson said he wanted to clear his name with Marvin, because he was afraid that when he got out Marvin would come after him. She told him not to worry, to call back later that evening or next day and Marvin would speak to him.

When Pierson called the next morning, Marvin was ready with pad and pen to make notes.

Pierson said he'd heard Marvin speaking on a couple of radio programs. Marvin responded hesitantly; he could not handle this with Hilari's dispassion. He didn't know what to say to Pierson. He wasn't even sure why he was allowing himself to talk to his daughter's murderer on the telephone. Pierson said he'd meant to talk to him for a long time. It had been on his conscience.

Marvin said there were things he didn't understand. He'd read his confession, Marvin said to Pierson, "and now you're denying you were ever in the house."

Pierson claimed that everything he knew about the house, "Detective Ben Hall had informed me of." Then, Pierson said, after he'd given his blood and saliva voluntarily, Hall told him they'd found his blood and saliva on the scene. "I told him I wasn't there, I had nothing to do with it," Pierson said to Marvin. He said Hall really scared him, said that he was guilty, that he was going to get the chair. Pierson said he failed the lie-detector test because he was terrified, because "I was being blamed for something I had no knowledge of."

Pierson related to Marvin how he had come to work for Stanley Steemer and there met Eddie Wasko.

Marvin asked him if he remembered his confession. Marvin reminded him of all the charges against him, including the rape charge, and told Pierson that if he had not accepted the plea bargain and gone to trial, he'd probably be with Wasko on death row—forgetting that Wasko's death sentence had been reversed. Marvin asked him why he'd pled guilty if he hadn't done anything wrong. Wasko was already in jail, Wasko couldn't hurt him, he could have laid the whole thing on Eddie and said he was innocent.

Pierson swore he could never do anything like that, the way the murder was described. He said he had wanted to go to trial because he was innocent, but that night in jail, when he was offered the plea bargain, his father was there, and he said he told his father he wanted to go to trial, to take his chances, but his father advised him to plead guilty, because, "my dad said if you go to trial I'll probably never see you again. My dad cried. I'd never seen my dad cry before. That was the only reason I took that plea bargain the way I did."

His blood and saliva on the scene? Pierson had no idea how it got there.

It was a protracted telephone conversation, lasting over an hour, with Marvin virtually putting Pierson on the witness stand again and interrogating him. Pierson said, over and over again, that he was in prison for something he didn't do, that Eddie Wasko had done it, and his entire life had been ruined because of it, his family had disowned him and when he got out he had no place to go. He was calling Marvin to clear his conscience, he said. He hoped Marvin would believe him.

Marvin didn't believe a word.

Today, Marvin struggles to free himself from the web of his own success at generating press and television publicity, at least to the point where he can begin to earn a living. His funds from the lawsuit have been substantially dissipated by unfortunate investments and because he has been living off that money for several years. He has worked only intermittently in the carpet business, never for more than a few weeks at a time. His core difficulty is that ever since the murder of Staci and his obsessive drive to see justice done, he has psychologically been unable to return to the mainstream of the world beyond murder and mayhem. His work with POMC—and not only with POMC but with victims of crime—keeps that flame burning within him. He finds it difficult to make any kind of business decision. He cannot figure out what to do with the rest of his life.

His most recent attempt at a business venture—a wholesale bakery—ended in disaster.

He is trying something else now with a part interest in a music store. It seems an unlikely venture for a baker and carpet layer, but it appears that he has found one corner of his existence not muddied by Florida's flood of major crime: music. He played violin as a child in school. Several years ago he took it up again, and it can be said that his first public performance was at the gates of John Pierson's prison. Later he joined Mort Glosser and his Corn Country band. He'd always liked country and western and bluegrass music. He plays at monthly jamborees in North Miami Beach, adding to his repertoire the mandolin and double bass. And since Marvin does not do things by halves, he has become the president of the South Florida Bluegrass

Association. There's no money to be earned at his music, but it lights up his life during its darkest moments.

Marvin Weinstein is virtually a walking encyclopedia of south Florida's major crimes. He can quote recent history and current events on armed robbery, rape and murder. He lives in an area well known not only for its shocking crime rate, but for its successful professional baseball, football, hockey, and basketball teams, and while your "average" man can reel off names of players, scores, team histories and statistics, Marvin knows nothing of these things, but can at the drop of a question, or even unsolicited, run through an updated scoreboard of the names of killers and rapists, their crimes and their sentences, the prosecution and defense attorneys, the judges and the names of next of kin of the victim—whom he will likely as not telephone and offer to help.

It is almost impossible to hold a conversation with Marvin on any subject but murder. His morbid fixation on this subject, a fixation not only on murder in general but on his own case, in which he continues to believe the justice system failed him by releasing Pierson so early—and even more than failed him, misled him, refused him the right to go before the Florida Supreme Court and present his case—fans the still hot embers of his anger.

And this stubborn refusal to let it drop, to forget it and get on with his life, continues to alienate Hilari.

Staci's bedroom is a shrine. Her stuffed toys are set on the shelf. Her little black shoes—the ones in which she could not be buried—are tucked away in the drawer of her dresser. He handles them lovingly. Her school papers lie about and he treasures the birthday card she made at school for him herself.

He has a color photograph of Staci's body just as he discovered her, lying murdered on her bed. It's a crime-lab photo. Hilari tore it to pieces once; carefully Marvin glued it all back together again.

Marvin sees Staci wherever he goes. He sees her in the supermarket, shopping. He sees her among the young girls at an ice skating rink. He sees her on the street, chatting to other girls in their early twenties, the age she would be now. He sees her image in the attractive receptionist at a doctor's office. Staci could do that job. He sees her in the young women holding their children by the hand as they stroll through the shopping malls, and always he thinks—that could be Staci, that *should* be Staci with her child, my grandchild. He realizes that John Pierson and Eddie Wasko killed more than just Staci; they killed the children she surely would have had, and her children's children, and so on down the line, entire generations of offspring that will not be born into this world because they killed Staci. A limb of the family tree severed from its base before it had time to bear fruit and the seeds of future generations.

All this he sees and understands, and he cannot make it disappear. Dearly he would like to reconcile his differences with Hilari if he but knew how to begin.

She lives modestly in a trailer park. "I love him to death," sighs Hilari, "but I can't live with him."

She has a bachelor of science degree in psychology but works sporadically at odd jobs: a waitress in a pizza restaurant, a barmaid. She doesn't mind. "I only went to college to please him," she says, "and he's so proud of me that my diploma has been hidden away somewhere in a drawer ever since I graduated."

No more. I shamed Marvin into framing it handsomely and hanging it on a wall in the living room.

He is proud of her. He loves her too, and worries about her, is concerned for her future, but down through the years of sadness and tragedy, of his fighting the justice system, he lost touch with her, lived for the dead and denied Hilari the love and parental support she so desperately needed all those years. Marvin knows that. Knows what he did and didn't do and that haunts him, visits him in his nightmares. Somewhere back there, when Staci was murdered and he lost his capacity to be a loving father, he lost his surviving daughter.

Maybe not irretrievably. He hopes that perhaps this book can prove to be a kind of catharsis for him, perhaps draw the poison from his system, give him the chance to pick up those scattered pieces of his shattered life and build a decent future of love and happiness for himself and for Hilari. He would like that.

To live for the living.